High-Risk Feminism in Colombia

High-Risk Feminism in Colombia

Women's Mobilization in
Violent Contexts

JULIA MARGARET ZULVER

Rutgers University Press

New Brunswick, Camden, and Newark, New Jersey, and London

Library of Congress Cataloging-in-Publication Data
Names: Zulver, Julia, 1990– author.
Title: High-risk feminism in Colombia : women's mobilization in violent
    contexts / Julia Margaret Zulver.
Description: New Brunswick, NJ : Rutgers University Press, [2022] |
    Includes bibliographical references and index.
Identifiers: LCCN 2021029937 | ISBN 9781978827097 (paperback) |
    ISBN 9781978827103 (hardcover) | ISBN 9781978827110 (epub) |
    ISBN 9781978827127 (mobi) | ISBN 9781978827134 (pdf)
Subjects: LCSH: Feminism—Colombia. | Social movements—Colombia. |
    Women—Colombia—Social conditions.
Classification: LCC HQ1552 .Z85 2022 | DDC 305.4209861—dc23
LC record available at https://lccn.loc.gov/2021029937

A British Cataloging-in-Publication record for this book is available from the British Library.

www.rutgersuniversitypress.org

Manufactured in the United States of America

They pulled out our fruits, they cut our branches, they burned our trunks, but they were not able to kill our roots.

-**ALIANZA MURAL** in Villagarzón, Putumayo

An abnormal reaction to an abnormal situation is normal behavior.

—**VIKTOR FRANKL**, 1959

Contents

Contents

Illustrations

Figures

High-Risk Feminism in Colombia

1

Introduction

• •

High-Risk Feminism
in Colombia

Anyela and I were sitting on a bus, traveling from Turbaco to Barranquilla, when she decided to share her story with me. We had met a few months earlier, when I first arrived in Colombia, and although we had spent lots of time together she had never chosen to open up to me about her past. Originally from Magdalena, she and her husband were displaced from the countryside to an urban center after her family members were murdered by paramilitaries. In that city, her husband was killed, and she had to move again, to El Pozón, a slum near Cartagena, with her children. There, she joined the Liga de Mujeres Desplazadas (League of Displaced Women) and moved into the City of Women. Her second husband was murdered on the doorstep of her house when their youngest child was only six months old. She told me about the early days of the City, when the women continued to be threatened by armed groups. Her words were clear: "Despite so much pain, so many violations, so much damage, the voice of us women has always survived."

We had woken up early and were en route to a rally, where women from all over the Caribbean coast would come together to express their support for the peace accords negotiated between the Colombian government and the Fuerzas Armadas Revolucionarias de Colombia (FARC). It was a moment of expectation, full of hopeful symbols: women wearing white, images of doves

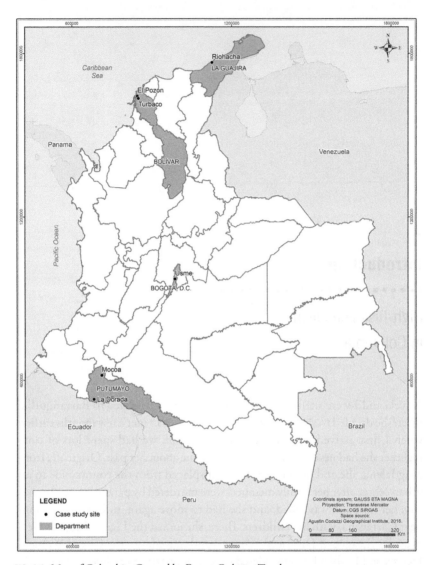

FIG. 1.1 Map of Colombia. Created by Francy Bolaños Trochez.

of peace, T-shirts bearing the message, "Sí."[1] Anyela told me she had been reflecting on what the day meant to her: "Behind every smile there is a story."

Years later, at the opposite end of the country, Sandra and I were sitting in the office of a local government employee in southern Putumayo, near the border with Ecuador. The oscillating fan on the desk created a background of white noise that at times made it hard to hear her, particularly when her voice lowered as she spoke about memories of the past. I asked her share with me how

FIG. 1.2 A mural painted by the Alianza outside the cemetery in San Miguel, Putumayo, reads: "Let us walk without fear, let us join forces." (Credit: author.)

she came to join the Alianza de Mujeres Tejedoras de Vida del Putumayo (Women's Alliance of Putumayo: Weavers of Life). She told of being kidnapped and sexually abused as a young woman. It was this experience that eventually led her to join the Alianza, where she was finally able to talk to other women about her experiences and find solidarity in group membership. For her, the traumas of the past were an intrinsic part of the reason why she joined the Alianza.

Being part of this organization is dangerous for Sandra today. Only a few months before, she told me, armed men had entered her house and told her that unless she stopped her community work and joined them, they would kill both her and her daughters. While our conversation focused on resistance and resilience, it was clear that times were tense. As soon as we left the building we were accompanied by her government-issued bodyguard, who followed us, a few paces behind, as we walked to a small restaurant located on the edge of the town's central plaza. The next time I met up with Sandra in late 2019, she was no longer living in the South; the threats had become too much, and she had been forced to move to the departmental capital.

Anyela's and Sandra's stories are tragic and painful. Ultimately, however, they are stories of resistance. Women's experiences of surviving destructive and devastating violence are unfortunately common in Colombia. The country is no stranger to conflict. Until recently, it was officially embroiled in the Western Hemisphere's longest-running war. At the time of this writing, the

Colombian Victims' Unit has officially registered almost 4.5 million women victims of the conflict (Unidad para las Víctimas 2020).

It is known that women suffered differently during the decades of armed conflict; they were often specifically targeted for violence, including, but not limited to, sexual violence (Meertens 2001, 2012; Centro Nacional de Memoria Histórica 2017). As the country's National Center for Historical Memory (2011, 26) outlines, "Women and girls—dehumanized, dispossessed of their own bodies—became territories to be colonized by all-powerful masculinities who declared themselves the victors through [acts of] brutality." This fits with Cockburn's (2004, 35–36) assessments about the gendered continuum of violence, whereby "men and women die different deaths and are tortured and abused in different ways in wars, both because of physical differences between the sexes and because of the different meanings culturally ascribed to the male and female body."

In 2016 the Colombian government signed a peace deal with the FARC, bringing an end to the fifty-two-year conflict with the left-wing rebel group. This was supposed to usher in an era of peace; the peace agreement itself is heralded as being the most gender-inclusive in the world (Meger and Sachseder 2020).

The research presented over the following chapters, however, is not bookended by the official end to the internal conflict with the FARC. Although 2016 represents a critical juncture in Colombian history, it has not brought an end to violent conflict, as Sandra's story—and those of so many other women—illustrates. While the immediate moment of post-accord peace brought about a temporary reprieve from hostilities (Tate 2017), in many parts of the country this tranquility has expired (Maher and Thomson 2018; Rettberg 2019; Meger and Sachseder 2020). Indeed, violence continues between other armed groups, FARC dissidents, narco-traffickers, the armed forces, and paramilitary successors. Social leaders have been murdered in alarming numbers (Prem et al. 2018; INDEPAZ 2019; Castro et al. 2020); feminicide is increasing around the country (Conexión Putumayo 2019; Tejedoras de Vida del Putumayo 2019; Parkin Daniels 2021); and female politicians face gendered threats and murder, including during the October 2019 departmental and municipal elections (Zulver 2019a).

In a perverse twist of fate, some of those women—often victims themselves—who came out to support the peace are now being targeted by armed groups for having become empowered (Arredondo 2019).[2] As another woman in Putumayo told me, "Women are being targeted . . . because we have *fuerza* and that is the biggest threat we pose. They don't want leaders; they want complete social control" (Zulver 2019b, see also 2021).

This book's story begins in the past, remembering incidents of women's high-risk collective action in Turbaco and Usme after women fled the paramilitary incursion into Montes de María and the Pacific Coast in the late 1990s and early 2000s. It then moves to a moment of relative calm—the moment at which I began my research—when many national-level and grassroots women's organizations were promoting a peace agenda (see Paarlberg-Kvam 2019). By the conclusion, however, we find ourselves in another moment of uncertainty: violence is returning to territories where it has a historical foothold, and in some cases it is directly targeting women who became empowered and are now empowering other women to make claims for gender justice. Nevertheless, these women continue to mobilize.

Some might assume that these women, in the face of the high risks of ubiquitous violence, during both conflict and postconflict moments, turn inward to the private domain of the household for protection and safety. Moreover, we might predict that owing to fear of violence, socially dictated norms around gender roles, and social isolation, they would lack the resources to mobilize. Indeed, this is a narrative that has been painted about the ways in which women behave during armed conflict, leading to an understanding in which women are represented as vulnerable and in need of protection (Carpenter 2005). There is a growing literature, however, that seeks to highlight the ways women behave during conflict moments, from small acts of resistance (Baines 2015; Sutton 2018), to participating as rebels (Kampwirth 2006; Viterna 2013; Trisko Darden, Henshaw, and Szekely 2019), to carving out new spaces for participation in politics (Hughes 2009; Tripp 2015; Berry 2018).

This book focuses on those local, grassroots women's organizations that choose to act collectively—and resist as feminists—in high-risk settings. Women's social movements in Colombia are very much visible in the streets, social networks, media, courts, and neighborhoods. The country has a long history of women's mobilization, particularly (in recent years, at least) around supporting the peace accords (Rojas 2009). The women I have worked with— the protagonists of this story—are not primarily peace activists, although most of them did and do support the peace process and, indeed, share feminist visions of peace (Paarlberg-Kvam 2019).

Rather, they have mobilized in the pursuit of gender justice. Their collective action is rooted in their gendered experiences of the conflict; as they came together, they were able to understand, for the first time, that women experience conflict differently because of their gender. Moreover, they began to understand that the same power dynamics that are pervasive during war also dictate everyday gendered inequalities.

In contesting these dynamics, however, they compound the violences to which they are exposed. These threats are twofold: women are daring to disturb imposed social order by mobilizing against armed groups, and they are transgressing socially acceptable gender norms by making demands for women's rights. Why do these women put themselves directly in harm's way by mobilizing? Why, when the response to acting collectively can be threats, stalking, violence, or even murder, do women decide to assume these risks? Many of the women survivors of conflict-related violence that I spoke with during my research refer to themselves as *berracas,* forces to be reckoned with. These women are the subject of this book.

The Argument

Why and how do women decide to risk their individual and collective safety by mobilizing for gender justice during periods of violence? Earlier studies have shown that severe repression, rather than causing demobilization, may actually stimulate collective action (Loveman 1998). I take the claim further: I argue that in conditions of conflict where risks are gendered, some women adopt feminist identities and frames of reference to resist violence, in both its gendered and generalized expressions.

My research with grassroots women's organizations shows that their gendered experiences of conflict can initially bring them together to meet their practical needs (access to food and shelter) but can then lead them to pursue strategic interests, including gender justice more broadly.[3] Over time, and through sharing their experiences and building a collective identity, their goals become bigger than meeting daily necessities and extend to critiquing the gendered power dynamics that caused them to suffer conflict differently in the first place. Not only do they develop a shared understanding of the dynamics that led to their particular experiences of conflict-related violence, but they also develop strategies and actions that make claims for gender justice both within and after the conflict moment. This behavior—feminist mobilization—transgresses traditional gender norms, particularly in *machista* Latin America, and thus attracts an additional level of risk, beyond that of everyday life in a conflict zone.

Armed groups employing a logic of militarized masculinity (Theidon 2009) do not look kindly on women's empowerment, particularly when this takes the form of resistance to the hegemonic imposition of violence. In mobilizing as feminists, women are running the risks not only of exposing themselves to retribution for contesting those who hold a monopoly on the use of violence, but also for disrupting a gendered social order more broadly. Feminist mobilization in contexts of high violence (that is, mobilization not imbued with social protections resulting from traditional understandings of gender roles) peels away yet another layer of safety and security for participants.[4]

Too often, women's action against violence is taken for granted or seen as something that automatically takes form. This book searches for explanations for women's high-risk feminist mobilization at the grassroots level, looking for evidence from the bottom up. Such an approach affords us the ability to understand women's decisionmaking calculations. Borrowing from cognitive psychology, however, we can see that when these women occupy a "domain of losses" (Kahneman and Tversky 1979, 269)—that is, a context of conflict where not participating collectively does not necessarily ensure protection from violence, and participating provides access to material and nonmaterial benefits—they are able to justify their potentially risky behavior.[5] The domain of losses women occupy is gendered; participation in a feminist organization offers members gendered "club goods" that are worth pursuing, given women's understanding of themselves in relation to the status quo of gendered violence.

This approach builds on Kreft's (2019, 221) findings of a relationship between "gender-differential outcomes and gender-specific violence in conflict." She draws on Tilly's (1978) work to conclude that women mobilize in response to the "*threat* that [conflict-related sexual violence] poses to them *as women* . . . regardless of whether they personally are victims" because they understand it "in distinctly gendered terms and as a violent manifestation of societal gender inequalities" (Kreft 2019, 222). Her work focuses specifically on conflict-related sexual violence, which women in Colombia clearly perceive as "a distinctly gendered violence that asserts male dominance over the social collective of women" (Kreft 2020, 3). However, while Kreft's (2019, 224) work is largely based on interviews with women working in national-level organizations, this book is grounded in the experiences of women at the grass roots. By adopting an ethnographic approach to research from the bottom up, I was able to gain certain insights into the day-to-day, lived understandings and experiences of resistance as they play out in violent contexts.

Until now, I have used the terms *conflict* and *violent contexts* fairly interchangeably. This is intentional. Indeed, Cockburn (2004) writes that war exists along a spectrum for women. Her work on the "continuum of violence" fits within a literature that talks about the "continuum of violence and conflict" (Moser 2001, 30) or war as "liminal" for women (Berry 2018, 178). It is also well known that everyday violence for women exists on the "knife's edge between public and private violence" (Hume 2009, 117); and Boesten (2014, 5) tells us that the "impunity of wartime sexual violence reflects peacetime values regarding violence and gendered violence." Still other research shows us how impunity contributes to the "multisided violence" (Drysdale Walsh and Menjívar 2016, 1) that normalizes brutal violence, including feminicide, even in supposedly postwar contexts (Sanford 2008; Menjívar 2011).

Indeed, one of the goals here is to further illustrate, using ethnographic research, that the conflict/postconflict binary is not necessarily relevant to women's lived experiences of violence.[6] Instead of adopting the language of "conflict" or "postconflict," I choose to frame women's mobilization in terms of "high risk." In doing so, I ask questions about what the continuum of conflict looks like on the ground—how it plays out in practice in women's everyday lives—and what the implications for women's mobilization are over time. I have taken inspiration here from Sandvik (2018), who, playing on the work of Arias and Goldstein (2010), suggests that we build a theory of gendered violent pluralism, whereby gendered violence can be an obstacle to organizing, women's organizing can be a response to gendered violence, and political organizing can be a cause of further gender-based violence.

Wood (2008, 555) notes that wartime can bring about the transformation of social networks, including the transformation of gender roles: "the transformation of gender roles during war is often reversed once war draws to a close" as social norms return to prewar moments. Similarly, Berry's (2017) work focuses on how women's mobilization was transformed during war in Rwanda and Bosnia, although she also questions the longevity of these gains over time, particularly given dynamics of patriarchal backlash. Indeed, the quantitative work undertaken by Webster, Chen, and Beardsley (2019, 256) does not find conclusive evidence that women's gains in empowerment during war persist beyond ten to fifteen years after conflicts end.

When violence continues to victimize women both in the context of civil conflict and in a purportedly postconflict moment, are these categories the most useful way to understand the contexts for women's lasting empowerment? By assessing the context in which they operate in terms of risk of violence—the risks of living in a territory controlled by violent armed actors, the risks of organizing collectively when these actors want total control, the risks of defying socially prescribed gender norms, and the risks of patriarchal backlash to empowerment—I use field-based evidence to add to the argument that the end of war and the signing of a peace agreement do not necessarily result in women's lives becoming more peaceful or less dangerous.[7]

This is a book about gendered resistance to violence over different moments of conflict cycles—moments of high risk—seen through a feminist prism that exposes the multifaceted and nuanced ways in which women experience and resist this violence. In doing so, it charts new territory not only by expanding our understanding of gendered mobilization during conflict, but also by asking questions about the limits to this mobilization and the creative ways in which women navigate new permutations of violence.

In addition to presenting an understanding of women's feminist mobilization as a function of risk, rather than war or conflict per se, I also paint a picture of the micro-level mechanisms that explain why women are willing to risk threats, violence, and death to pursue gender justice. To shine a light on these dynamics, I draw on years of research with grassroots women's organizations, with the goal of explaining why and how women choose to resist the violent contexts in which they live. In answering these questions, the book also provides broader insights into how exposure to conflict can propel women toward pursuing gender justice and how mobilization expands beyond traditional conflict/postconflict binaries. It thereby gives a more granular understanding of the dynamics of patriarchal backlash along the continuum.

The chapters that follow examine four cases of communities of women whose lives have been irreparably affected by Colombia's conflict. Yet despite vulnerabilities and the high risks of challenging a violent social order, these women choose to resist and demand gender justice. The aim is to showcase the various forms of agency that women have, adopt, manipulate, create, modify, and employ in their daily lives when living under the shadow of brutal and targeted violence.

To begin, I look at how existing studies on social movements have grappled with the high-risk collective action question. These studies do not adequately factor gender—both as a basis for specific threats and as providing a set of benefits worth mobilizing for—into their analysis. I then engage with literature on women's mobilization in conflict to demonstrate that our understanding of why women engage in risky activities is not adequately theorized. It is at the intersection of these bodies of literature that this book makes its contribution.

Existing Perspectives on High-Risk Collective Action

According to classical social movement theorists, people do not choose to participate in social movements if there is risk involved in doing so (Olson 1965). This is the commonsense explanation: people will not engage in activities that expose them to personal danger because doing so is irrational (Muller and Opp 1986). For action to be justifiable, the participant would have to have the expectation of a positive and measurable outcome that would outweigh the cost of action. Risking death or likely personal injury, therefore, defies the logic of collective action.

The empirical research in this book, however, clearly shows that this is not the case. I am not the first to try to explain why individuals mobilize in high-risk situations. In *Freedom Summer*, McAdam (1988) investigates just this question. In a separate publication, he notes that "certain instances of activism are clearly more costly and/or risky than others" (1986, 67). He concludes that those people engaging in high-risk action must be biographically available, that is, "relatively free of personal constraints that would make participation especially risky" (71). This by itself is not a satisfying explanation; the implication here is that a person who engages in a rational choice–based calculation of costs and benefits and decides to mobilize anyway is not, in fact, as susceptible to the risks of participation as someone else.

Loveman's (1998) study on human rights defenders mobilizing in the Southern Cone despite authoritarian repression further seeks to answer this question, noting that participants were not free of McAdam's (1986) personal constraints. She engages in a review of the literature on social movement theory in her attempt to explain action. Initially, she rejects a purely rational choice explanation for participation, because "fear" as a psychosocial process is not formally theorized. Moreover, she notes,

> If risk or cost is calculated as a high probability of "death," while benefit is calculated at a minimal probability of "maintenance of honor" or "respect for human rights," how is this "ratio" to be assessed in the grammar of rational calculation in order to predict the outcome? If the likely result of action is death, rational choice models would predict inaction, unless they determine ex post facto, with reference to the individual's behavior, that the first order preference is a certain "value" that requires such a sacrifice. This, of course, is tautological. (Loveman 1998, 481)

One of Loveman's key points is that participants mobilize in response to, and not despite, repression. This is in keeping with Calhoun's (1991) identity-based explanation that action is the result of commitment to an identity that involves participation. There exist nonmaterial benefits (or goods), Calhoun argues, that lie in the conception of oneself (identity) and that are generated from the performance of an action (and not necessarily even from the success of the action). Other social movement scholars further assert that identity has explanatory power, whereby moral, political, and social contradictions that emerge from repression catalyze action (Calhoun 1991; Gould 1995; Melucci 1988; Viterna 2013). Snow et al. (1986) further explain this phenomenon in terms of the interpretation of grievances, which is to say, the way that the repression and subsequent mobilization is framed.

Moving beyond purely identity-based explanations for mobilization, Goodwin and Pfaff (2001) call for the development of what they call "emotional sociology." For them, many of the key causal factors emphasized by social movement analysts "derive much of their causal power from the strong emotions that they embody or evoke among actors" (Goodwin and Pfaff 2001, 283). When it comes to emotion and high-risk social movements, then, there is value in assessing Hochschild's (1983, 50) notion of "emotion management." Her key idea is that people "induce or suppress feeling in order to sustain the outward countenance that produces the proper state of mind in others" (1983, 7). Goodwin and Pfaff (2001) point out that Tilly's (1978) repertoires of collective action, in fact, require a great deal of emotion management. They state that "when protest is extremely risky or dangerous, fear may inhibit collective action (or certain forms of collective action), and so it must be suppressed or at least mitigated, not necessarily in purposive or self-conscious ways, if such action is to occur at all" (Goodwin and Pfaff 2001, 284). The important point here is that those who mobilize in a context of risk are not confused, irrational, or mistaken about the risks of their participation. Rather, people have ways to actively manage emotions such as fear.

For example, in an article that examines why human rights defenders in Russia mobilize despite considerable risks to personal safety, van der Vet and Lyytikäinen (2015) note that a participant's decision to become a high-risk activist involves more than a rational choice: "Participation often involves a deep emotional engagement and, in dangerous environments, a management of fear despite the high costs" (2015, 983). Emotions can be seen as a logical explanation for joining and maintaining membership in high-risk movements: "For example, ongoing participation in 'high-risk' movements typically requires the mitigation of participants' fears of violent reprisals against one's self or family, or of losing one's job. [Goodwin and Pfaff (2001)] . . . show that factors and processes that movement analysts have typically invoked for other explanatory purposes—including networks, mass gatherings, rituals, and new collective identities—also helped participants deal with their fears (sometimes as unanticipated consequences of these processes) and thereby helped sustain participation in these movements" (Goodwin, Jasper, and Polletta 2001, 19).

Beyond individual-level factors, other scholars engage with social network theories in attempts to explain high-risk mobilization (della Porta 1988; Gould 1995; Loveman 1998; McAdam 1986, 1988; Wickham-Crowley 1992). For example, they would assert that activists must have access to certain basic resources to start a mobilization. These resources can be institutional links or personal links to churches, political parties, unions, universities, or nongovernmental organizations. Connections of this sort can offer resources such as funding, information, and physical and symbolic space (Morris 1984). Taking a resource mobilization position, Loveman (1998, 484) uses her case studies in the Southern Cone to highlight the need for access to external financial and material capital to sustain mobilization in repressive conditions.

Alternatively, other scholars advocate for a political opportunity structure argument. Without examining the political opportunities on offer, simply having access to resources, existing social networks, or sociopolitical space cannot sufficiently explain when social movements emerge (McAdam et al. 2001; Tarrow 2011; Tilly 1978). Rather, as Tarrow (2011, 169) notes, the political opportunity is "external" to the potential actor in a social movement, meaning that even weak actors can take advantage of changing opportunities to mount their mobilization. In this way, Loveman (1998, 485) sees political repression and increased human rights violations as creating new political opportunities for previously unmobilized actors: "excessive abuses by the state may *directly stimulate* the emergence of *certain types* of contentious collective action," meaning that as grievances skyrocket, people "mobilize *in response to* . . . severe repression" (emphasis in original).

Research about El Salvador (Viterna 2009; Wood 2003, 2015), the Southern Cone (Loveman 1998), West Germany (Opp and Roehl 1990), Northern Ireland (O'Hearn 2009), Jordan (Moss 2014), Palestine (Alimi 2009), Egypt (Rizzo, Price, and Meyer 2012), the West Bank (Khawaja 1993), and Liberia (Press 2014) represent but a few of the efforts that have used case studies to explain mobilization in high-risk contexts. Most of these rely on some combination of identity, political opportunity structure, or resource mobilization explanations. The lines of thinking explored, however, are not enough to explain women's gendered mobilization in high-risk moments. I agree with Loveman's (1998, 485) assertion that participants "mobilize in response to, *not despite*, severe repression"; however, I do not think that her research provides a sufficient answer to the question of why women mobilize as feminists.

As mentioned, this book is not the first to grapple with the question of why people choose to mobilize in high-risk settings. Logical questions might emerge, however, around the notion of high risk: Does this imply that there are variants of low-risk or medium-risk feminist mobilization? If women were guaranteed to face extreme violence, would they still participate in high-risk collective action? The reasoned thinking about the relationship between repression and mobilization is that it falls on a normal distribution curve (an inverted parabola). Indeed, Van Dyke (2003, 229) suggests that repression might have a curvilinear effect on protest: "some arrests may anger activists and mobilize them for additional protest." Severe levels of repression, however, may effectively prevent mobilization. This argument is further articulated by other scholars, within an emphasis on the model of political opportunity structure (Eisinger 1973; Brockett 1991; Khawaja 1993; Opp 2009). Without experience of repression, people do not necessarily feel a need to mobilize against it. As repression begins, people resist until they assess that it is too dangerous to continue. Then mobilization would likely trickle away.

What I propose here, however, is that prospect theory (Kahneman and Tversky 1979) can provide more insight into when people choose to mobilize in the face of risk. This theory—borrowed from behavioral economics—is based on the idea that people think in terms of their expected gains (or utility) relative to a reference point (that is, this very moment) rather than in absolute terms. Thus when women consider that their actions may result in violent retribution, they make this decision not from a point of complete safety but rather from existing conditions of insecurity. Given that not mobilizing does not necessarily offer them protection and does not allow them access to the potential material and nonmaterial gains of acting collectively, women make the decision to assume a certain level of risk.

Chapter 2 further engages with this approach to explain why and how women participate in high-risk feminism despite the violence that can be incurred by doing so. It assesses these questions through a gendered lens, looking at the specific power dynamics that catalyze this mobilization. This is one of the unique contributions this book makes, not only to studies of collective action but also to studies of civilian agency and to wider understandings of women's agency during conflict and postconflict moments.

Existing Perspectives on Women's Mobilization during Conflict

This book is premised on the idea that employing a gendered lens is imperative to an understanding of high-risk feminist mobilization. By no means, however, is it the first to grapple with the varied roles that women take on in conflict situations.

Recent scholarship on civilian strategies during conflict or war aims to explain how people are able to make decisions and exercise agency despite the violent contexts in which they live (Masullo 2015; Arjona 2016; Kaplan 2017; Krause 2018; Justino 2019). These scholars are clear that, against the odds, civilians are able to engage in strategies that effectively resist, negotiate, and withstand violent stakeholders' actions. Some scholars have applied a gendered lens to their work. Baines's (2015, 2016) work complexifies understandings of victimhood, for example, by documenting how women abducted by the Lord's Resistance Army in northern Uganda were able to exert political agency, even in the face of violence. Sutton's (2018, 134) work on women who were detained by the state during Argentina's Dirty War documents the micro-resistances they enacted—for instance, "lifting one's hood to see the surroundings, lending a comforting hand to a fellow captive, making sounds to communicate with other detainees,"—and notes that "any and all forms of micro resistance were liable to be met with brutal forms of retaliation and punishment, and thus entailed considerable risk." As Krause (2019, 1468) tells us, "Civilian agency is gendered," although no systematic analysis of the gendered dimensions of civilian agency and nonviolence currently exists. While this book does not necessarily engage with the language of "civilian agency," it nevertheless offers important insights into the ways that women choose to resist, defend, and protect themselves in unforgiving contexts.

Other literature on gender and conflict shows that women are not merely passive victims during war. When it comes to understandings of women's mobilization during conflict in Latin America, the example with which researchers often begin is the Madres de Plaza de Mayo (Mothers of the Plaza de Mayo), the heroic image of mothers in politics (Jaquette 1994). During the military dictatorship in Argentina (1976–1983), a cross-class group of mothers engaged in peaceful protest to find their children who had been disappeared by the state. They marched around the statue at the Plaza de Mayo in Buenos Aires, calling on the military junta to give them information about their children. They did so despite the great personal risk this implied: the dictatorship was notoriously violent against anyone who dared to dissent. Moreover, they had personal knowledge of the violence they risked because of what had happened to their family members.

Navarro (1989) explains that the Mothers of the Plaza de Mayo were able to engage in collective action against the repressive state because they created a new political opportunity by mobilizing from their social location as mothers. That is, acting as mothers allowed the women to "achieve new identities and roles" (Jaquette 1994, 225). Elshtain (1996), for example, theorizes about the transformations that these mothers underwent as a function of their mobilization. She says that, in fact, it was their mobilization—the act of coming together in the first place—that gave them the ability to manage their emotions and generate change through action. By talking about human rights, they were "afforded . . . a framework within which to canalize their grief—to make it do political work. And those Mothers who seemed to me to be coping best were those who had been able to transcend somewhat the vortex of personal devastation and make common cause, through human rights efforts, with their fellow Argentines and human rights activists internationally" (Elshtain 1996, 141). More than just a "sorority bound by loss" (Elshtain 1996, 131), the Mothers became a force to be reckoned with, by using their disobedience to transform their maternal roles (supposedly powerless and weak) into a strategic strength that could confront a brutal dictatorship.

The Mothers perceived themselves as less likely than fathers to face repression, for example. Despite this, it is important to note that they did not think they were safe; they were keenly aware of what the regime was capable of doing. They knew that they had a certain cultural legitimacy to mobilize as mothers looking for their children but also recognized that the regime would not necessarily avoid repressing them, as was evidenced by the disappearance of three of the founders and the French nuns.

There are clear criticisms that come with essentializing women's roles to those associated with maternity. Ruddick's (1989) seminal work, *Maternal Thinking*, ponders whether maternal actions and efforts could be used as a resource for peace.[8] Jaquette (1994, 255) questions whether, despite the shift from practical to strategic gender interests, women can be "citizens if they always act in the interest of *others*." That is, this shift may be geared toward the greater goals of feminism, but not in a "feminist way." This may not be a bad thing, she notes, as in certain societies it might be rational to take advantage of the powerful rhetoric of "political motherhood" (Jaquette 1994, 228).

We can find clear examples of when women participate during conflict in ways that bend gendered stereotypes: for example, women-as-revolutionaries (in Latin America, see Moghadam 1997; Luciak 2001; Stephen 1997; Kampwirth 2004, 2006; González and Kampwirth 2001; Viterna 2013, 2006; Molyneux 1985; Lobao 1990; Trisko Darden, Henshaw, and Szekely 2019; in

Colombia specifically, see Barrios Sabogal and Richter 2019; Herrera and Porch 2008).[9] There are two different camps when it comes to this body of literature, which correspond to Moghadam's (1997) two models of revolution: one in which traditional gender roles are reinforced (the patriarchal model) and one in which women's emancipation is fundamental to the project (the emancipation or modernizing model).

In the first stream, women participate as revolutionaries in a way that corresponds to traditional gendered division of labor.[10] Shayne (1999, 99) documents the ways that women played strategic roles in the Salvadoran Civil War yet ultimately concludes that they were not fully acknowledged (particularly by their male comrades) as actors in the revolutionary process. Viterna (2013, 5) also notes that in some cases, rather than breaking gender barriers, women combatants are seen as pawns in larger struggles for power and emerge in the aftermath of warfare "traumatized, resource-poor, and with great difficulties in meeting the basic necessities of life." In all, despite women's ability to act as revolutionaries, Molyneux (1998, 72) notes that participation in these types of movements rarely involves the pursuit of "gender-specific interests."

On the other hand, there is a body of work that focuses on distinctly feminist mobilizations born out of experiences of revolution (see Shayne's [2004, 10, 159] work on "revolutionary feminism"). As interviewees from Kampwirth's (2004, 2) fieldwork explain, women who participated in revolutions did not join the guerrilla struggle with the goal of revolutionizing gender relations. Years later, however, they found themselves critical of the sexual inequality that existed within the guerrilla forces (despite the guerrilla's public commitment to reduce inequality at large within their society) and began to come together as feminists.

If women do not participate on one side of conflict (as combatants), there is a tendency to position them in opposition to it, as antimilitarists or peace activists (Cockburn 2007). This line of thinking about women's organizations in violent contexts is based on concepts of their peacefulness and how their roles as peacemakers and peacebuilders can serve society more broadly. Indeed, this thinking is included in the underpinnings of the United Nations Security Council's (2000) Women, Peace and Security agenda.

At the international level, Moosa et al. (2013) acknowledge that women have a unique ability to build peace at local levels, and others (Krause, Krause, and Bränfors 2018) note that peace accords with the active participation of women are more likely to be successful over time. In her article on gender, conflict, and peacebuilding, Arostegui (2013, 535) notes that in the aftermath of conflict, women often become activists and use their experiences to "reshape societies, rewrite the rules, and advance women's rights." She further proposes that "the trauma of the conflict experience also provides an opportunity for women to come together with a common agenda."

In Colombia, Restrepo's (2016) study explores the ways in which some women overcome their victimhood, emerging as leaders in peacebuilding, despite the significant risks associated with the ongoing violence. I agree wholeheartedly with her assessment that "against all odds, these unsung [women victim] leaders have proven to be powerful agents of change." Where I diverge, slightly, is in her framing of women leaders as "capable of healing, empowering, and even reconciling broader society." I hesitate to necessarily link women with healing and peacebuilding, even if this is an outcome of the mobilization. Indeed, I argue that much of the recent work on Colombia's women's organizations focuses on peacebuilding (for example, Rojas 2009; Restrepo 2016); mobilization around gender justice is not usually the central focus of study.[11]

Indeed, Aroussi (2009) presents a feminist critique of the stereotypical associations of women and peacefulness that are often included in the literature, suggesting that these are mythical and linked to maternal ideologies and sociological and biological traits. Her argument suggests that we tend to focus on women as nurturing peacebuilders (or mobilizing on behalf of others) and that this does not allow the necessary space to understand where women's agency fits within this narrative (see also El-Bushra and Gardner 2016; Goetz and Jenkins 2016). The high-risk feminism framework offers this space, allowing for an analysis of the motivations with which women justify their mobilization. These are not necessarily related to the wider landscape of healing society more broadly. It is important to see women's mobilization as an act of resistance to protect themselves, and not necessarily in the interest of others. While Restrepo aims to change the narrative of women as needy, helpless victims by painting them as potential peacebuilders, my research shows that a further step can be taken: women can overcome victimhood and claim a feminist agency to resist the specific violences they face. This is a specifically feminist project, not necessarily predicated on the greater good of peacebuilding.

Before continuing, it is important to break down the use of the category, "women." Crenshaw (1991, 1243) was one of the first to academically discuss the importance of intersectional analysis. She notes that racism and sexism do not exist on "mutually exclusive terrains" and that there is a need to consider these "intersectional identities . . . [of] women of color." When considered apart, and "in the context of violence against women, this elision of difference in identity politics is problematic, fundamentally because the violence that many women experience is often shaped by other dimensions of their identities, such as race and class" (1991, 1242). Her work focuses on the intersections of race and gender, with the goal of highlighting the need to "account for multiple grounds of identity when considering how the social world is constructed" (1991, 1245). Rodríguez Castro's (2021, 15) work on decolonial feminisms in Colombia draws on Quijano's (2000) colonial matrix of power to document how rural women face violences that are related not only to structures of patriarchal capitalism but also to the "racial white hegemony constructed during colonialism."

In the Colombian context, we cannot speak of "women" as a homogenous category. Women both understand violence and suffer it based on their multiple identities, including race and ethnicity (Marciales Montenegro 2015; Acosta et al. 2018), sexuality (Centro Nacional de Memoria Histórica 2015, 2019), and geography (rural versus urban) (Appelbaum 2003; FIP 2017; Rodriguez Castro 2021), among others.[12] Their expressions of feminism are contingent on these intersecting identities (Gargallo Celentani 2012).

High-Risk Feminism

There is a specific interplay between the social dynamics that facilitate and spur action and the various gendered opportunities and constraints under which women experience and act against violence. The problem with the abovementioned streams of literature is that they do not capture both the specifically gendered identities of the participants involved and the ways in which a high-risk environment influences action in creating a "domain of losses." The organizations studied in this book mobilize not just against war and resulting violence but also against gendered violence and the gendered impacts of war. Doing so puts them at risk for continued violence.

To be sure, one can ask, What does gender have to do with it? Playing with counterfactuals: Are men (and mixed groups) not mobilizing in the face of violence and displacement, as well? The immediate answer is yes. As demonstrated see in the empirical chapters that follow, men and mixed groups did mobilize in El Pozón, Usme, and Bajo Putumayo. The women discussed here could have mobilized with them. Furthermore, they had grievances that could have led them to mobilize as mothers (protecting their children from violence) or as popular feminists (critiquing economic injustice from a gender- and class-based perspective). Notably, however, they did not. Kreft's work might lead us to believe that there is something about the individual-to-collective threat framing of conflict-related sexual violence that sparks women's mobilization. I would argue, here, that using the lens of high-risk mobilization and prospect theory allows us to see how women calculate their potential gains given their current position in a domain of losses (that is, where the risks of gendered violence are not controllable through nonparticipation in mobilization). The potential to benefit from the particular gains that are afforded by joining a women's organization, then, is what sparks mobilization.

High-risk feminism is an original framework that applies a gendered lens to a composite of social movement theories to examine women's mobilization in high-risk contexts. What makes this framework unique is its examination of feminism as coloring women's mobilizational strategies in these settings.

High-risk feminism combines resistance to violence with a gender justice project. It is novel in the sense that it does not rely on narratives of women as vulnerable victims, maternal peacebuilders, or female combatants in a largely male revolutionary movement. Rather, it casts them as protagonists in their own stories: by coming together with other women living in the same domain of losses, participants learn to contextualize their experiences with gendered violence within a larger frame of women's rights. Their subsequent actions are self-serving (in that they allow for participants to reap material and nonmaterial benefits of participation) but also contribute to a wider societal project of gender equality. High-risk feminism is about women gaining agency and using it to try to change the dominant power dynamics that color their daily lives. This feminism, however, is not necessarily premised on a peace project; it is about creating an identity and building social capital around a broader understanding of gender justice that can actually help them to survive.

The component parts of the framework can explain the adaptation of a mobilizational strategy within these violent contexts; the dynamic interactions between the mechanisms explain action—feminist mobilization. The four pillars of the framework (collective identity building, social capital generation, legal framing, and acts of certification) further allow for an understanding of mobilization that is able to consider the importance of emotions and lived realities in action.

The high-risk feminism framework draws on different social movement theories to construct a comprehensive way of understanding high-risk mobilization under a specific set of circumstances, shaped by the power dynamics of gender relations. This book outlines the high-risk feminism framework, further contributing to existing social movement theoretical developments to fill the gaps in the literature—especially as they relate to strategies of feminist resistance—and creates a platform of analysis for contemporary situations of women's mobilization in high-risk contexts.

As mentioned earlier, the existing ways in which women's mobilization is studied do not account for feminist mobilization against gendered dynamics of violence, particularly when the act of mobilizing itself further puts a target on participants' heads. High-risk feminism thus provides descriptive utility: how do we explain what is going on when we see women (who we might not expect to organize) acting collectively? Indeed, high-risk feminism is premised on the idea that contexts of high risk give rise to identities shaped by fear and trauma (that is, identities borne of a domain of losses). In turn, identities can be transformed into mobilizational identities that seek agency amid feelings of impotence (Lerner and Keltner 2001). In the chapters that follow, I draw on social movement theory to explain this feminist mobilization; my reading of these theories is firmly grounded in a feminist understanding of the many gendered power dynamics that exist in contexts of high violence.

Many regions of Colombia, despite the recent peace process, continue to feature pervasive violence and risk, which are experienced in differential ways by marginalized groups such as displaced women. How such groups respond, resist, and actively construct a space protected from pernicious forms of gender violence is the topic of the book. The ways in which women leverage their identity, draw on social ties, and pursue strategic collective action as feminists to resist violence and construct peace has to be understood; whether "feminist" is consciously adopted or rejected as a label (a question that is discussed below), the ways in which the women in this book mobilize are a function of the power dynamics they are governed by and aim to contest and disrupt.

While there exists research that speaks to the ways that women can actively participate in forging peace in their daily environments, feminism as a mobilizational strategy is not widely theorized within the literature on women and conflict/postconflict. High-risk feminism is based on the idea that whether danger comes in the form of physical threats, murder, torture, disappearance, displacement, targeting activists, or revictimization, women who may not otherwise have engaged with feminism draw on repertoires and modify them according to the specific situation. They do not necessarily mobilize for peace, per se, but for gender justice. These repertoires include collective identity building, construction of social capital, framing techniques, and certification practices, all of which are outlined in chapter 3. To make this set of mechanisms operational, I draw on McAdam et al.'s (2001) book, *Dynamics of Contention*, and further incorporate empirical data gathered during fieldwork.

To get to the point where women can overcome barriers to mobilization (such as fear of violent reprisals), however, they need a specific type of leader to frame why engaging in collective action is justifiable. A charismatic leader has the ability to frame the material and nonmaterial benefits of mobilization to potential participants. When everyone occupies the same domain of losses and inaction does not necessarily offer protection, displaced women can be convinced that there is value in joining a collective that affords them agency in an otherwise dire situation.

The second-wave feminist notion that the personal is political captures the concept that relationships usually conceived of as personal are, in fact, shaped by larger power relations in society and that experiences and frustrations previously understood as individual are, in fact, shared by other women. This book articulates an understanding of a highly violent context whose unique and gendered dimensions impact women in a manner differently from men. I use the term "gendered lens" to suggest it is being written from a point of view that appreciates the need for critical reflection on socially constructed power relations when analyzing women's mobilization. I do not, however, take a uniquely second-wave view.[13] Indeed, Rodriguez Castro reminds us to avoid the pitfalls of reproducing colonial feminist discourses, in which "'genderwashing' operates by excluding racial and ethnic experiences by homogenizing women's experiences through using *only* a 'gender lens'" (2020, 15–16; emphasis added). Rather, an intersectional understanding of the influence and intersections of gender, race, culture, and class will also be examined (Gargallo Celentani 2012; Vergara Figueroa and Arboleda Hurtado 2016; Acosta et al. 2018; Rodriguez Castro 2020, 2021).

In terms of theorizing high-risk feminism, I turn to Jasper (2010, 965), who notes that social movement theorists are moving away from grand theories, seeking rather to bridge the gaps between materialism and structuralism. He predicts that the future of social movement theory will be based in approaches that offer a cultural and emotional theory of action. He notes that "serious efforts to grapple with agency must remain close to agents' *lived experience*" and that we "must add emotions and moral visions to the cognitive apparatus that all frameworks have tried to adopt" (973). This book uses methods that aim to give meaning to an understanding of women's mobilization in high-risk contexts, thereby contributing to social movement theory.

What's in a Name? Feminism and Mobilization

In this book I employ the concept of feminism both deliberately and cautiously; in Latin America, the word and the concept are contested on multiple levels.[14] Understandings of feminism are varied, depending on time, and place, "in the wrongs to which it responds and the methods it mobilizes to address them" (Cockburn 2013a, 28). Rodriguez Castro's (2020, 2021) work on decolonial feminist struggles is essential reading when it comes to understanding what it means to construct "feminisms from below" in Colombia. Citing Bastian Duarte (2012, 153), she reminds us, that "feminist discourse in Latin America has also been implicated in a 'racist, classist, and heterosexist bias' through a monopolization by the 'white and mestiza urban middle-class elite'" (Rodriguez Castro 2020, 2). Indeed, reflecting on the First International Seminar, "Afrodiasporic Feminist Conspiracy," held in Cali in 2011, Vergara Figueroa and Arboleda Hurtado (2016, 125) note, "Although most of the leaders of these organizations did not see themselves as feminists prior to the conference, their narratives and actions demonstrated their deep commitment to overthrow gender and ethno-racial inequalities. There is a strong sense of agreement about the fact that our main intellectual and political concerns relate to the deconstruction of essentialist and controlling images used to represent Black/Afro-descendent Women."

Some of the women's organizations I have worked with readily adopt a feminist label, while others reject it with a wave of the hand. A woman in Mocoa told me, "No, we don't really think of ourselves as feminists or antimilitarists (*antimilitaristas*), we believe in social fabric . . . and how we transform ourselves."[15] Other organizations I have worked with find the concept loaded with neocolonialist overtones that do not mesh with their organizational ethos; they reject "suit-wearing feminism" in favor of contextually grounded intersectional brands of feminism "in a woman's body and face." My conversations with some organizations were seemingly similar to those of Rodriguez Castro (2020, 16), whose interlocutors also qualified their understandings of feminism as a "form of resistance and re-existence" by necessarily linking them with other identifiers, including Black, popular, campesina, or agrarian. This is, in part, owing to a strong middle-class Colombian feminist movement that struggles to recognize diversity, including racial and ethnic experiences (Lozano 2016, in Rodriguez Castro 2020).

Gargallo Celentani (2012, 125, 129) notes that Indigenous and Afro-Latina women have multiple and interesting understandings of concepts such as empowerment, feminism, and women's rights and that they might reject adopting the label "feminist," not because they disagree with the concept but rather because they see "feminist NGOs" as imposing projects that do not include their community/ancestral practices, or they reject the idea of "hegemonic feminism as a political movement."[16] Moreover, their intersecting identities often link them to other, mixed-sex groups from whom they do not want to distance or isolate themselves, particularly given shared histories of racialized violences (Gargallo Celentani 2012; Marciales Montenegro 2015)

On the other hand, some groups whole-heartedly self-identify as radical feminists. A member of the Liga in Turbaco told me, "There are various types of feminism, and the Doctora [leader of the organization] is a radical feminist. . . . Here, there are women who say, yes, we are feminists! There are others who say no. But the organization itself is feminist in its very essence. We support women's rights." When I asked if she was a feminist, she replied, "Me, yes. I am a feminist. I am studying it a lot right now."[17] It was the leader of the Liga who first introduced her to the language of feminism when the organization began in the late 1990s, and this framing of the organization's strategies and activities remains strong to the present day.

I do not wish to replicate unequal, colonial power dynamics by assigning a label to a group or organization that has deliberately and consciously decided not to identify with this concept. The choice to self-identify as a feminist can be a loaded and political decision, and one that cannot and should not be essentialized or simplified merely to facilitate my own academic understandings and explanations of women's mobilization. Far from this, I am using the word as qualitative descriptor to highlight, at a profound level, the women's organizations studied here. They promote women's rights in a context where they have identified gendered power dynamics that negatively impact daily life, experiences of conflict, access to justice, and lived realities of peace. Cockburn (2012), found that, when asking women about their analyses of violence and war and why they choose to organize as women, "the answers I hear add up to a kind of feminism—that is to say not a set of genes but a set of ideas, a political ideology." She continues to define her understanding of antiwar feminism: "It involves a critique of the meaning and operation of power itself—women often choose to organize in prefigurative ways that exchange 'power over' (domination) to 'power to' (capability)." In each chapter, I attempt to use empirical data to explain women's understandings of their strategies and actions and to use their own words to draw conclusions about their agency.

While this caveat about the use of the term *feminism* is important to state up front, the this book examines feminist mobilization in high-risk contexts, in that it reflects a "deep commitment to overthrow gender and ethno-racial inequalities" (Vergara Figueroa and Arboleda Hurtado 2016, 125). More than simply women who mobilize for peace or for their children (neither of which are ignoble causes, to be sure), this book focuses on the women whose experiences with the violence that comes from war catalyze them into a mobilization for gender justice more broadly.

Research Design

In selecting case studies for this book, I chose to work with organizations whose members have suffered multiple types of violence, including displacement, and who continue to live and work in violent contexts. This is in keeping with work that cautions against focusing only on women's experiences of conflict-related sexual violence and looks at the broader effects of, for example, forced displacement (see Meertens 2012). To ensure comparability, the groups in chapters 4 and 5 possess similar qualities, including size, socioeconomic status, ethnic makeup, experiences of displacement, experiences of sexual/physical violence, and time since establishment. In keeping with Mills's (1843) indirect method of difference, and by selecting within the parameters of the possibility principle (Mahoney and Goertz 2004), I also chose a case wherein a group of displaced women (in Riohacha, La Guajira) possess a similar set of characteristics (violent social context, experiences with displacement, ongoing violence, and profiles of potential participants), but have not formed any type of organization nor engage in collective action.

In the final chapter, I reflect on the Alianza in Putumayo, an umbrella organization made up of dozens of small-town, grassroots women's organizations. The women of these organizations suffered—and resisted—similar types of violence in this southern province. Their case of high-risk feminism illustrates the durability of women's resistance repertoires—that is, their mobilization over time—along the continuum of conflict, reflecting on the questions posed by Berry (2017, 2018) about barriers to postwar gains and putting qualitative meat on the bones of Webster, Chen, and Beardsley's findings (2019) about the temporal limits to women's empowerment.

The units of analysis for this study are the women's groups themselves. These groups are formed of individuals whose collective discourse is representative of the opinions and beliefs of the organization as a whole. Naturally, there are power dynamics within each group. Empirical evidence was collected from all ranks within the organizations and has been collated and triangulated to present a comprehensive narrative.

With regard to the type of research undertaken in these chapters, it is useful to recall Taylor's (1998, 360) comment: "The goal of those who advocate for feminist research is to make women's experiences visible, render them important, and use them to correct distortions from previous empirical research and theoretical assumptions that fail to recognize the centrality of gender to social life."

Accordingly, the research methods employed in this book were selected based on their ability to shed light on experiences, voices, and opinions that are not always included—or at least included effectively and constructively—in mainstream analyses of high-risk settings. Indeed, while investigator neutrality is important in qualitative projects, it would be disingenuous not to admit that the project design was done in such a way to facilitate the "challenging of gender inequality and empowering [of] women" (Taylor 1998, 358). Using ethnographic methods and adopting a grassroots focus gives granular insight into the daily experiences of women living in violent contexts.

This process of using different methods and sources to gather and substantiate evidence has been cited as "one of the central ways of validating qualitative research" (Richie 2003, 43). In her chapter "Negotiating the Muddiness of Grassroots Field Research," Viterna (2009) notes that triangulation can sometimes be difficult when a lack of formal or informal documentation exists (especially, for example, when factions of the organization are illiterate or only basically educated). She suggests that in these situations, comparing interview data with statements of past behaviors, comparing past with present actions, and conducting interviews with associated actors (about the interviewees themselves) can be a way to "check" statements (Viterna 2009, 293).

Data for this current project were gathered during research trips that span five years in four different regions of Colombia: Turbaco (Bolívar), Usme (Bogotá), Riohacha (La Guajira), and Mocoa and Bajo Putumayo (Putumayo). The fieldwork took the form of interviews, participant observation, archival work, qualitative data analysis, and process tracing. I then used triangulation to gain a hermeneutic understanding (that is, an understanding that considers written, spoken, and other data holistically) of the situation of women's mobilization in Colombia. To protect their safety, I have removed identifying information and used pseudonyms for almost all interlocutors in this book; with their permission, the exceptions are the leaders of the Liga, Afromupaz, and the Alianza, whose names are widely published in various academic and non-academic literature.[18] El Pozón, Turbaco, Usme, Riohacha, Mocoa, and La Dorada are real places, and I refer to them as such, to avoid confusion with other published accounts. La Soledad is a pseudonym—as a relatively small and identifiable neighborhood, interlocutors asked that I not use its true name when writing about their community.

Research took place over time. I first met the Liga in 2015, when peace was very much in the air but not yet consolidated. Efforts continued in earnest the following year, during which time the country voted in a national plebiscite, ultimately rejecting the proposed version of a peace agreement. By the time I began to spend time with the women of Afromupaz in 2017, the peace deal had been amended and pushed through Congress. It was a hopeful moment: the women were working closely with the Alcaldía de Bogotá to materialize their collective reparations. It was in late 2017 and early 2018 that I began to spend time with women living in informal neighborhoods outside Riohacha in La Guajira. These interactions were overshadowed by uncertainty; armed groups were present in the neighborhood and had threatened Estefania, my main contact, and her family. When I first went to Putumayo in 2018, the women I spoke with were highly concerned that violence was returning to the department. Driving around La Dorada and the wider municipality of San Miguel with Sandra, we were accompanied by her government-issued bodyguard, assigned to her after she had received multiple threats from members of armed groups. When I returned a year later, she had fled to Mocoa, after the threats became too serious for her to stay.

This research over time offers us unique insight into how women participate in violent contexts that do not always fit within the formal definition of an armed conflict. The timeline of the Colombian conflict is neither static nor linear; it is increasingly apparent that the end of hostilities with the FARC brought about a reconfiguration, rather than a cessation, of violent hostilities between armed groups. What this book offers, then, is an examination of women's mobilization during moments of conflict, moments of relative calm, and moments of patriarchal backlash. As such, its findings can shed light on the violence women face not only during conflict moments but also during other high-risk times during which they are exposed to brutal and gendered violence.

Chapter Outline

Chapter 2 outlines the theoretical underpinnings of high-risk feminism. It conceptually defines "high risk," to proceed with an understanding of what this term means in the context of the high-risk feminism framework. It then looks at the dynamics of the charismatic bond to explain how a charismatic leader can convince potential participants to overcome barriers to mobilization (fear of violence) by highlighting the material and nonmaterial benefits of doing so within a domain of losses. I then circle back to discuss how prospect theory allows us to understand high-risk collective action that might initially seem irrational.

Chapter 3 engages with the four pillars or strategies of the framework—collective identity, social capital, framing, and certification—to illustrate how women mobilize in high-risk environments.

Chapters 4, 5, and 6 apply the high-risk feminism framework to the book's case studies (Turbaco, Usme, and La Soledad). All chapters give detailed case backgrounds and engage with past literature to outline how mobilization has been understood over time. More centrally, however, the chapters engage with the high-risk feminism framework. The main emphasis is women's mobilization within that framework, based on data gathered from fieldwork. I examine each of the mechanisms in turn. I also use each chapter to further refine the explanation for why women engage in high-risk feminist mobilization. Chapter 6 presents La Soledad, a negative case that provides "inferential leverage" about the casual mechanisms of high-risk feminism as a strategy of feminist resistance (Collier, Mahoney, and Seawright 2010, 100).

The conclusion turns to the case of the Alianza in Putumayo; this case examines high-risk feminism over time. It highlights a scenario where women who actively mobilized for women's empowerment during the conflict are now being targeted for this social mobilization in an area where armed groups want social control, and for transgressing gender norms that do not look favorably on women's empowerment. This final chapter offers reflections about the utility of high-risk feminism to social movement theory more generally. It makes overall comments about both why and how women mobilize in contexts of high risk. It provides a summary of findings and an overview of the book's contribution to theory. It postulates on potential comparative cases that could further nuance and circumscribe the utility of high-risk feminism.

The chapter situates high-risk feminism in the global context, wherein international agendas increasingly recognize women's unique experiences of war and promote women in what the United Nations Security Council (2000) has called their "important role" in peacebuilding. It suggests that there is room to complicate our essentialized understandings of women's roles in conflict and postconflict settings, particularly when such roles can expose them to more danger. Finally, it ends with a discussion of what the localized experiences and expressions of high-risk feminism in Colombia can offer to our understandings of feminist movements and leadership more broadly.

2

Why Women Mobilize in
High-Risk Contexts

● ● ● ● ● ● ● ● ● ● ● ● ● ● ● ● ● ● ● ●

The established paramilitary order . . .
implied a specific model of being a
woman that reproduced traditional and
patriarchal gender arrangements.
Women had to accommodate to what
traditional culture would expect of
them: they were restricted to the private
sphere, to their homes, to raise children,
to take care of the house, to be disci-
plined and to show respect to male and
paramilitary authority. Within this
framework, all behavior and practices
that did not conform to the model were
considered "transgressive" and therefore
stigmatized. . . . They were also labelled
as "gossipers," and for that reason . . .
they were punished and subjected to
public scorn: "Women were punished
because they were very gossipy. [The
paramilitaries] did not like to see a group
of women sitting anywhere."
—Centro Nacional de Memoria
Histórica (2011, 83–84)

Engaging in nonviolent collective action during wartime can be dangerous. Armed groups seeking social and territorial control in Colombia did not look favorably on attempts by civilians to resist and reject violence, although there is variation both in civilians' experience of resistance and in armed groups' established orders (see Masullo 2015; Arjona 2016; Kaplan 2017). For the most part, however, these experiences have not been analyzed or differentiated using a gendered lens, either generally (Krause 2019) or in the case of Colombia.[1]

When women mobilize under imposed social order, they run additional risks. The transgression of accepted gender roles and norms means that their work is interpreted as doubly subversive. And when women mobilize for gender justice, they add yet another layer of risk to their collective action: not only do their feminist goals challenge armed groups and the militarized masculinities they perform, but they also challenge the status quo. A lens that can account for gendered power dynamics can reveal that women are exposed to violence not only as a strategy of territorial and social control but also as an expression of backlash to their refusal to kowtow to imposed gender norms.

The violence that women in Colombia faced during the armed conflict was multifaceted and meted out by various actors, including paramilitaries, guerillas, and the armed forces. Sexual violence was prevalent—more than 34,000 events have been registered with the country's Victims, Unit (Unidad para las Víctimas 2020). Scholars of sexual violence delineate different motivations for rape in conflict. Wood (2018) notes that it can either be a top-down strategy of war (a policy) or a tolerated behavior that leadership does not prevent from happening (a practice). In a similar vein, Davies and True (2015, 497) find that sexual and gender-based violence in conflict contexts—and particularly rape—has two main explanations: either it can be an opportunistic crime facilitated by the conflict itself, or it can be used for the purpose of "war gain or plunder," a strategy that facilitates access to resources and power.

Swaine (2018) reminds us that conflict-related violence extends beyond sexual violence and rape and occurs throughout and into the aftermath of conflict (2018).[2] Boesten (2014) asks us to interrogate whether sexual violence in wartime has the same social "roots" as rape in peacetime, breaking down binaries of "extraordinary" versus "ordinary" sexual aggression. In the Colombian context, Meertens (2001) and Lemaitre and Sandvik (2013, 2014) further show that displacement has deeply gendered implications. For many of the women I encountered in my research, homicide also has gendered implications, insofar as when men are killed, their widows were left without income and with children to care for.

To return to Cockburn's (2004, 30) gendered continuum of violence, when we examine armed conflict through a gendered lens, it becomes apparent that gender relations "[produce] effects at three interrelated sites: first, the specificity of male and female bodies; secondly, their relative positioning in society;

and third, the gender ideologies in play." Beyond becoming victims simply for occupying contested territories, women were also subject to highly gendered social orders. This is evident in the quote from the Centro de Nacional Memoria Histórica report at the beginning of this chapter; women who did not conform to accepted gender roles were stigmatized and ultimately punished.[3] We saw that even the act of women sitting together was considered transgressive: women who "gossiped" were a threat to imposed order. These dynamics were not isolated to San Onofre (where the above observation was made); these logics of social order dominated in other parts of the country as well, including in Montes de María, La Guajira, Putumayo, and other areas (Centro Nacional de Memoria Histórica 2010, 2011, 2012). When women dared to contest these established orders, they exposed themselves to retributive punishment. This is one of the factors that makes high-risk feminism high risk.

I have argued elsewhere that the violent imposition of social order that punishes women for taking leadership roles continues today in Colombia, particularly in areas where paramilitary successors violently battle for territorial control (Zulver 2021). While male social leaders are more likely to be killed for their activism (Prem et al. 2018), women social leaders are targeted with additional violences: sexual violence, threats to their families, and defamation campaigns that question their ability to participate in social life (see Tapias Torrado 2019). Moreover, targeting and enacting violence against a woman social leader seeks to undermine a social and political process based on years of her overcoming barriers to participation. As an interlocutor once told me for a journalistic article, "When you lose a woman leader, you also lose an entire process of political empowerment that was able to break stereotypes to get her to that role" (Zulver and Janetsky 2020).

Yet despite the risks associated with doing so, the women I spent time with during the research for this book continued to mobilize and make demands for gender justice. They did so during the dark days of the paramilitary incursion in the late 1990s and early 2000s, after the demobilization process resulting from passage of the Justice and Peace Law in 2005, and into Colombia's so-called postconflict era, following the signing of the peace agreement with the FARC rebels.

When the risks of mobilizing could be death or grievous bodily harm, why do some women choose to engage in grassroots mobilization anyway? While we might expect women to protect themselves from further exposure to violence (that is, not to mobilize), against the odds, we see groups of women organizing in the streets of marginalized, dangerous neighborhoods to defend their rights and promote gender justice. Most of the women I met during my research had never participated publicly in any sort of organization before; it was their experiences with the conflict that catalyzed their actions. In this way, some women are mobilizing because of, not despite, the violence they face. Rather than presenting an obstacle or disincentive to mobilize, violence gives rise to a specific kind of gendered resistance in which some women make gendered calculations about particularly gendered risks.

Gendering High-Risk Collective Action

A long academic tradition investigates this very question (see, for example, Loveman 1998; McAdam 1986, 1988). What this book uniquely adds is its application of feminism as a strategy of resistance in the face of high risk. Moreover, it combines the use of two existing theories to explain how women move from inaction to action: combining the charismatic bond (whereby a charismatic leader creates a specific bond with potential participants) and prospect theory (whereby taking on a level of risk is framed as justifiable within a domain of losses) allows us to see this shift in participants' behavior.

As outlined in chapter 1, however, the question emerges, What does gender have to do with it? Indeed, men mobilize in risky settings too, in their roles and identities as activists, union members, workers, students, Indigenous people, Afro-Colombians, and environmental defenders, among others. Yet what I find interesting is that the women discussed in this book had the option to mobilize with mixed organizations or not to mobilize at all. For them, deciding to mobilize with a group of women was, and continues to be, a deliberate decision. When it comes to high-risk feminism, their gendered mobilization was a response to gendered violence and brought with it risks that are shaped by gendered social order.

That women participate in mobilization in a context that has the potential to attract retributive violence requires explanation. Cockburn (2004, 28) notes that gender is about "relation" and that studies of preconflict, conflict, and postconflict moments require that we use a gendered lens to understand the power dynamics at play and how these are relational. Indeed, such feminist analysis observes that "the differentiation and relative positioning of women and men is seen as an important ordering principle that pervades the system of power and is sometimes its very embodiment" (28).

The women whose stories feature in this book are—or became over time— keenly aware of the gendered power differentials that govern the contexts in which they live. Indeed, Kreft (2019) argues that victims of conflict-related sexual violence come to frame their experiences of conflict as a threat against all women and are thereby moved to participate in collective action in their communities. I would go a step further, however, to argue that when women choose to resist, they are seen as transgressing rigid social orders, which, in turn, makes them targets for ongoing and retributive (backlash) violence. The risk of violence clearly presents a barrier to mobilization. What dynamics are at play that catalyze action in a way that can effectively overcome these barriers? Why are women willing to expose themselves to compounding gendered violences to pursue gender justice?

Women's engagement in high-risk feminist mobilization has to do with the creation of a bond between an auspicious leader and a population looking for leadership. This dynamic is consistent with what Madsen and Snow (1991) call the "charismatic bond," a connection forged between a particular type of leader and a community struggling to cope. Leadership is key to explaining the specific types of mobilization outlined in this book. A leader must have the ability to convince people to mobilize, despite the risks associated with doing so. She does so by highlighting that in a domain of losses (where even inaction does not guarantee safety), the nonmaterial benefits of collective identity and belonging make it worthwhile. Moreover, she orchestrates collective actions that lead to small successes over time; in this way, participants are reassured that their participation can modify their day-to-day experiences of conflict; this deep, personal, lived relationship with violence reaffirms an individual's participation and encourages new recruitment. It is important to highlight that once a bond is built between a leader and her followers, the nonmaterial benefits and incremental successes of participation reinforce continued participation. The ensuing collective action is shaped around ideas of gender justice—projects that aim to ameliorate the situation of women by restoring their ability to live dignified lives.

Defining High Risk

For the most part, in the areas where I conducted fieldwork between 2015 and 2019, extreme violence was no longer a feature of everyday life. In Turbaco, Usme, and Riohacha, women's daily lives were much safer than they had been a decade and a half earlier, when they first began to mobilize. Despite this, mobilizing for gender justice was still not a safe activity, even at the time of research.

In 2010 María Eugenia was kidnapped and raped for her leadership role. It was shortly after I made my final visit to Riohacha in 2018 that Estefania called to tell me she had moved to Medellín after a violent incident, when armed men broke into her house and tried to harm her because of the cases of sexual violence she denounced to the authorities through her role in a local victims' committee. Violence began to increase in the wake of the 2016 demobilization of the FARC and attacks against social leaders increase in numbers (see INDEPAZ 2021), and many of the women I still communicate with privately share that they are increasingly worried about their safety and that of their family and that "things are going back to how they were before." In this book, accordingly, I draw on Cockburn's (2004, 43) continuum of violence to provide evidence that different moments of conflict (prewar, war, postwar) are overshadowed by the gendered power relations of war: "To consider one moment in this flux in the absence of the next is arbitrary."

My research was, in part, historical, insofar as my interlocutors spoke to me about violences of the past and about how, despite these adverse contexts, they decided to come together with other women in the pursuit of gender justice. The research also took place in a changing context of risk. While looking to the past, and even looking at the changes that have taken place since I conducted my research, I have often been struck by Nordstrom's (2004) understanding of "the tomorrows of violence." Violence, she notes, "isn't a passing phenomenon that momentarily challenges a stable system, leaving a scar but no lasting effects after it has passed. Violence becomes a determining fact in shaping reality as people *will* know it, in the future. Part of the way violence is carried into the future is through creating a hegemony of enduring violence across the length and breadth of the commonplace world, present and future" (226). These tomorrows—and the very fact that they are possible—shape the high-risk nature of the feminism that this book discusses. This is why my definition of high risk is not confined to a conflict context. Rather, *high risk* is a qualitative label I give to situations where violence—both lethal and nonlethal—is a possibility.

What exactly does high risk entail? For Loveman (1998, 487), what differentiated normal collective action from the high-risk variety in the Southern Cone was the characterization of a what Corradi, Fagen, and Garretón Merino (1992, 1) call a "culture of fear," wherein "the intentional propagation by a regime of a climate of uncertainty, insecurity, and terror aims to paralyze forms of collective action. Threats of persecution, arrest, torture, disappearance, or assassination of opponents of the regime are meant to create insurmountable obstacles to collective action; they exacerbate existing incentives to free ride" (Loveman 1998, 487).

For the purposes of this book, a subjective definition of *high risk* is applied (see Ball 2005). Do participants themselves consider that they are engaging in activities that put them and their families at risk of harm? These harms can—and have—been documented over time and include displacement, disappearances, torture, sexual violence, and murder. What is important is whether the conditions on the ground are such that an individual perceives that engaging in collective action is a dangerous activity. "High risk" is a continuous concept, not a binary one, and one that varies across time and space for differently positioned individuals.

Numerous scholars note that understandings of gender-based violence should be grounded in women's own experiences (Menjívar 2011). For example, "new violence" (Wilding 2010, 719), everyday forms of violence (Hume 2009b; Hume and Wilding 2015) and "enduring" violence (Menjívar 2011, 18) are deeply tied to gendered power dynamics, both in conflict settings, postconflict moments, and contexts of urban violence. Indeed, Hume and Wilding (2015, 94) push back against attempts to disconnect "gender violence" from "violence": "this forced compartmentalization not only misses that violence against women takes multiple forms . . . but it also reveals a certain reduction of gender analysis to women and, by default, to what happens in the private sphere." Boesten (2014, 7) further encourages us to think about continuums of violence in terms of the "underpinning norms, values, and institutional structures that normalize certain violence and exceptionalize others." Thus my use of the term *high risk* in this book is based on the situated knowledge of those women with whom I spent time over the years—which is to say, it takes into account their day-to-day experiences, practices, fears, and understandings of the ways in which certain acts and actions they undertake will necessarily involve assuming a level of personal risk.

Making a critical identifier contingent on (subjective) context opens itself to criticism; if violence exists on a continuum, does this mean that high-risk feminism also exists on a continuum? If this is the case, are we likely to see variations of high-risk feminism along this scale, including low- and medium-risk feminism? Just as Loveman (1998) studied incidents of human rights organizations mobilizing in high-risk settings yet did not expand her findings to human rights organizations mobilizing in low-risk settings, there is value in applying the high-risk feminism framework as a tool not only for description but also for explanation. Indeed, Loveman (1998, 478) reflects on McAdam's (1986) work, noting: "the mobilization dynamics of high-risk movements are likely to be qualitatively different from those of low-risk movements." What is important about a high-risk context is the way in which it gives rise to a particular type of leader who is able to form a special bond with participants. Indeed, as Madsen and Snow (1991, 143) note, when it comes to the charismatic bond, "the right moment comes when the incipient followers, feeling rather abruptly unable to cope with the fundamental problems, are ready—and indeed anxious—to assign responsibility for solving these problems to a relative proxy."

Over time, women living in domains of losses develop identities based on fear and trauma; their day-to-day lives are characterized by uncertainty and a lack of power to control their surroundings. This, in turn, can shape feelings of impotence that leave the individual particularly primed to follow a leader who promises the ability to regain agency over one's own life, effectively changing people's perceptions from fear to anger (see Lerner and Keltner 2001), or—in the case of the research presented in this book—from fear to resistance.

Madsen and Snow (1991, 143) argue that psychological crisis is essential to the emergence of a charismatic bond and that the contextual crisis is relatively abrupt: "A more prolonged crisis would have the effect of wholly undermining self-efficacy—not even through a proxy could control be regained," resulting in a response of despondency and withdrawal. In the case of high-risk feminist mobilization, I do not entirely agree with this assertion. Rather, I think that the leader's active use of prospect theory to frame the benefits of mobilization within a domain of losses is key to overcoming the barriers to mobilization. This initial mobilization does not necessarily rest within a circumscribed temporal aperture, at least in terms of how long an individual has lived within said domain of losses.

The authors named above do not detail the characteristics of a community likely to form a charismatic bond with a leader. I argue, however, that there is something about the new neighborhoods where women find themselves that facilitates their mobilization. Indeed, these women did not mobilize as parts of women's organizations when they were living in their houses in the *campo* (countryside), though these areas were also at risk of paramilitary and guerrilla violence—it was from these locations that women were displaced in the first place. What about coming together in new settings made their mobilization possible?

Neighborhood and Social Context

Most of the women I interviewed had lived in rural areas before being displaced to different urban centers. While they were not always isolated on their farms, they were not necessarily living in close quarters with others. Their new neighborhoods therefore facilitated mobilization, as the physical barriers to entry (for example, travel) were removed as an obstacle to participation. Whereas before they may have only seen other women in similar situations of vulnerability when they went into town (to market or to church, for example), once they were displaced, they lived in densely packed neighborhoods and slums. This agglomeration effect, then, is directly related the forming of kinship bonds and social networks: getting to know one's neighbor was not just an act of friendliness, but one of survival. Without engaging in networks of communal cooking or childcare, it would have been impossible for many of the new residents of El Pozón to make ends meet, feed their children, or build shelter.

Indeed, as Bantjes (2007, 12) observes, Marx and Engels note of working-class culture that physical proximity "guarantees face-to-face relationships that facilitate common concern." In the absence of aid from anyone else, people help one another out, building a sense of community solidarity. While Marx saw these communities as "spontaneous expressions of the communist spirit" (Bantjes 2007, 12), for displaced women they serve as the initial source of coming into daily contact with other women suffering similar and ongoing violences.

Second, as a collective, these women operate in the same domain of losses, which they discover only when they are in physical proximity to one another. They may not know or identify this shared condition until it is revealed through the experiences of finding solidarity, voice, and resistance, as directed by the charismatic leader. Interviewees in Turbaco, for example, discussed their first realizations that they were not alone in their struggle: "When we started to talk, we realized that each of us wasn't alone. This is something crucial, fundamental. . . . It was the process that gave the organization its strength" (in Thomas Davis and Zulver 2015). Living in the same neighborhood allowed individuals to come to the realization that they were all living in an environment in which, to avoid (further) violence, their decisionmaking should involve minimizing losses instead of strictly maximizing gains (see Elster 1987). Such a realization becomes important in the context of how leaders frame mobilization.

Third, for many of these women, living as displaced people in their new neighborhoods was the first time they interacted with aid organizations. These interactions left much to be desired when it came to specifically women's issues. Both Patricia Guerrero and María Eugenia Urrutia, leaders of the organizations explored in the following chapters, told me that the aid organizations in El Pozón and Usme did not recognize the differential impact that conflict has on women and women's specific needs following displacement. The victims in question were able to see this with their own eyes and, when presented with an alternative—that is, mobilizing as women, for women—were more inclined to do so.

In the Madsen and Snow (1991, 142) context, then, a specific community of individuals who no longer feel they can cope is ripe for the appearance of a charismatic leader in whom they can place their faith. In this way, the charismatic bond is a "product of circumstance" whereby a would-be leader must "provide for [her] audience through a combination of personal attributes and seemingly effective actions."

Charismatic Leadership

Feminist leadership is a central feature of high-risk feminist mobilization. It is not, however, just any leadership that functions as a necessary condition for mobilization. Yet within social movement studies, understandings of leadership remain unconvincing in terms of explaining why women engage in high-risk collective action. For example, McAdam's (1982, 47) studies of mobilization suggest that leaders are recycled from other movements: in the context of a political opportunity, there is a need for recognized leaders, who can be "called upon to lend their prestige and organizing skills to the incipient movement." Leaders, for McAdam, come from existing organizations, which form the base of a new insurgency. Without someone with prior experience to guide collective action, an aggrieved population will lack the capacity to act, even if they have the chance to do so. This is a resource-based explanation, with the existing skills (such as organizing, education levels, personal connections, and experience) representing the resources that the leaders bring to the new movement.

Approaching the leadership question from a different angle, Erickson Nepstad and Bob (2006) ask, When do leaders matter? Like others, they note that the significance of leadership in collective action is relatively understudied (Morris and Staggenborg 2004; Eatwell 2006; Ganz 2009, 2010; Robnett 2013). Consequently, they note that scholars talk about recruitment, resource mobilizing processes, protest events, and frames without referencing the leaders who invent these strategies. As a potential solution, Erickson Nepstad and Bob (2006, 1) make reference to "leadership capital," a broad term that has cultural (knowledge, skills, and abilities), social (ties to activist communities), and symbolic (charisma, respect, and moral authority) aspects. Like McAdam (1982) and Morris and Staggenborg (2004), however, they hypothesize that leaders will be more likely to successfully mobilize preexisting organizations (rather than establish an organization from scratch) at opportune political movements, providing they have leadership capital (Erickson Nepstad and Bob 2006, 8).

These existing studies on leadership and social movements prove insufficient to explain the high-risk action studied in this book. Notably, my research shows that not all leaders have previous organizational experience, as McAdam (1982) might suggest. It is also not enough to uncritically posit that a "good" or "strong" leader can convince a community to mobilize, particularly when this involves exposing oneself to ongoing and augmented dangers. Leaders need to be sufficiently persuasive to encourage mobilization, meaning that they need to be seen as legitimate in the eyes of the community. Moreover, as theorists from the resource mobilization tradition tell us, a leader also needs to be able to gain access to (at least basic) organizational and other resources to make sustained collective action possible (McCarthy and Zald 1977).

There is value here in returning to Max Weber's trifold typology of leadership. For him, the third type of leader that will rise in a time of crisis is a charismatic leader.[4] A charismatic leader gains legitimacy on the grounds of "the devotion to the exceptional sanctity, heroism, or exemplary character of an individual person, and of the normative patterns or order revealed or ordained by [her]" (Weber 1978, 215). Baker (1982, 335) says that to move beyond Weber, "scholars need to construct empirically based typologies that can tap the kinds of leadership within [social movement organizations] over time and can also relate organizational characteristics to expected bases of authority." This is one of the theoretical contributions that this book makes: an investigation of feminist leadership in high-risk settings where we would expect aggrieved individuals not to mobilize.

In his study of agricultural workers in California, Ganz (2009, 8) notes that "in times of crisis, particularly talented leaders may become symbols of hope, sources of inspiration for their constituents." He further explains that leadership, organization, and strategy are the factors that allow small groups of actors (the Davids) to win against their adversaries (the Goliaths). In terms of leadership, he tells us, "The greater an organization's strategic capacity [the ability to devise good strategy], the more informed, creative, and responsive its strategic choices can be and the better able it is to take advantage of moments of unique opportunity to reconfigure itself for effective action. An organization's strategic capacity . . . is a function of who its leaders are—their identities, networks, and tactical experiences—and how they structure their interactions with each other and their environment with respect to resource flows, accountability, and deliberation" (8).

Eatwell (2006, 153) acknowledges that the theory of charisma has moved on very little since Weber's formulations. His discussion of fascism in twentieth-century Europe points out the shortcomings of the Weberian charismatic figure but concludes that there is no need to do away with the concept in its totality. Thus, despite Ganz's (2010, 528) throwaway comment that we have moved beyond the need to talk about charismatic leaders, this is not necessarily the case when it comes to high-risk feminism. While our definition can perhaps move beyond Weber's archetypal definition (and will do so descriptively throughout the remainder of this book), for the purposes of high-risk feminist mobilization we can talk about the need for a charismatic leader.

Just as it is unsatisfying to posit that a good or strong leader can convince a population to mobilize, it is further insufficient to uncritically state that a charismatic leader is able to do the same task. What Madsen and Snow add to the discussion is the context in which these charismatic leaders emerge. They further focus on the nature of the "following which rallies to the emergent leader's banner" (1991, 1). If it is assumed that individuals do not make irrational decisions, it must also be assumed that the followers of a charismatic leader—in the present circumstances, those who choose to join a high-risk feminist organization—see it as within their best interests to do so (see Muller and Opp 1986). What is it, then, about the followers that makes them willing to expose themselves to risk through mobilization?

Here, Madsen and Snow (1991, 15) outline the charismatic bond. The crux of this concept is that people are willing to accept a proxy control as part of a strategy of psychological self-preservation. That is, "[People] in despair restore their own sense of coping ability by linking themselves to a dominant and seemingly effective figure—a leader who seems to be acting in their behalf, but also seems to be not beyond their influence (if only because that leader is "known" to be devoted to their interests and therefore reachable through petition and supplication)."

During this process, the individual bonds with the leader and develops a group identification with other followers. This bonding "with the leader, and also with the group, restores a sense of security and of competency, which ultimately may provide the foundation for renewed autonomy" (Madsen and Snow 1991, 15). Potential leaders, then, must be able to fix (or at least be perceived as able to fix) the problems that are associated with the stress or chaos. They must possess strong rhetorical skills and "project an aura of knowledge, strength, and effectiveness" (Madsen and Snow 1991, 21). By incorporating Ganz's (2009) argument about strategic capacity and the ability to creatively mobilize resources, we see that a charismatic leader has the unique ability to mobilize a population that otherwise might not have participated in collective action.

In high-risk contexts, women worry about the ongoing threat of violence in its many forms. The idea of mobilizing as women necessarily implies exposing oneself to even more violence. In the case of displaced women in Colombia, leadership is the key factor in explaining the "why" dynamic of mobilization. Research for this book also shows that strong leadership is an important factor for the establishment and early days of an organization. Without the leadership of Guerrero (of the Liga) and Urrutia (of Afromupaz), it is unlikely that these organizations would have come into existence. This, of course, involves hypothesizing on counterfactuals. With that said, the women in Riohacha living in similar circumstances to those in both Turbaco and Usme have not mobilized. Crucially, they also lack a source of charismatic leadership.

The way rank-and-file members of the organizations speak about their leaders falls within Weber's (1978) definition of a charismatic leader. When I once asked a member of the Liga what would happen if Guerrero was were no longer able to lead the organization, she became visibly upset and replied, "I can't even think about that. *La Doctora* [Guerrero] is a fundamental part of the organization and we love her very much. She has offered us love and kindness and we all recognize the skills that she has. She is a very wise woman and everything that we do as an organization, we ask her to give her point of view on it first. There is a good team within the Liga but it wouldn't be the same without her."[5]

It is problematic, however, to say that we can explain the "why" of high-risk feminism social movements based on the random or lucky appearance of a charismatic leader, without whom the organization would either cease to exist or never would have been created in the first place. Indeed, from a feminist point of view it is important to avoid the pitfalls of idealizing a single leader figure, particularly as this might pose risks for a wider feminist agenda, given that strict and hierarchical understandings of leadership may be at odds with the more egalitarian visions of the future promoted by feminists. Robnett (2013, 5), for example, contrasts different levels of leadership between Black men, Black women, and white women within the civil rights movement and notes that "leadership . . . is often comprised of multiple levels" and is "determined largely by socially constructed and culturally embedded understandings of who should lead." Speaking about radical feminist and lesbian-feminist groups, Baker (1982, 325) outlines a "radical antibureaucratic view of leadership" premised on an understanding of every woman's potential capacity for leadership, which can be developed over time, thus creating a feminist "power" that is based not in logics of domination but in "a transferable source of energy or initiative."

Within the context of high risk, there is a need for a charismatic leader who has the foresight to develop a charismatic bond through creative and strategic framing of the benefits of doing so, and of turning fear to anger or resistance. What is key in the case of high-risk feminist mobilization is a leader's ability to frame participation as justifiable to potential members. To a certain extent, this also involves successful strategizing and the ability to accrue at least basic resources for mobilization. Such recruitment is particularly tough in a high-risk situation, where it is difficult to convince people to take part in an activity that may expose them to further expressions of violence.

What this book adds to the discussion, then, is an articulated and empirically grounded discussion of the dynamics that constitute the charismatic bond. That is, by examining how a charismatic leader convinces participants to act we can better understand why women mobilize despite the risks that doing so naturally entails. Moreover, it attempts to take away some of the saintlike zeal with which scholars sometimes speak about charismatic leaders and replace this with contextualized explanations and descriptions of how these leaders are able to build bonds with a community in need. Ganz (2010, 4) succinctly summarizes this by noting that "commitment to a shared future and the consequence of a shared past transform an exchange into a relationship." Indeed, during research, I sometimes found myself struck by some of the tensions I witnessed between leadership and members of the organizations. These observations are further articulated in the empirical chapters to reflect on the implications of the sustainability of charismatic leadership over time and to account for different models and understandings of leadership that do not necessarily conform to hierarchical or vertical power structures.

As the upcoming empirical chapters document, members of the Liga de Mujeres Desplazadas provide multiple examples of how Guerrero always offers them *cariño* (love. affection, care), especially in times of need, and fights for their dignity.[6] Afromupaz members refer to Urrutia as a "very humane person" and their "mother hen figure."[7] Moreover, in the case of both leaders, participants and institutional officials alike speak of their specific and creative abilities to connect and link institutions and organizations in a way that others do not.[8]

Leadership is crucial for explaining high-risk feminist movements. Yet it is not just leadership as a good in itself, but rather a leader's ability to create a bond with participants in order to spur action, as will be outlined in the following section.

Building the Charismatic Bond: Using Prospect Theory to Spur Action

Overcoming the barriers to high-risk feminist collective action requires the presence not only of a charismatic leader but also of a bond the leader is able to create with her followers. Indeed, as Viterna (2006, 6) notes, a movement's power lies in its ability to amass participants, and therefore understanding how individuals initially come to participate in a movement is key to better understanding the occurrence of social mobilization. How does a charismatic leader convince a group to mobilize in a high-risk context?

Borrowing from the world of behavioral economics, prospect theory offers a useful tool for understanding a charismatic leader's framing strategies. First outlined by Kahneman and Tversky (1979), and later revised by the same authors (1992), prospect theory provides insight into why people show inconsistent preferences when the same choice is presented in different forms. The key elements of the theory are a value function that is concave for gains, convex for losses, and steeper for losses than gains, and a nonlinear transformation of the probability scale, which overweights small probabilities and underweights moderate and high probabilities (Kahneman and Tversky 1992, 297–298).

As Weyland (2004, 40) observes, "people act quite differently depending on whether they face gains or losses." Prospect theory centers on the contention that "actors view outcomes not in terms of their final utility but as losses or gains relative to a reference point. This frame helps organize information and guide behavior" (Schenoni, Braniff, and Battaglino 2020, 39). When compared with expected-utility theory, it allows for a "positive rather than normative account for human behavior under conditions of risk" (Schenoni, Braniff, and Battaglino 2020, 39).

Other scholars have drawn on behavioral economics, including prospect theory, to explain people's preferences for action during conflict. For example, Voors et al. (2012) examine the causal effect of exposure to violence on behavior, including proneness to risk-taking. Using survey data from Burundi, they found that people who had experienced or been exposed to violent attacks displayed more altruistic behavior and were more risk-seeking (ibid., 943). On the other hand, another experiment in Afghanistan found that people who have been exposed to violence value a "certainty premium," which may be at odds with prospect theory explanations (Callen et al. 2014, 125). Still others use an appraisal tendency approach to assess how emotions trigger changes in the actions people take, both to respond to the event and into the future. Lerner and Keltner (2001, 148) found that fear and anger have opposite effects on risk perception and that the sense of certainty and control associated with anger led angry individuals to make risk-seeking choices. They note that different appraisals of certainty and control define both fear and anger and that these two emotions activate "sharply contrasting perceptions of risk" (Lerner and Keltner 2001, 156).

In the case of high-risk feminism, charismatic leaders are skilled at turning frames of fear into frames of anger and resistance. They can convincingly show women that when operating in the domain of losses, joining a women's organization allows for potential benefits, whereas not joining does little in terms of obtaining a higher certainty premium. What prospect theory adds to this book, then, is the understanding that women operating in the domain of losses value incremental material and nonmaterial benefits over inaction, which does not actually guarantee safety. Nonparticipation is an option, but a person can still be targeted for further violence even if not participating, given the generalized context of conflict; and the potential benefits of participation (emotional and identity based) are accrued through participation and not as mobilizational outcomes. Therefore, while participation in a women's organization might make someone a target, it becomes preferable to nonparticipation because everyone is operating in the same domain of losses, and benefits come only to those involved and not to the community as a whole.

The reward system here is not outcome based but actions based. It is the role of the charismatic leader to show participants that they will get something out of joining (that is, before they have experienced this). As such, participants' calculus for action is more based on trust (inherent to the charismatic bond) than on what the leader has promised will come true. The right leader can overcome the perceived risks of mobilization, and individuals will most likely remain involved if they begin to perceive (and acquire) the rewards of solidarity.

According to the women I interviewed, this framing was not an a priori understanding before they joined their respective organizations. Indeed, one of Guerrero's main observations when she first arrived in El Pozón was that although women were sad and defeated, they had no understanding of the larger dynamics of their displacement within the context of the civil conflict (Sandvik et al. 2014, 75), and thus they could not shift beyond frames of fear. As Nussbaum (2001) says, we make choices based on values we experience via emotion. It is the job of the charismatic leader to demonstrate to a potential participant that there can be positive and reaffirming emotions that result from participation in collective action. Similarly, Ganz (2010, 6) tells us that "social movement leaders mobilize the emotions that make agency possible." He notes that a choice to act despite fear constitutes courage, and we get courage from hope. We get hope from "credible solutions . . . reports not only of success elsewhere, but direct experience of small successes and small victories." In the Colombian context, the stakes are arguably much higher than those experienced in Ganz's study, which focused on Californian agricultural workers. For this reason, the strategic use of prospect theory by a charismatic leader is key. Framed this way, Ganz's idea of small successes and small victories remains salient. How do these play out in the case of high-risk feminist mobilization?

Nonmaterial Benefits: Belonging and Meaning

What benefits do leaders like Guerrero and Urrutia present to convince potential participants to mobilize? Kahneman and Tversky (1979, 1992) note that behavioral economics observes inconsistent patterns of behavior when the same choice is presented in different forms. Women joining high-risk feminist organizations do not encourage others to do so by highlighting the fact that their membership will expose them to more danger; rather, they emphasize the benefits of coming together to pursue shared goals that aim to improve their quality of life as women.

Here, we can borrow here from Muller and Opp's (1986) work on rational choice and rebellious collective action. The authors note that from a conventional rational choice perspective, people who engage in this behavior would appear to be acting nonrationally, particularly given that free-riding is an option and the benefits of the outcome will apply to all (not just participants). Given that citizens do participate in this behavior, however, the authors note that there must be other incentives that form part of their cost-benefit calculation—"private personal rewards that the individual can expect to receive only by participating." (Muller and Opp 1986, 472). Building on earlier work by Tullock (1971), Silver (1974, 64) refers to these incentives as "psychic income" and talks about the value of "the individual's sense of duty to class, country, democratic institutions, the law, race, humanity." In sum, these authors note that a rational choice model should include the private psychological benefits (private interest theory) of participation.

In the previous chapter, I spoke about identity as a mobilizing factor for collective action in repressive situations. Leaders sell potential participants the idea of collective identity as a nonmaterial benefit (or psychic income) to participation. Leaders were able to recruit participants by explaining that collective action would not only give meaning to their daily struggle but would also foster a sense of belonging or solidarity. This sentiment is echoed in Wood's (2015, 279) study of participation in the Salvadoran Civil War: "In the early years of the war, when the circumstances of risk and the uncertainty of material benefits meant that other reasons for acting were insufficient, acting against the state—in defiance, in outrage, for revenge, for justice, against the fear that could be paralysing—brought emotional 'benefits' to exactly that subset of campesinos who participated."

Madsen and Snow (1991) also note that joining a group that follows a charismatic leader forges bonds between the leader and the participant and between the participants themselves. Emotions matter, as do feelings of belonging to a group. Tied in with this is the concept of giving meaning to daily struggle. O'Hearn's (2009, 498) study of cultures of resistance in Ireland notes that emotions are important to the construction of collective contention because "affective emotions facilitate respect and trust, which enable effective leadership and solidarity." This solidarity generates the morale necessary to continue to act collectively. Goodwin's (1997, 55) Freudian approach (which employs a "libidinal-economy perspective") to group ties posits that "[group members] form a collective identity on the basis of their common attachment—emotional as well as cognitive—to a project, leader, or ideal."[9] Beyond simple measures of shared interests of goals, ideologies, or frames, "groups . . . may be held together . . . by powerful affectual ties of empathy, friendship, and camaraderie that spring from, and are reinforced by, face-to-face interactions" (Goodwin 1997, 55). Finally, Wood (2003, 235) offers us the concept of "pleasure in agency": "that positive affect associated with self-determination, autonomy, self-esteem, efficacy, and pride that come from the successful assertion of intention."

Still others note that emotions are mobilized and framed by leaders to recruit potential participants. Gould's (2015, 259) idea of "emotion management" suggests that activists try to induce emotions when they think they are good for the overall cause, actively working to generate feelings such as "outrage, excitement, joy, guilt, hope for the future, solidarity, and/or commitment to the cause," while simultaneously attempting to mitigate fear, depression, or hopelessness. Tarrow (1998, 112) includes emotions in his ideas of collective action frames, noting that emotions can be used to orient people, and that they can "[convert] passivity into action." Benford (1997, 419) continues with the instrumentalization of emotions or feelings, noting that leaders can use this "vital social movement resource" strategically.

Gould (2015, 259) aptly notes, however, that studying emotions as just another resource in the framing toolkit of the social movement entrepreneur risks skimming over some of their "bodily noncognitive, non-instrumental attributes." In the case of high-risk feminist mobilization, there is something to be said about individuals' feelings of validation that emerge from group membership. Not only were their experiences of violence and displacement painful, but there were others who experienced the same thing and wanted to come together to share the burdens of trauma. An interviewee from Afromupaz recounts the extreme sadness she experienced when her daughter died: "I didn't know anyone. I suffered alone." When her son-in-law was murdered during the time I was conducting fieldwork, however, "it was hard, but not as hard because I had the support and strength of Afromupaz."[10] This is another illustration of the utility of Goodwin's (1997, 66) perspective, which he notes "is especially useful for understanding the discipline and commitment . . . of activists who are involved in . . . high-risk movements."

The words of an interviewee in Turbaco serve as a motto across cases: "The pain of one is the pain of all" (in Thomas Davis and Zulver 2015). When Guerrero entered the neighborhood, she began to coordinate group conversations for women about women's issues and problems. This was an "attractive discourse" to the displaced women who had "already felt direct discrimination for being women, as well as the disinterest of other civic organizations in regards to their specific problems as women" (Sandvik et al. 2014, 17). Indeed, the official written narrative of the Liga notes that the first years of the organization were dedicated to "creating consciousness" and developing "mutual trust between group members" (Sandvik et al. 2014, 17). Guerrero's actions illustrate her capacity as a leader to demonstrate potential nonmaterial benefits of participation— "psychic income": the ability to connect, bond, commiserate, and share. In doing so, participants develop bonds of friendship. "It is [these] affective ties that bind and preserve the networks in the first place, as well as give them much of their causal impact" (Goodwin, Jasper, and Polletta 2001, 8).

As well as a feeling of belonging, participation gives meaning to daily struggles. Ganz (2009, 12) notes that "the intrinsic rewards associated with doing work one loves to do, work one finds inherently meaningful, are far more motivating than extrinsic rewards. For social movement leaders, whose work is deeply rooted in what moral philosopher Charles Taylor calls their 'moral sources,' their work is not a job but a 'vocation' or a 'calling.' As such, its rewards are intrinsic and highly motivating." In the case of displaced women living in precarious situations, there is a value in resisting the daily violences to which they are exposed. This requires an active reframing of fear into anger, and then resistance. Indeed, this could be seen as similar to Wood's (2015, 268) emotional in-process benefits—those "emotion-laden consequences of action experienced only by those participating in that action"—which serve to express "moral outrage, [assert] a claim to dignity, and [give] grounds for pride." Participation gives meaning to suffering: "to express rage at the arbitrary and brutal violence of authorities [is for some] . . . a necessary expression of being human," and this impels action despite high risk and uncertainty (Wood 2015, 268).

For women living in high-risk conditions, the ability to mobilize and make claims for dignity and gender justice is a good in itself. Leaders use this as a recruitment tool, especially when all participants are acting in the same domain of losses. If nonparticipation does not guarantee safety, and participation can bring feelings of agency, belonging, identity, and dignity, why would a person choose not to participate? There is a cascade element to this: as Goodwin and Jasper (2015, 53) highlight, once the initial activists form a group and begin to think of themselves as a movement, they try to recruit others to join their cause.

Success of Incremental Gains

A full explanation of the why of women's participation in high-risk feminist movements requires a look at the successes of incremental gains. While leaders initially recruit participants based on the leveraging of nonmaterial benefits such as identity and emotions (belonging and meaning), there is also something to be said about the way that they frame the successes of incremental gains over time.[11] That is, while participation in a high-risk feminist movement will quite likely not end the situation of violence in the community, it may bring other successes. These successes are club goods—they are only available to participants, thus eliminating the free-rider problem.

Gamson (2015) suggests that it is useful to think of success as "a set of out-comes, recognizing that a given challenging group may receive different scores on equally valid, different measures of outcome." He designs a schema that classifies outcomes as falling into two basic clusters, "one concerned with the fate of the challenging group as an organization and one with the distribution of new advantages to the group's beneficiary" (2015, 414). "New advantages" can be assessed from the perspective of the group, and the aspirations it held at the starting point of the mobilization (Gamson 1990, 34). When it comes to high-risk feminist mobilization, what do these successes look like?

A previous study of the Liga notes that over time, the women:

> showed . . . their appreciation of community organizing as having a positive effect on their lives. They mentioned not only the material gains, especially having their own house, but also a sense of community and a transformation of negative ideas about women and their role in politics and society. Some also pointed to a stronger sense of their own value, and the consequent renegotia-tion of family relations While acknowledging the many difficulties, they also considered that challenging the system is a possibility, resources can be mobilized to do so, and danger can be carefully managed to eventually achieve common goals (Lemaitre and Sandvik 2015, 24–25).

My own research confirms as much, as detailed in chapter 4. What is missing from the Lemaitre and Sandvik assessment, however, is that these benefits allow women to overcome barriers to mobilization—including frames of fear—specifically related to violence.

As noted earlier, Nussbaum's (2001) work highlights the logical role emo-tions can play in decisionmaking. Moreover, Ganz (2009) underscores the need for small successes to generate the hope necessary to overcome fear of mobilization. He asks, how does David (the ostensibly powerless participant) beat Goliath (the powerful participant)? Through strategic and creative fram-ing strategies, he notes, Davids are able to generate motivation: "Motivation enhances creativity by inspiring concentration, enthusiasm, risk taking, persis-tence, and learning. We think more critically when intensely interested in a problem, dissatisfied with the status quo, or experiencing a breach in our expectations. And when we have small successes, they can enhance our creativ-ity, in part because they generate greater motivation" (Ganz 2009, 12).

In a context in which violence is perceived as ongoing and constant (indeed, along a continuum), the hope for a better tomorrow is crucial. To encourage women to participate in a high-risk feminist organization, then, leaders and early risers focus not on (escalating or declining) violence writ large, but rather on a possible world in which action leads to certain protections from violence. The City of Women, in Turbaco, is an example of this. Over time, the women of the Liga dedicated themselves to a specific project—building a housing development. The women knew that owning a house would not necessarily put an end to the daily violences they face, nor prevent paramilitary groups from targeting them, but it offered them a mitigated "tomorrow of violence." That is, building houses would do something to improve their quality of life, despite not being able to eradicate exposure to violence. One member of the Liga told me definitively during fieldwork, "We had the dream of building a dignified house . . . and we could only achieve this through [participation in] the organization."[12] Her statement was in response to my question about why she had continued to participate in the organization after the murder of the husband of a fellow Liga member while he was working for the organization. This interlocutor is committed to the idea of achieving a better future through participation in the organization. The success of achieving a goal—of homeownership—is seen as an incremental gain that justifies continued participation in the Liga over time.

Interestingly, during research I also found that a lack of recent successes contributed to a sense of mobilizational fatigue among members of the Liga. After a meeting of the technical committee, an interviewee privately shared that she feels "stretched too far" and that there is a feeling of frustration among members who do not feel that they "get anything" out of their membership. For example, while women now have a house, they do not have an income to pay for gas, electricity, or food. Moreover, the last time I spoke to members of the Liga about whether they had advanced in their collective reparations process (in 2018), they continued to express disappointment and frustration at the stagnation of the process. This fatigue is perhaps consistent with Epstein's (2015) work in the 1990s on the decline of the women's movement in the United States. She notes that "movements are fragile; the glue that holds them together consists not only in belief in the causes that they represent, but also confidence in their own growing strength" (348). This confidence in growing strength seems, in the case of the Liga, to be directly related to ongoing successes over time.

Conclusion

High-risk collective action presents a puzzle that requires investigation: Why do people choose to expose themselves to potential harm or even death? When women engage in high-risk collective action, they are faced with gendered barriers. These are layered with additional and intersecting barriers based on race and ethnicity, geography, class, (dis)ability, and sexuality, among others.

This book seeks to understand, explain, and document why women in Colombia choose to engage in behavior that potentially puts them at a higher risk for violence. As a feminist contribution, it is deeply interested in how gendered power dynamics influence and shape these behaviors and decisions. I posit that the way these Colombian women overcome barriers to risky collective action can arguably be applied to mixed or men's organizations as well. With that said, in the case of the research presented in this book, gender as a site of power is deeply implicated in women's decisions to participate in the pursuit of gender justice under violent circumstances. I hope that an understanding of how a "high-risk" context is gendered, and how mobilization incurs a potentially gendered response, makes clear that the barriers that women overcome to engage in this type of collective action are shaped by gendered power dynamics. To repeat the quote that begins this chapter, the paramilitaries "did not like to see a group of women sitting anywhere" (Centro Nacional de Memoria Histórica 2011). The assumption that women simply sitting together signaled nefarious behavior that required suppression and punishment illustrates the context of high risk in which women engaged in mobilization.

In a domain of losses, a charismatic leader can compellingly frame the benefits of joining a collective, despite the potential risks this might incur. Indeed, prospect theory tells us that when people find themselves in a losing situation, they are more willing to take risks. This is because the perceived benefits of group membership outweigh the potential for retributive violence, understood in relation to the everydayness of conflict-related violence, which is not avoided through nonparticipation. Armed groups who impose hegemonic, militarized masculinities on the populations they attempt to control mete out violence not only to those who dissent or oppose their incursion but also to the controlled community more generally.

However, a charismatic leader can effectively shift frames of fear to frames of anger or resistance. Indeed, behavioral economics demonstrates that fear and anger have opposite effects on risk perception; people expressing fear viewed risk pessimistically, while angry people express optimistic risk estimates and engage in risk-seeking choices (Lerner and Keltner 2001). The majority of the women in this book had never previously participated in a women's organization. It was through the special bond they developed with the leader that they were able to reframe the world around them, and began to understand the violences they experienced not as inevitable but as unjust and worth taking a stand against.

3

The High-Risk Feminism Framework

• • • • • • • • • • • • • • • • • • • •

> Cada una por su lado no iba a lograr
> nada. (Each one of us by herself wasn't
> going to achieve anything).
> —Interview, City of Women,
> 29 September 2016

Having outlined the "why" of women's high-risk collective action, I now turn to explaining the "how" of their mobilization. What tactics and strategies do women living in contexts shaped by violence and conflict use to express their grievances and meet their goals of gender justice? Within the dynamic of the charismatic bond, how do these strategies reinforce participants' ongoing justification for actions that may expose them to increased risk? Four strategies—or pillars—make up the high-risk feminism framework: collective identity, social capital, framing techniques, and certification.[1]

Recent academic literature and international frameworks—including, for example, the United Nations Women, Peace and Security agenda—have increasingly focused on the ways in which women play fundamental roles in bringing about the ends of conflict and engaging in peacebuilding in postconflict moments. Such a lens is hugely important and represents a growing recognition that women experience conflict and postconflict moments differently from men, based on the gendered power dynamics that govern war. It further recognizes the unique and important role that women can bring to decisionmaking spaces, including those around ceasefires and peace processes (see United Nations Security Council 2000).

Yet the women I spent time with during research for this book do not necessarily frame their mobilization in terms of peace. While peace was important to them and formed part of their lexicon when discussing both their grievances and their hopes for the future, the language they used more often was centered around justice—gender justice. In thinking about this book, then, it did not seem legitimate or authentic to represent the mobilizations I was studying as falling neatly within the category of "women as peacebuilders." I wanted to find a way to discuss their mobilization not in terms of instrumentalizing their potential to reweave community fabric but rather, in terms of the demands they make on wider society—in both conflict and postconflict moments, for gender equality, for reparations, for security, and for feminist peace.

Even when we focus on women as peacebuilders, this type of mobilization is often considered something that simply materializes or happens naturally. Such thinking assumes women's inherent predisposition toward peacefulness, which is often linked explicitly or implicitly to grand narratives of maternal predilections (see Ruddick 1995). The nuts and bolts of how women actually overcome the barriers to mobilization is rarely articulated. Moreover, not all women are peaceful, and many do not fit within the women as victims/men as perpetrators binary (see Sjoberg and Gentry 2015; Sjoberg 2016).

The previous chapter provided answers to some questions: What spurs some women into action, while others prefer to stay at home? What conditions must be present so that women are willing to engage in high-risk collective action in the pursuit of shared goals, when others stay inside to avoid potential backlash or retributive violence? This chapter examines a different question: When women do decide to engage in high-risk collective action, what strategies do they adopt?

In *Regimes and Repertoires,* Tilly (2006, 35) asserts that, "like a jazz trio or an improvisatory theatre group, people who participate in contentious politics normally can play several pieces, but not an infinity." Social movements are often characterized by varying repertoires of collective action—that is, the recurrent, and historically embedded character of contentious politics. For Tilly (2006, 35), repertoires can vary over time and space, but "on the whole, they innovate within limits . . . already established for their place, time, and pair." McAdam et al. (2001, 138) further convey the idea that the term *repertoire* implies that people making public claims adopt scripts they have performed or at least observed before (although different circumstances require different improvisations of the original). They "rework known routines in response to current circumstances. In doing so, they acquire the ability to coordinate, anticipate, represent, and interpret each other's actions" (McAdam et al. 2001, 138).

When it comes to women specifically—as detailed in the previous chapter—high-risk collective action is necessarily shaped by the gendered power dynamics that govern the context in which they mobilize. Violence and resistance to this violence do not take place in a vacuum. Women strategically assess the contexts in which they live and develop tactics and strategies to both protect themselves and react in ways that do not elicit violent response from armed actors. At the micro-level, for example, research has shown how women in Uganda did their cooking in the early morning so that the smoke from their fires mixed with mist and thus did not alert potential violent actors of their whereabouts (Baines and Paddon 2012). In parts of Nigeria, women working in the market established an informal phone chain and would call one another when they could sense that violence was imminent (Bonkat 2014). Sometimes they used their local languages to share sensitive information, as they knew that potentially violent actors would not understand (Bonkat 2014). In my own research, I saw that women in Putumayo strategically choose to not wear identifying clothing when moving around certain parts of the territory, or they change their transportation routes based on where they know armed actors might be (Zulver 2021). Even silence can be strategic: where women know that impunity is rife and access to legal redress is unlikely, keeping quiet can be a tactic of protection (Hume 2009; Hume and Wilding 2019).

High-risk feminism is not simply about self-protection, however. It is also about making claims on gender justice more broadly. Thus the repertoires that emerge out of gendered high-risk collective action involve the development of a "feminine collective consciousness . . . through years of conflict" (Skjelsbaek 2001, 58).

Accepting that women use learned patterns of action implies that daily social life, existing social relations, shared memories, and the logistics of social settings are important in understanding the forms of contention. Drawing on Tilly's (2006, 43) understanding of repertoires, the women's movements in contexts of conflict are both cultural and structural, resting on "shared understandings and their representations in symbols and practices (that is, on culture), but also [responding] to the organization of their social settings" (2006, 43). As the empirical chapters that follow make clear, however, these understandings of the value of collective action do not come a priori and must be nurtured, first by a charismatic leader, then (as the charismatic bond develops) by participants themselves.

The high-risk feminism framework operates on the premise that past and present mobilization can be connected not only by a context of risk (a domain of losses) but also by a series of learned rhetorical and mobilizational acts and tactics constitutive of a repertoire of action. These compound over time, so that once the initial barriers to mobilization are overcome, women are willing to continue mobilizing, as their involvement has become integrated into their identity. In concert, these experiences mold and shape the ways in which certain strategies are used, based on lessons learned from previous mobilizational efforts. It is charismatic leaders who are able to write the initial scripts of repertoires of action, translating them to fit the local context.

Moreover, it is charismatic leaders who are able to devise effective strategies and accrue mobilizational resources in a way that is essential to the ongoing actions of the organization. McCarthy and Zald (1977, 1213) highlight the utility of adopting a resource mobilization approach, which "examines the variety of resources that must be mobilized, the linkages of social movements to other groups, the dependence of movements upon external support for success."Ganz (2009, vii) further talks about "strategic capacity" and the ways in which the underdog (the David) can sometimes use strategic resourcefulness to compensate for lack of actual resources when fighting a Goliath. As demonstrated in the following chapters, charismatic leaders have been able to develop effective strategies for mobilization that are able to mobilize resources in times of great scarcity.

For example, Patricia Guerrero (leader of the Liga) writes that when she first arrived in El Pozón, she met with displaced women who were suffering, sad, and fearful but did not have an understanding of the wider gendered dynamics of power that had led to their displacement. She discusses initiating a dialogue—one that continues to this day—to explain the linkages between the wider context of conflict and the impact it has on women's daily lives. She began to run meetings in which she would talk to women about their experiences and about their rights as women and as victims. As part of this discussion, she was able to awaken consciousness about the potential for creative strategies of resistance against this violence (Sandvik et al. 2014, 75). Guerrero was exercising what Ganz (2009, 14) would call "strategic capacity" through the depth of her motivation, the breadth of her salient knowledge about the situation, and the robustness of her reflective practices.

Resistance in the case of the high-risk feminism is the act of rejecting marginalization caused by conflict, including the ways in which it manifests as gendered violence. The high-risk feminism approach explains that the successful employment of particular strategies by women (as directed by charismatic leaders) allows them to mobilize as feminists to defend and secure rights, overcoming significant barriers in the process. Those strategies include creating collective identity, building social capital, legal framing, and engaging in acts of certification. The rest of this chapter is dedicated to outlining these component parts of high-risk feminism. That the women discussed in this book choose to shape their mobilization around the pursuit of gender justice is of particular interest and is discussed throughout the rest of the chapter and in the following empirical case studies.

Consciousness-Raising Creates Collective Identity

When charismatic leaders emerge in a particular neighborhood, they first have to show potential participants that their collective action is compatible given certain identities they share. In a domain of losses, these are often based around shared experiences of fear, trauma, and victimhood. As outlined in studies by Moser and McIlwaine (2001), this fear can serve to motivate or to paralyze. The subsequent adoption and transformation of their identity as displaced women and victims of conflict-related violence is an active strategy of the organization, as "activists have to work hard to get a certain category of people to think of themselves as belonging to a group with distinctive problems and interests" (Whittier 2015, 115). Indeed, as noted in the previous chapter, the shift from frames of fear to frames of anger—or, in this case, resistance—makes all the difference in terms of willingness to run risks (Lerner and Keltner 2001).

Such behavior is consistent with Friedman and McAdam's (1992, 157) work on collective identity and activism, which considers different existing theories to explain the life of a social movement. The authors look at the concept of collective identity itself as an incentive that encourages an individual's participation in a movement. Defining collective identity as a set of communally held values, attitudes, commitments, and rules for behavior to which an individual ascribes, they posit that the act of joining a movement implies that the individual sees value in assuming the shared identity. Collective identity, therefore, functions as a selective incentive—or as noted in the previous chapter, nonmaterial benefit—that motivates participation.

When it comes to high-risk collective action, though, individuals are faced with higher barriers to participation. Loveman (1998, 482) asserts that in a high-risk setting, sometimes mobilization becomes "the only choice." This is clearly an exaggeration (and arguably does not do justice to the agentic capacities of those who choose to mobilize both because of and in spite of the risks associated with doing so): women are perfectly able to choose not to mobilize, and indeed many do make this choice. When they do choose to mobilize, then, the strategies and tactics they adopt require attention and analysis.

For example, Calhoun (1991, 51) discusses the issue of identity in collective action, noting that "bravery to the point of apparent foolishness is essential to many social movements, especially the most radical." He goes on to say that given the low odds of a desirable outcome, the lengthiness of some actions, and the high risks of involvement, those who engage in radical actions are held to be either psychologically crazy, acting on inadequate information (completely unaware of historical precedents), or forced into seeming bravery by being involved in a situation with no room for individual will. These explanations, however, are falsifiable. Rather, he states, "The risk may be borne not because of the likelihood of success in manifest goals, but because participation in a course of action has over time committed one to an identity that would be irretrievably violated by pulling back from the risk" (Calhoun 1991, 51). Loveman (1998) notes that identity can both influence and be influenced by the process of struggle; and Calhoun (1991, 52) is more explicit in explaining that "identity is, in many cases, forged in and out of struggle, including participation in social movements." A person's embeddedness in social networks can impact whether that person participates in collective action: "Personal ties are particularly important for sustaining contentious collective action in extremely repressive contexts because they provide a foundation of constructing the types of dense and insulated social networks required for effective resistance" (Loveman 1998, 482, citing Wickham-Crowley 1992).

The construction of collective identity is an active strategy of high-risk feminism. Part of understanding high-risk feminism involves recognizing how collective identity is created and why it brings perceived utility to members. Taylor and Whittier (1992, 169) note that movements are able to establish consciousness by attaching meaning to their group affiliation and collective action. These authors use the example of the lesbian feminist movements to track how different communities have been able to generate a collective identity that encourages the group to engage in a wide range of social and political actions that challenge the dominant system (170). They further state that when examining any politicized identity community, it is necessary to analyze the social and political struggle that created this identity.

High-risk feminism is also characterized by the pursuit of gender justice. That is, women build collective identities around a shared set of world experiences that are shaped by their condition as women. To draw a parallel: Padilla's (2001, 94) work in popular neighborhoods in Lima, Peru, shows that "women who are actively involved in popular organizations gain gender consciousness which, through activism, leads them to develop gender identities." Whittier (2015, 115) explains further: "Participating in consciousness-raising groups, activist organizations, and political actions such as boycotts or pickets gave women a new interpretation of themselves and the events around them." Molyneux (1985, 232–234) famously outlines the distinction between practical and strategic gender interests when looking at women's political subjectivities in the context of mobilization. She details how women who originally mobilize for a practical need (such as housing, food, or childcare) gain consciousness about the broader arena of their subordination, and transform their protest into a broader quest for gender equality, thus pursuing what she calls "strategic gender interests." The creation of collective identity, as part of high-risk feminism, allows for this pursuit of strategic gender interests.

Taylor and Whittier (1992, 114) explore the idea of boundaries in terms of locating some people as members of a group, thereby creating a group consciousness, a phenomenon that "imparts a larger significance to a collectivity." This concept of consciousness refers to the interpretative frameworks that a group uses in its articulation of a struggle against a dominant order. In the case of high-risk feminism, this can be as simple as showing women that they are not alone in their suffering and that others have also experienced various acts of violence during forced displacement. That is, "Although participants construct their consciousness interactively in a movement context, individuals internalize it.... At root it is about seeing oneself as part of a group, a collectivity. The mechanism by which this is accomplished is the construction of group boundaries, or symbolic and material distinctions between members of the collectivity and others" (Whittier 2015, 119).

There is something to be said about informing women that not only are their situations traumatic and painful, but that as individuals (and sometimes, as a collective) they are considered to be legal subjects in need of protection and reparation (see Lemaitre et al. 2014; Lemaitre and Sandvik 2015; Sandvik and Lemaitre 2015). Interviewees consistently revealed that before joining a high-risk feminist organization, they were aware that they were living in near-unbearable situations, but they did not necessarily know that legally qualified as victims.[2] Holston (2008) has written about "insurgent citizenship," an understanding of citizenship that rests on the idea that participants understand, desire, and demand their right to rights. This citizenship requires a conceptual elaboration in addition to an experiential elaboration.

Identity formation and the ascription of value found in collective identity involves both an understanding of the lived reality of being a woman in a violent context and the conceptual understanding that the risk of mobilizing is seen as appropriate, given the perceived greater risk of not mobilizing. Essentially, both experientially (through lived experience) and conceptually (through a desire for gender equality), women are able to join together in a type of collective action in which they can frame and justify the high risks of mobilizing as being in their best interests. This is captured by McGarry and Jasper (2015, 1), who call collective identity a "banner" under which people can be mobilized, one in which "identification can follow from collective action as well as contribute to it."[3]

The formation of collective identity is key to the success of high-risk feminist mobilization. That women are better able to minimize their losses by adopting a strategic and feminist identity of resistance facilitates high-risk feminist mobilization. That women are able to see that they are not alone in their struggle, and that they are validated in rejecting the conditions of marginality and violence to which they are exposed, is a product of participation in this same organization.

Building Social Capital

Beyond simply creating collective identity and building collective consciousness, women participating in high-risk feminist organizations add substance and value to these connections. Putnam (2000, 19) defines social capital as the "connections among individuals—social networks and the norms of reciprocity and trustworthiness that arise from them." He outlines the ways in which social capital can be simultaneously a private good and a public good, bringing benefit to both the individual involved in a specific network and to the community at large.

Social capital varies, with bonding social capital and bridging social capital representing the most important distinctions. The former is about bringing people together, for "undergirding specific reciprocity and mobilizing solidarity," and can involve providing social and psychological support for members of a community (Putnam 2000, 20). Bridging capital, on the other hand, is about creating linkages to external assets and for information diffusion. Bonding social capital has the potential to make a group insular and antagonistic to out-groups. In certain situations, though, it can have positive social effects. This is the case for women living in high-risk contexts: coming together as a collective allows for solidarity, healing, and belonging. Putnam (2000) notes that a group can bond and bridge at the same time. Organizations such as the Liga de Mujeres Desplazadas and Afromupaz link themselves to state institutions and international donors to get the support and resources women need.

In her gendered continuum of violence and conflict, Moser (2001, 41) articulates the idea that assessments of the impacts of violence on a country and its society's capital can provide insight into the true cost of violence. The more assets an individual or a community acquires and the better they manage them, the less their vulnerability and exclusion. Social capital, for Moser (2001, 43, quoting Narayan 1997), is defined as the "rules, norms, obligations, reciprocity, and trust embedded in social relations, social structures, and a society's institutional arrangements that enables its members to achieve their individual and community objectives." This definition recognizes that social capital "is generated and provides benefits through the membership of social networks or structures" (Moser and McIlwaine 2001, quoting Portes 1998). In situations of high levels of violence, Moser (2001, 44) posits, the relationship between violence and social capital is highly complex: "violence can erode productive social capital when it reduces trust and cooperation within formal and informal social organizations that are critical for a society to function."

Many of the women fleeing gendered violence in Colombia arrive to their new homes without knowing anyone else. Fear of further violence can erode women's ability to connect with one another and with their community and shape their expectations of the future. For this reason, leaders try to build social capital as a strategy of resistance in high-risk feminist mobilization. In communities where residents describe their lack of trust in terms of lack of social fabric, women's groups have the potential to forge new networks that have the dual purpose of producing a private good (the benefits of support and kinship gained by individual membership) and a public good ((re)creating relationships with state institutions, which may eventually serve to lessen the structural violence that may have given rise to contexts of high violence in the first place). Here, the benefits of bonding social capital become evident.

We can again draw on Gould's (2015, 254) emotion work: "More than *manage* emotions—a term that implies a preexisting emotional state that then is amplified or dampened—the emotion work of movements frequently *generates* feelings." The active building of social capital fills this same role. Padilla (2001, 103) refers to the way women who participate actively in a community generate an increase in their self-esteem and in their development of a sense of empowerment, as well as other consequences like "happiness, feelings of accomplishment, and satisfaction."

The idea that consciousness-building strategies employed by women's groups build social capital constitutes "connecting, empowering, and integrating people and organizations" and can serve to build communities that are resilient in the face of pervasive violence (Colletta and Cullen 2000, 113). In the context of high-risk feminism, participation in women's organizations brings personal satisfaction that then provides the incentive for women to continue to remain active in the organization, thus increasing that organization's capacity. At the beginning, this social capital falls under the bonding category. With time, and as groups become established, they begin to engage in bridging social capital with state institutions and other organizations.

Moreover, the bonds of being part of a social network provide communal services that an individual alone might not be able to access, particularly when the presence of the state is weak. This particular phenomenon is not unique to high-risk settings. For example, certain literature shows that over the years women have come together in collectives that focus on cooking or providing childcare when they are unable to individually find the resources to survive (see Fernandes 2007; Safa 1990, 357; Schroeder 2006). What changes in the case of high-risk conditions, however, is that the bonds of trust with neighbors and community members do not necessarily a priori exist. Meertens (2001, 140) notes that women who have fled displacement are often seeking anonymity in their new homes so that they cannot be revictimized.

Finally, being part of a community of women who have also experienced (and continue to experience) the violences that come with conflict situations can be considered a good in itself. Learning that one is not alone in one's suffering and being able to share stories and memories that have previously been too painful to recount, is an integral part of healing. Building social capital—forging a context in which women feel safe (physically, psychologically, and emotionally) to connect to other people—can be considered one of the strategic acts of feminist resistance that forms part of high-risk feminist mobilization.

Meertens (2001, 142) notes that the female victims of displacement are often widows and have to dedicate themselves to taking care of their children, which "leaves no time for emotions or for memories, so the necessary mourning for the loss of their loved ones is postponed almost indefinitely." This remains true outside of the context of displacement; gendered violence (sexual, physical, or psychological) is widely known to be underreported. Especially in a context where the perpetrators of this violence still have social dominance, it is not surprising that victims are reticent to report or even discuss their ordeals. Being part of a group and growing the bonds of confidentially and security is therefore a strategy that facilitates empowerment for women who have been disempowered through (often repeated) acts of violence and victimization.

Indeed, in postconflict contexts, Porter (2016, 36) tells us, "When the voices of women and men are suppressed, silenced, excluded, or ignored, agency is undermined. When space is created for these stories to be told, and they are listened to respectfully, not only is dignity affirmed, but the possibility of a gender-sensitive approach to responding to these stories is enhanced. . . . Listening to stories that are told about individual versions of trauma and personal experiences of violence requires compassionate responses if these stories are to be given significance in individual, communal, and national narratives on the violent past."

In terms of bridging social capital, we can see the ways in which the organizations studied in this book try to create alliances with state institutions and other purveyors of resources. This is particularly evident when it comes to the collective reparations process. There is a critical need for organizations to create linkages with national and international actors if they are to finance projects, which is fundamental to their ability to generate incremental material benefits over time (Lemaitre and Sandvik 2015, 13). The empirical chapters of this book specifically examine the role of networks, including funding bodies, and the way the Liga, Afromupaz, and the Alianza successfully negotiate these relationships.

Creating social capital, therefore, represents a strategy that empowers women and gives them back their agency. This involves both solidifying the norms of trust and reciprocity that facilitate sharing and healing, as well as establishing efficacious connections with actors who provide external resources. This is essential to a gender justice project in the context and aftermath of conflict.

(Legal) Framing Adds Value to Collective Identity

Snow and Benford (1992, 137) articulate the idea that social movement actors draw on collective action frames that "underscore and embellish the seriousness and injustice of a social condition" and "articulate a narrative that constitutes a liberating interpretive framework." Ryan and Gamson (2015, 137) state that "facts take on their meaning by being embedded in frames, which render them relevant and significant or irrelevant and trivial. The contest is lost at the outset if we allow our adversaries to define what facts are relevant. To be conscious of framing strategy is not to be manipulative. It is a necessary part of giving coherent meaning to what is happening in the world, and one can either do it unconsciously or with deliberation and conscious thought."

High-risk feminist organizations perform such actions: participants unite to draw attention to the social injustices they have faced and create a narrative of consciousness in an attempt to rectify these injustices. Their understanding of gender justice moves beyond the conflict moment to encompass questions of how and why women experience conflict differently from men in the first place. Leaders encourage and teach participants to use legal measures to underscore and legitimize what they have suffered.

Snow et al. (1986) seek to explain support for and participation in social movement organizations by expanding on Goffman's (1959) idea of framing. "Frame alignment processes" link individual interests, values, and beliefs in such a way that they become compatible with the activities, goals, and ideologies of social movement organizations. Framing explains the nuts and bolts of how a social movement adds value to its associated collective identity.

For Goffman (1959), a frame is a way for individuals to locate, perceive, identify, and label occurrences within their life space. Doing so allows experiences to gain a certain meaning and then directs further action, both individually and collectively. Snow et al. (1986, 467) critique the static view of participation adopted by many social movement theorists: "Just as movement activities and campaigns change with developments in a movement's career and environment of operation, similarly there is variation in the individual's stake in participating in new or emergent activities. Decisions to participate over time are thus subject to frequent reassessment and renegotiation."

Enloe's (2000, xiv) work notes that when a government or international organization assumes that girls and women are "somehow less valuable, less responsible, less fully citizens than boys and men," it follows that the officials within these governments and organizations "treat threats to women and girls as trivial, as not worthy of serious attention." My research in both El Salvador and Colombia has shown that to combat this, women's organizations invest time in registering injustices with the legal mechanisms of the state (Zulver 2016). This has the dual function of seeking justice for those whose rights have been violated and also making these cases visible within a framework set out by the same state that then has the responsibility to investigate them. In this way, legal framing legitimizes women's victimhood by using the state's own language.

The first step of this strategy is to use collective identity processes and bonding social capital creation to get women to identify not just as a displaced, but also as victims. Indeed, as Krystalli (2020) notes, in Colombia the term *victim* identifies a powerful legal category that is linked to access to reparations through the country's transitional justice architecture, and one that is deeply tied up in questions of power and strategic activism (Krystalli 2020).[4] Victimhood for many women in Colombia is about conflict-related sexual violence, displacement, and other violences that lie along the continuum of violence, reflecting the crosscutting nature of dominating, militarized logics of masculinity. Women's experiences of Colombia's armed conflict are shaped by their gender identities, as exemplified in a haunting sentence included in one of the Centro Nacional de Memoria Histórica (2011, 26) reports: paramilitary actors in the north of the country saw women as "territories to be colonized by all-powerful masculinities."

The coming chapters highlight the ways in which high-risk feminist organizations encourage group members to register their victim status with the Victims' Unit. They also make claims with other legal mechanisms, including taking their cases to international human rights bodies such as the Inter-American Commission for Human Rights. By framing their experiences as illegal acts that are not being seriously considered by the state, members and leaders are able to direct at least some of their mobilization resources toward confronting a system that should be able to make a difference in the ways they experience violence. They do this by calling on women to make demands on state institutions to comply with their duties (that is, claiming their right to rights) and by using the state's own language and mechanisms to define their experiences as unjust within the outlined rights and responsibilities enshrined in law (included in Colombia's 2011 Victims' and Land Restitution Law, known as the Victims' Law).

In the Colombian case, this strategy has been well documented in Lemaitre and Sandovik's study of women's movements' use of legal norms within the transitional justice context (Lemaitre et al. 2014; Sandvik et al. 2014; Sandvik and Lemaitre 2013, 2015). The report, *De desplazados a víctimas* (From displaced people to victims), outlines the strategic adoption of the label "victim" by people who had previously not considered themselves as such (Lemaitre, Lopez, et al. 2014, 15). By doing so, they framed their identities within the new Victims' Law, which qualified them for transitional justice measures offered by the state. In this way, they were better able to negotiate their inclusion and presence in institutional spaces. Despite current feminist concerns with the language of victims as opposed to survivors, in Colombia, "women who identify as victims [echo] that the label of 'victim' is a site of politics that allows particular kinds of claims to emerge. 'Victim' indicates that someone suffered harm, that there is a victimizer, and that there ought to be a process for remedy and reparation" (Krystalli 2020).

This framing strategy signifies that violence against women is not just perpetrated by the expected actors—the armed groups imposing militarized masculinities—but also by the judicial and legal arms of the state that fail to prevent, investigate, and respond to women's experiences with violence. This is what, in the context of Ciudad Juárez in Mexico, Ensalaco (2006, 418) calls the "failure to exercise due diligence" in terms of failure to investigate and prosecute, and what Sanford (2008, 113) sees as differentiating the term *feminicide* from *femicide*.[5]

Certification as Contentious Action

What remains, then, is certification, the action item. Certification refers to the "validation of actors, their performances, and their claims by external authorities" (McAdam et al. 2001, 145). Processes of certification explain why members of social movements spend energy in "public affirmations of shared identities: marching together, displaying shared symbols, acting out of solidarity" (147). Certification should be distinguished from ideas of the intrinsic value brought by social capital and collective identity. Solidarity in terms of certification, in fact, is about making a successful claim of collective worthiness, and of gaining recognition as a credible political player with the capacity to make a difference. When it comes to high-risk feminism, certification is the public expression of the worthiness of the pursuit of gender justice.

The certification pillar further addresses the question of why women participate in high-risk collective action despite the potential risks incurred by doing so. Indeed, acts of solidarity—marching in the streets, engaging in *plantones* (sit-ins) in state buildings, and making claims before state and institutional officials—have the potential to bring further suffering to participants and leaders by making them publicly visible and recognizable figures. At the same time, however, these acts shine a light on their grievances. When members publicly frame certain types of violence as illegal, and certain responses from the state and judiciary as remiss or negligent, this is an act of certification. When women call on the Inter-American Court for Human Rights because the state is not guaranteeing the protections it is obliged to provide, this is an act of certification. When women hold press conferences with national and international media sources, this is an act of certification. In fact, as I have written elsewhere "being visible," ironically, can in fact be a tactic of self-protection. In the context of a resurgence of extreme violence in Putumayo, for example, women who engage in tactics of "being visible" are able to draw widespread attention and solidarity to the violence they face (Zulver 2021).

Claiming a voice and a right to rights is key to transforming a group from being politically and socially invisible to becoming a legitimate force with whom other actors (the state, institutions, individuals, the international community) will engage in dialogue. Certification provides an active way for women's organizations to continually define and redefine themselves in relation to their immediate perceived dangers, and make their identities public, therefore demanding a response (or highlighting a lack of response). Making an act public is a tactic of presenting the group as legitimate and thereby requiring answers, actions, and explanations.

A charismatic leader sees that engaging in acts of certification is one of the ways to bring about an incremental gain that encourages continued participation over time and generates new recruitment. For example, building a City of Women was not only a physical, but also a symbolic act by which the Liga showed women their ability to make their daily lives safer. The material benefits of the City are obvious, and the nonmaterial bonds of pride and satisfaction at completing an action further add justification to a woman's decision to participate in a potentially risky undertaking. Ironically, by becoming tactically visible, the women feel that they make themselves safer, as acts of aggression would not go unheard or unseen and would require response.

Conclusion

This chapter and the previous one have explained why women who we might expect not to mobilize do, in fact, act collectively in high-risk contexts. A charismatic leader has the ability to convince potential participants of the material and nonmaterial benefits of participation within a domain of losses. That is, when inaction does not guarantee safety, and action has the ability to create a sense of agency over the "tomorrows of violence"—shifting from frames of fear to frames of resistance—women can justify their actions. The strategies are able to bring about the material and nonmaterial benefits required to encourage participation in the first place and to facilitate ongoing mobilization over time.

The more complex reading of the dynamics at play, however, show that the presence of a charismatic leader does not reveal the whole picture. Indeed, it is the bond between the leader and the participant—and then among the participants themselves—that allows participants to overcome barriers to mobilization and also sustains action over time. This bond is reflexive and recursive; once people decide to participate, their identities becomes fundamentally tied up with the collective. This is where the pillars of action (the "how") allow the participant to experientially understand why they should continue to mobilize and encourage others to do the same. There are benefits to doing so, both material and nonmaterial, and these supersede the potential for opting for a lower risk of violence, especially when the social context does not guarantee that nonparticipation is linked to increased safety.

This is to say that a charismatic leader is not a puppeteer in charge of the entire fate of the collective. Indeed, leaders may initially play a strong role in generating participation, and then continue to direct action in ways that they think have the potential to bring about success. The bonds between participants become a good in themselves (part of the "psychic income"). Moreover, when past mobilization has led to material gains, women might expect ongoing material gains in the future. In periods without material gains, psychosocial benefits can sustain mobilization. This combination of nonmaterial benefits and incremental gains creates a positive feedback loop, leading to ongoing and dedicated participation. Indeed, Madsen and Snow (1991, 147) discuss the evolution of the charismatic bond, noting that over time followers lose some of their emotional fervor and become more committed to the movement than to the leader.

Why women join and remain in organizations over the years can be explained, then, by some combination of expected or delivered material rewards, psychosocial support, and attachment to an identity. Continued participation and continued exposure to risk become part of the way that women define themselves and are able to exert agency in what is otherwise a dire situation. During fieldwork, one woman expressed why she feels obligated to continue with her work: "I have to keep moving forward. After everything we've suffered . . . I don't have any option but to continue my work. . . . I have to keep going."[6] What she was expressing here is that her life project is now so strongly tied up with high-risk feminist mobilization that abandoning the project is unthinkable. Indeed, Elcheroth and Reicher (2017, 100) argue that "collective identities in the aftermath of violence . . . represent the bonds of solidarity and sociality that are left over once many, if not most, of people's ordinary social connections have been broken. . . . As a consequence, one typical feature of identities re-shaped by violence is their rigidity: by giving up alternative ways to define themselves, people also lose . . . their capacity to navigate flexibly between a variety of relevant identities." During conflict, new identities and patterns of mobilization emerge out of extraordinary circumstances and then become the norm. Auyero (2003, 2) expands on this in his work about contentious identities: even after the revolts subside, protestors with no previous experience of collective action think of these episodes in personal terms—"their lives have radically changed."

Especially given the protracted dominance of militarized masculinities within conflict settings—those that exist along Cockburn's (2004) continuum of violence—high-risk mobilization is a way that women can gain control over their own lives. Mobilization is sustained because it has proved successful in the past, and this reinforces its ability to modify the uncertainty of violence that women might otherwise feel is inevitable. In the final chapter of this book, I discuss the case of the Alianza, an organization that has mobilized for gender justice at different moments over the past two decades. By looking at its ability to reignite specific tactics and strategies during distinct moments of conflict, the longevity and durability of its mobilizational repertoires become evident.

4

The Liga de Mujeres Desplazadas

• •

Creating a Site of Feminist Resistance in a Conflict Zone

> Women and girls—dehumanized, dispossessed of their own bodies—became territories to be colonized by all-powerful masculinities who declared themselves the victors through [acts of] brutality.
> —Centro Nacional de Memoria Histórica (2011, 26)

> We ask the goddesses to give us the strength and health to reach the end of this wonderful journey of civil resistance in the midst of war, which has given full meaning to our lives, and whose primary evidence is the City of Women.
> —Patricia Guerrero

Colombia's Caribbean coast was a theatre of war during the country's armed conflict, with violence reaching brutal heights between 1997 and 2005, when the Autodefensas Unidas de Colombia (AUC; United Self-Defense Forces of Colombia) paramilitaries enacted a bellicose campaign against the FARC guerrillas and those they considered to be their sympathizers. The violence during this period was so intense that the National Center for Historical Memory (Centro Nacional de Memoria Histórica 2011, 24) refers to the AUC's offensives as creating the *ruta del terror*, the route of terror, in their search for "indisputable authority"; they used massacres, disappearances, public torture, displacement, rape and sexual violence, sexual and domestic slavery, and threats as a way to achieve total social control.

This chapter focuses on the Liga de Mujeres Desplazadas (League of Displaced Women) and its struggle to build a more peaceful, secure, and gender-just existence in the midst of this violence. The Liga is made up of women who suffered, resisted, and ultimately survived the route of terror inflicted on the region. Indeed, *la ruta* was itself gendered; the specific violences that women suffered during the AUC's control of the Caribbean region reflect the "violent repertoires and protocols of social regulation . . . promoted by the commanders of [the paramilitaries] . . . to achieve its goals" (Centro Nacional de Memoria Histórica 2011, 307). Paramilitaries inflicted violence against women as a way to consolidate the traditional gender roles that were central to their bloody campaign in the north of Colombia (19). Those who resisted—including women leaders—were targeted and murdered for their transgression of gender roles.

Women from all over the north of the country were forced to flee the terror being wrought in their communities. Many arrived at El Pozón, a slum on the outskirts of the city of Cartagena. Homeless, traumatized, and often newly widowed, these women arrived with their children and found themselves the victims of new types of violence at the hands of other paramilitaries and criminal gangs who fought for control of these deprived areas.

In 1998, however, a group of women came together under the guidance of Patricia Guerrero to build their dream of a dignified life, their *sueño de una vida digna*. At first, this involved creating social bonds of trust and belonging, which, in turn, facilitated the formation of a collective identity. With the nonmaterial benefits of participation established, they then turned their attention to building the City of Women, the Ciudad de las Mujeres, a manifestation of their mobilization. The City is more than a physical space that provides housing; for the women of the Liga, it is also a symbolic representation of their mobilizational agency. The City represents their feminist resistance to violence in the middle of a conflict zone. The members of the Liga mobilized not just as mothers or as victims of the conflict but also as women in the pursuit of gender justice.

Today, the organization maintains a membership of around 160. Many live in the City, but some live in other poor neighborhoods close by. In the City, the women own the deeds to their houses, but many live with male partners. Family homes are mixed, with nieces and nephews, biological children, stepchildren, and grandchildren often living together under the same roof. Every interviewee described economic hardship. While they own their property, many do not have the resources to pay for electricity or water. The women work informally, selling food, fruits, vegetables, and minutes for mobile phones or sewing or cleaning for others. No one I interviewed is engaged in formal employment. Violence continues to plague the neighborhood, even after the official demobilization of the AUC paramilitaries in the mid-2000s.

Particularities of Case Study and Methodology

The chapter draws on fieldwork I conducted with the Liga de Mujeres Desplazadas between July and November 2016, as well as additional research for a journalistic report in 2015 (see Thomas Davis and Zulver 2015). The women of the Liga have serious ongoing security concerns, and it took effort to make initial contact, as members were understandably wary to allow a stranger into their community. After a series of phone calls and text messages, one of the leaders eventually agreed to meet my colleague and me at a small shopping mall on the outskirts of Cartagena. We met this leader outside a shoe shop in the blistering midday Caribbean sun, and any remaining tensions melted away as she greeted us with a warm hug and an invitation to the City of Women. We caught a local bus that took us out of Cartagena, through bustling suburban centers and eventually into lush, quiet housing developments. We got off at the final stop, which dropped us off on the Avenida Guerrera—the Avenue of the Woman Warrior.

This visit was my first of many subsequent trips to the City. I spent these visits hanging out with the women of the Liga: sitting on porches, helping make the midday meal, drinking ubiquitous cups of sugary *tinto* (coffee). When there were tasks to be done, I helped with shopping and running errands. Many of the conversations I had with the women were held while traveling on busses and in taxis, with vallenato or reggaeton music blasting over the radio.

As a function of spending time together, I was sometimes asked to help with various organizational tasks. For example, I helped organize the logistics for a conference held in the provincial government buildings and gave a speech about the collective reparations process. I spent time with the woman in charge of the Liga's social media accounts, showing her how to update Facebook statuses and create a Twitter account. At one point, I taught a class on sexual health and reproductive rights to a group of teenage girls living in the City. Through the time we spent together, personal relationships developed, allowing me to better understand the nuances of the daily challenges these women encounter.

Despite these relationships, it was important for me not to engage in retraumatizing research practices throughout this project. The women do not have reliable access to health care, let alone mental health services, and traumas of the past sit just below the surface. When possible, I tried to fill in historical details of violence in the region by reading existing documents. Information was largely drawn from a detailed report about the Liga written by a group of academics and lawyers (Lemaitre et al. 2014) and the National Center for Historical Memory's (Centro Nacional de Memoria Histórica 2011) incredible report on women and war in the Colombian Caribbean.

As in all research conducted for this book, my position as an academic from the Global North impacts the power dynamics I have with interlocutors. Sachseder (2020, 175) notes of her own research with participants with similar backgrounds in Colombia that such interactions are "exposed to multiple problematic influences and colonial power dynamics," including those related to socioeconomic status, ethnicity, and race. This is yet another reason it was important for me to engage in slow research, which allowed for the creation of relationships of trust over time.

The Liga is made up of a number of different chapters—in Cartagena, Turbaco, San Jacinto, and Carmen de Bolívar. Over the course of fieldwork, I spent time with women from all of these chapters, but the vast majority of evidence presented in this book comes from my time with the women of the Turbaco chapter, most of whom now live in the City of Women. While the historical and contemporary risks to which these women are exposed differ based on geography (rural versus urban), one unifying element of the Liga is its pursuit of gender justice in the face of violence.

The Liga de Mujeres Desplazadas: Narrating Experiences of Terror and Resistance

Displacement and Arrival in El Pozón

During the paramilitary incursion in the late 1990s and early 2000s, the northern part of Colombia witnessed a particular intensity of conflict-related violence. The departments of Antioquia, Atlántico, Bolívar, Cesar, Chocó, Córdoba, Magdalena, and Sucre—where the majority of members of the Liga come from—experienced hundreds of thousands of episodes of violence, including forced displacement, kidnapping, disappearances, homicide, physical violence, sexual violence including rape and torture, and recruitment of child soldiers (Unidad para las Víctimas 2020).

Interviewees were quick to recount their stories of displacement from various areas in rural sectors of the north of the country to vulnerable urban neighborhoods. Anyela's story in the first chapter of this book is an example of how some women were displaced multiple times, suffering compounding violences over time. Another woman and her husband—both residents of the City of Women—told me their story of being present at one of the worst massacres of the Colombian conflict. The massacre at El Salado, a small town in the Montes de María region, took place over three days in 2000, as paramilitaries attempted to oust and kill guerrilla fighters and their sympathizers. They brutally murdered dozens of townspeople and raped, injured, and tortured more than one hundred others. Thousands fled to nearby towns in the aftermath of the massacre (Rohter 2000). The people I interviewed described loading a car with their possessions and driving away with their children, just before the massacre began. They have never been able to go back to their home, where they ran a small store together.

A third woman recounted the story of having to live in hiding for many months during the height of the conflict. A resident of Carmen de Bolívar, a town in the heart of Montes de María, she was targeted by paramilitaries for being a community leader who condemned their violent actions. She told me how she would spend every night staying at a different friend's house, so that they could not find her and kill her while she slept.

Stories like these are unfortunately common among the women who have been displaced and now reside in the City of Women. Their exact experiences are distinct, and their stories are deeply personal, but the reality itself is constant. Women and their families were forced to pack up what they could and flee their homes at a moment's notice, or risk extreme violence.

Yet the urban slums where they arrived were also places of "necessity and anguish" (Sandvik et al. 2014, 15). The word *pozón* refers to a large well, or water source. The name is apt in the case of this neighborhood in Cartagena. During the rainy season, the streets flood, leaving the women and their families vulnerable to the elements. Women told me that the walls of their temporary homes were made of cardboard, pieces of corrugated metal or plastic, or wooden pallets. These materials would rot over time, leading to the disintegration of structures, further exposing families to the coastal weather. They were unable to store food and constantly struggled to keep their foam mattresses dry.

El Pozón also represented a space of lawlessness—there was little police presence, and interviewees spoke about experiencing break-ins, robberies, threats, and violent encounters with violent actors. The neighborhood was characterized by insecurity that ranged from theft and vandalism to physical harm and sexual abuse (see also Lemaitre 2016). One woman told me the story of how a group of men repeatedly assaulted her sexually before stealing her wallet.

These conditions in the slum put women in situations of extreme vulnerability. Ongoing insecurity, as well as risks of natural threats like floods and heavy rains, left women and their families at constant risk of danger. Residents of El Pozón lacked access to basic services such as water, electricity, sewage, and medical attention (Sandvik et al. 2014, 19). One interlocutor told me in an interview, "Our situation was very depressing . . . it was practically inhuman."[1]

The Roots of the Liga: Patricia Guerrero and the Charismatic Bond

Despite the precariousness of their new neighborhood, the cramped living situation had the effect of bringing women in similar situations of displacement into close proximity with one another. For many, who had previously lived on farms in rural areas, this was the first time they found themselves in close quarters with other women suffering the same sorts of violence that they had. Not only did they share similar stories of displacement, but they also shared daily and ongoing exposure to continuing forms of vulnerability at the hands of gangs and paramilitaries present in the neighborhood. Their ability to locate themselves as part of a wider network of displaced victims was a new experience, one that was in many ways comforting.

One of the original leaders told me the story of the first action taken by a group of neighbors that would eventually become the Liga: In El Pozón there was a group of eight women who met regularly to share food in a communal kitchen, an *olla común*. This way, each woman would contribute what she had—one carrot, one potato, a scrap of chicken—and could guarantee that there would be a meal available to share with her children.

Over time, the women's actions expanded beyond food to other areas of daily life. For example, they came together to pool the little money they had to take a woman to the clinic when she fell ill. Sadly, owing to the absence of medical attention, the woman did not survive. An interviewee told me, "For us, this was an incredibly sad moment . . . and the first [conscious] action we took as a collective was to find a coffin so that we could give our *compañera* a proper burial."[2] This event, interviewees recounted, consolidated their understanding of their shared situation of vulnerability and brought them closer together as an informal support system.

Around this time, a feminist lawyer named Patricia Guerrero arrived in El Pozón with the idea of providing legal aid to desperate women. Through her connections with a religious leader, she was able to make the acquaintance of the group of women who had come together to bury their neighbor. She began to have conversations with them about the specific ways in which their experiences of displacement were shaped, in part, by their roles as women. According to Guerrero, while the women expressed sadness and resignation at their situation of suffering, they had never contemplated the larger complexities of their gendered roles as victims of the armed conflict (Sandvik et al. 2014, 75). She began a basic dialogue about the situation, origin, and causes of their displacement, framing the discussion in terms of women's rights and gender justice. "I was able to ignite a fire in their hearts, showing them the enormous discrimination against women in the conflict. And I would say to them, 'Look what we have to do now: we have to organize!'" (Nobel Women's Initiative 2016).

This discourse was appealing to the women involved, as they felt that the gendered particularities of conflict and displacement were ignored by other social organizations active in El Pozón. For example, aid given by the Catholic Church at the time did not provide condoms or menstrual hygiene products in the handouts they gave to women. In a zone where women were highly vulnerable to ongoing sexual abuse, the Church judged and stigmatized women who had become pregnant. Moreover, most of the grassroots organizations in the neighborhood were run by men, who did not adopt any gender focus in their requests for aid. Sometimes, male leaders would provide aid in exchange for "sex with the most vulnerable, desperate displaced women" (Sandvik et al. 2014, 82). Guerrero and the new women leaders felt that the existing community organizations were built on patriarchal models that did not have room for organized, feminist women: "From that moment on, we decided to manage our own humanitarian aid, whose meaning would be re-defined by [the very women it was intended to reach]" (84).

The idea of a women-only organization was particularly appealing to other women—it consolidated a collective identity that allowed them to feel that they were not alone in their situation of displacement. They could come together around a shared understanding that "the pain of one is the pain of all" (quoted in Thomas Davis and Zulver 2015). It was during this time that Guerrero also began developing a narrative that framed women as operating within a domain of losses, within which inaction did not protect a potential participant from either the daily grind of poverty or the ongoing risk of violence. That is, since not joining the Liga did not guarantee safety, the potential benefits of membership justified running extra risks to one's safety.

The group began to meet more regularly, and membership increased as women started to bring their friends and neighbors to meetings. Multiple interviewees spoke to me about the relief they felt at realizing that their situation—in the domain of losses—was not unique, and that other women were having the same struggles as they were. They found solidarity in shared experiences and were attracted to the meetings, which gave meaning to their daily hardships in the slum. They also felt comfort in knowing that the violences from which they had fled were, sadly, not unique. While they knew that mobilization might expose them to heightened levels of violence, Guerrero was able to frame collective action as justifiable, given the potential for accrued benefits over time.

Beyond convincing women to mobilize under high-risk conditions, Guerrero also developed an effective strategy for mobilization. She was able to draw on her skills as a lawyer to facilitate a discussion around women's and victims' rights, and she had the ability to organize meetings for these women. In a domain of losses, as a charismatic leader she had a special ability to accrue base-level resources to facilitate these early iterations of mobilization.

Material and Nonmaterial Benefits of Collective Action

The first years of the Liga were focused on creating and building gendered consciousness, mutual confidence, and collective identity. Guerrero spent time educating the women about their legal rights, as women and as victims. She effectively created a charismatic bond; women living in the violent slum were receptive to the presence of a leader who offered them reasons to be hopeful about the future. Group membership expanded over time, growing to other slum communities, including another settlement of displaced people in nearby Turbaco. They had their first *encuentro* (gathering) in 2001, in which workshops about women's rights continued to contribute to the creation and strengthening of a collective consciousness.

It was also in 2001, however, that the women began to receive their first threats from groups associated with paramilitaries. Over time, the threats became more acute: "[The] struggle for organizational autonomy and a position in the community worsened the threats against women, the violation of group leaders, the following [that is, stalking], and the persecution: with more social and political empowerment came more threats of sexual violence" (Sandvik et al. 2014, 85). Such threats and violence "were associated with the transgression of gender norms, or definitions of man and woman, that were central to the project of paramilitary order in the north of Colombia" and led to the selective assassination of many women leaders in the region (Centro Nacional de Memoria Histórica 2011, 16).

It was in this year that unknown perpetrators raped two members of the Liga, and some of the women's sons were forcibly recruited as child soldiers. Lists with the names of women were posted on lampposts near Liga-run daycare centers, threatening rape and murder if the women did not leave the area within twenty-four hours. These threats came from paramilitary groups in the neighborhood, who did not like the ways in which women were beginning to stand up to their situations of vulnerability, violating traditional gender norms and defying the groups' claims to total social control.

Armed groups would send pamphlets with images of firearms and make threatening phone calls to members of the Liga. An interviewee recounted how used vulgar language, and: "[They told us that they] knew who we were, and that they were watching us. . . . They told us that they were going to 'disappear' us. . . . I imagine that as we were forming as a group, gaining consciousness, and empowering ourselves about our rights, [they felt threatened because] we knew that we had rights that we wanted to gain access to. . . . We became a stone in their shoes."[3]

By this time, however, collective identity building was underway. As one interviewee told me, "We didn't want to faint. . . . We wanted to keep going! We knew that together, united we could achieve anything."[4] This togetherness can be seen as a nonmaterial benefit of participation in the organization. The woman interviewed here was directly expressing her understanding that participation facilitated a sense of protection: being united meant that despite ongoing risks, there was a collective hope that a group of victims offered some level of insulation from violence.

In her position as leader, Guerrero was able to frame the women's gendered risks in a way that appealed to them. In terms of the tenets of prospect theory outlined in chapter 2, she highlighted the increasing benefits of group membership and the decreasing value in being alone, or not joining the organization. That is, she showed the women that nonparticipation did not necessarily guarantee safety and that the potential emotional and identity benefits derived from participation were valuable assets that could improve their lives. These benefits are not the outcome of mobilizing; they derive from the act of mobilizing. Therefore, while participation might make a woman a more visible target to paramilitaries, for example, taking action was preferable to inaction because everyone was operating in the same domain of losses (high-risk context). In this way, in the early days of the Liga, Guerrero was able to convince women that it was to their advantage to act collectively in the pursuit of gender justice, despite the threats and violence they experienced.

Throughout this time, Guerrero encouraged the women to share their stories of displacement and sexual violence with one another and to officially register these crimes with state institutions. An interviewee noted, "When we started to talk, we realized that each of us wasn't alone. This is something crucial, fundamental. . . . It was the process that gave the organization its strength" (Thomas Davis and Zulver 2015). It was around this time and in this context that the women began to frame their mobilization in terms of their dream of living a dignified life: a life free from the multiple and gendered sources of marginality that threatened their day-to-day existence.

Successes of Incremental Gains: Fulfilling the Dream of a Dignified Life

In 2003 Guerrero won a scholarship to study human rights at Columbia University in the United States, during which time she made the acquaintance of Senator Patrick Leahy, of Vermont. This support eventually materialized as a United States Agency for International Development grant to build sustainable housing for the members of the Liga. Interviewees corroborated: "When *la Doctora* [Guerrero] came back from Washington, we had a meeting all together. She told us the surprise, and we cried with happiness. We had the initial drop [in the bucket] to start with a housing project."[5] The potential to own one's house represented an opportunity to overcome the vulnerabilities of living in precarious makeshift housing in El Pozón. Owning the deed to a house eliminated the threat of eviction by a landlord. Moreover, "the theme of housing for these women is not just a theme of richness or poverty, but one with an

FIG. 4.1 A plaque in the City of Women reads: "We thank Doctora Patricia Guerrero, founder, ideologist, and creator of the Liga who, through her ardent labor, dedication, love, care, and untiring struggle, was able to make the dream of a dignified life into a reality." (Credit: author.)

important symbolic dimension" (Lemaitre et al. 2014, 20), particularly given the violent histories of forced displacement from the homes they had left behind.

This is another example of how Guerrero was able to mobilize resources for the organization. The success of a charismatic leader is dependent on "a mixture of style and substance, of promise and performance" (Madsen and Snow 1991, 145). Part of Guerrero's success as a charismatic leader was based on her ability to mobilize resources. She was able to make good on the promises she made to her followers, encouraging and reinforcing ongoing participation among the women of the Liga, despite the risks associated with doing so.

And so the women of the Liga set to work, building their dream of a dignified life. From January 2004 to March 2005, they helped prepare the terrain, fabricate cement bricks and build the houses. Yet despite the successes of their construction project, the women of the Liga were still not free from threats. To intimidate the women, cars filled with unknown men frequently drove around the neighborhood, taking photos and filming videos.

The violence came to a head when Don Julio, the husband of one of the Liga members, was murdered while guarding the women's brick factory overnight. In the aftermath, some of the women left the City, fearing for their lives. Those who stayed told me this event was a critical juncture in the Liga's history of the Liga. One interviewee said, "This was one of the events that actually strengthened me. I did not have a house, and I had to keep believing in what we were doing, that we were going to be able to move ahead and achieve our goals. They [the armed group] wanted to destroy us, to undo our structure . . . so we would splinter, and the organization would go away. They wanted to finish us. We were able to move forward, though."[6] Another told me:

> We had a dream of building dignified housing, and the organization was able to achieve this. Through the organization, we were able to move forward. Yes, I was very scared. In fact, in some of the days following the murder of Don Julio I didn't come to work . . . but eventually I returned. The idea is to fight, to resist. The *compañera* Simona [Julio's wife] told us "my husband and I fought for this project. They want us to stop, to end this dream that we have. But they are not going to stop us. . . . We have to move forward, united." And this gave us the force to continue.[7]

Despite ongoing threats and further acts of violence, disappearances, and murders, the women continued the construction process. When finished, the City consisted of ninety-eight houses, covering five blocks. The City has electricity, drinking water, garbage collection, and sewage. The women talk about the days when they began to move into their houses. One interviewee described the process of allocating houses: "'We made little cardboard houses and put them in a big box, and you reached your hand in and pulled one out. . . . What number are you in? You're my neighbor! It was an amazing experience'" (quoted in Thomas Davis and Zulver 2015).

FIG. 4.2 A block of houses in the City of Women. (Credit: author.)

Building and living in the City of Women was an act of resistance consistent with high-risk feminism. The risks of building the City were real. The belief that the pain of one was the pain of all, however, allowed the women to continue. Each small success created a feedback loop of continuing participation: When the women learned that they had received funding, they were motivated to begin work on building. When they bought the land for the city, they were inspired to creatively solve the obstacles they encountered. When they saw the emotional strength of their friend whose husband was murdered, they were determined not to give up hope, even in the face of violence. The City provides evidence of how material benefits also strengthened resolve to participate in the Liga.

Ongoing Violence in Turbaco: The Domain of Losses Continues

Despite all the undoubtable progress made since the Liga's roots in El Pozón, life in the City is not without struggle. Turbaco—the municipality in which the City is located—remains characterized by violence to this day. Even after the City had been built, the threats and violence continued. The AUC officially disbanded in the context of the Justice and Peace Law of 2005, and the Government of Colombia claimed that more than 30,000 paramilitaries had handed in their weapons. Despite this, "critics have demonstrated that the paramilitary demobilization process was deeply flawed from its inception and enabled successor paramilitary groups to emerge throughout Colombia" (Maher and Thomson 2018, 5). These paramilitary successors are often referred to under the umbrella label "Bacrim" (*bandas criminales*, criminal gangs); while this label distances the new iterations of these armed actors from their predecessors, their modi operandi are similar, including their use of extreme violence, an anticommunist agenda, and their involvement in the illegal drug trade (6).

It was around this time that Bacrim groups like the Aguilas Negras "declared the 'stupid women organizers' of the Liga a military target, and threatened the women with sexual violence" (Thomas Davis and Zulver 2015). As Saab and Taylor (2009) explain, this behavior is consistent with Bacrim's fight for over control in marginalized neighborhoods in the wake of the demobilization of the AUC. Just like their paramilitary predecessors, mobilizing and empowered women threatened the new groups' projects of dominance (see also Zulver 2020). Guerrero notes, "A community that demands rights and makes itself visible is more difficult to intimidate and displace. So a threat becomes a tool [for armed actors] who start to lose control over their territories. I think that in the case of the League of Displaced Women, it was because we were carrying out this resettlement in an area controlled by paramilitarism. We are women who dare to put a stick in the wheel and obstruct organized crime" (Nobel Women's Initiative 2016).

FIG. 4.3 A member of the Liga sells food at an informal stand in the City of Women. (Credit: author.)

Continuing incidents of violence lead the women to comment that their dream of a dignified life is not yet complete. Aside from direct risks to their safety, the women continue to face the vulnerabilities that come from a lack of financial security. While they own their houses, the ability to earn enough income to pay for food and bills (water, electricity, gas) is far from guaranteed. They do not have affordable transportation, nor do they have access to health care.

Despite ongoing challenges, however, the story of the Liga is one of feminist resistance—resistance to the experience of displacement, to the various sources of marginality and insecurity in El Pozón, to the lack of state support or protection, and to the threats and acts of aggression carried out by paramilitaries, Bacrim, and even the state. Against all odds, participants built a City of Women, which for them represents the fulfillment of a dignified life. They did so in light of a narrative based in feminist values and the pursuit of gender justice, as has been elaborated through their creation of collective identity and social capital, and strategic use of framing and certification. In such a way, the high-risk feminism framework explains how and why these women choose to mobilize, despite the risks entailed—both historically and in the current climate of insecurity.

El Pozón and then Turbaco represented a social context in which displaced people were forced to live and operate in a domain of losses. When Guerrero, a charismatic leader, arrived, however, she was able to frame mobilization as a way to give women back some agency in their lives, to modify their "tomorrows of violence" (Nordstrom 2004, 223). She did this by highlighting—and then making good on—the material and nonmaterial gains of acting collectively. Over time, these incremental successes compounded, giving women proof that their participation was worth the risk of exposure to increased violence.

The following section provides empirical evidence on how the Liga has transformed its narrative from one of helpless victimhood to one of political agency and survivorship. Indeed, there has been a shift from frames of fear to frames of feminist resistance. This strategic resistance can be illustrated using the high-risk feminism framework. Each of the pillars of this framework are highlighted in the deliberate and feminist resistance employed by the Liga both historically and contemporarily.

The City of Women is far more than just a physical city. It is an attitude and an ongoing act of certification. In the time I spent with one of the leaders of the Liga, she frequently referred to the organization's strategy of feminist resistance. When I asked what she meant by this, she replied, "Despite so much pain, despite so many violations, so much damage, the voice of us women has always survived. We have decided not to silence ourselves. Because of this, together, each of the members of the Liga decided to implement a strategy, an agenda of justice, where we will denounce crimes. [This strategy also means] that we have to stay united, together. And to demand our rights. . . . This is our form of peaceful resistance."[8]

Another interviewee was even more direct about what she meant by peaceful resistance: "The act of building a city in the middle of an [armed-group] controlled zone is an act of peaceful resistance. Especially despite the threats, especially as Don Julio was killed here. Despite all of that, we used our voices and our actions to build peace in the middle of a war. Especially for women like [another interviewee] who survived massacres [at El Salado], living in the City of Women is a sign of hope for the rest of Colombia."[9]

Although these interviewees use language related to peace, they are actually talking about feminist resistance rather than just antimilitarism.[10] They are showing how their experiences of violence—including gendered violence—catalyzed mobilization (see also Kreft 2019). This is not simply about broader goals of societal peace, but rather about visions of gender justice that were made collective through their engagement with the Liga.

For Guerrero and the women of the Liga, however this resistance has not been without barriers: "To get anything, anything at all, you have to fight for it—fight with sit-ins, fight by knocking on their doors. You knock on the door, they open it, they close it in your face, you knock again, they open it, they close it in your face again, you knock on the door, they open it, you push it open" (in Thomas Davis and Zulver 2015). Participating in these learned patterns of behavior is, at times, exhausting, but the women continue in the knowledge that in the past such determination has proved efficacious and that—despite having to deal with rejection—success is still feasible in contemporary conditions. This is in keeping with the idea of incremental gains over time. Success comes through participation, not as a necessary outcome of mobilization. This not only eliminates Olson's (1965) free-rider problem but also encourages people to join, as they see others enjoying the benefits of participation. When it comes to a strategy of resistance, high-risk feminism provides the tools with which to accurately account for action.

Discussion

Collective Identity

In August 2016, the Liga hosted a meeting to discuss the organization's goals and challenges. Sitting in the air-conditioned ballroom of the Bolívar government offices, the departmental director of social development said in her keynote speech, "We have to recognize ourselves in each other's stories."[11] This mantra has rung true for the women of the Liga throughout its history; in gaining a collective identity, they weave together stories of victimization and stories of resistance to create a narrative that unites them in their struggle.

One of the first strategies Guerrero undertook when she arrived in El Pozón was showing women that they shared experiences of violence and framing these in terms of their identities as women. By encouraging them to identify as women victims of the conflict, she allowed them to reflect on how gendered power dynamics influenced their experiences of violence and displacement. This is emotional work, consistent with Jokela-Pansini's (2016, 1475) observation about women human rights defenders in Honduras that "the activist's emotional connectedness with the network and its practices . . . is essential for constructing collective identities."

The early meetings of the Liga in El Pozón in the late 1990s focused on learning about one another's stories, to understand the histories and experiences they shared. The act of coming together in meetings and learning showed the women of the Liga that they were not alone in their suffering and that they had a lot in common with other displaced women living in the neighborhood. Many women told me that it was in meetings with the Liga that they were able—for the first time—to talk about the violence they had experienced in their hometowns and communities. These were deeply cathartic experiences for these women. It became apparent that "the pain of one is the pain of all"—that despite coming from different parts of the coast and having deeply personal memories, they were united as women survivors of the conflict. Over time, this helped generate a collective identity that took away the loneliness and isolation that came with displacement.

Being part of the Liga also highlighted for women how their experiences of conflict were based on the gendered social roles they occupy in society.[12] Kreft's (2019) work has found that the women mobilize in response to the threat that conflict-related violence poses to them as women, collectively speaking. That is, rather than focusing on individual threats, women mobilize in response to threats in terms of their potential impact against all women. One of her interviewees noted that without the conflict context, many women would still be in their houses or on their farms "without any questioning of their position as women. And . . . the need to leave because they were displaced, that turned them into citizens, and it helped them to understand their position as women" (230).

These findings also ring true in my research settings. As the Liga began to meet more regularly, word spread quickly throughout El Pozón. Other women in the same situation of displacement, poverty, and misery also wanted to join a group that framed understandings of their gendered experiences of conflict in such a way as to create agency and a sense of personal control. Another leader of the Liga discusses her experience in this way: "I began to meet with the Liga seventeen years ago, in Turbaco. I began because I was living in horrible conditions in the municipality where we arrived as victims of forced displacement. When I learned about the Liga—that there was a group of women teaching other women—and that they were looking for more women . . . I showed up. The group had a focus on women's rights, and I identified strongly with this work. . . . I wanted to remake myself."[13]

These realizations about their positions as women are not automatic. The experience of building collective identity is a deliberate strategy of high-risk feminism, one that is precipitated by a charismatic leader, and then through engagement by the members themselves. Finding a collective identity and a collective voice helped underscore the gendered ways in which women had suffered, but this required coming together in meetings to learn how to see themselves in one another's stories. These nonmaterial benefits to participation—sharing experiences of pain and forging a sense of togetherness—are accrued through ongoing mobilization, not as an outcome of action itself.

Social Capital

The strategy of building collective identity allows women to transform how they think about themselves, positioning them as part of a group with distinctive problems and interests. Generating social capital, then, is about giving meaning to these collective identities and creating norms of reciprocity and solidarity that foster a sense of empowerment. Beyond weaving a narrative of collective identity that united them, the women of the Liga quickly learned that being part of an organization provided them with multiple benefits, both emotional (identity based) and material.

As collective identities were established, the women learned to trust one another and began to participate in other Liga activities. Being part of the Liga offers a sense of belonging, developed through bonding social capital. One interviewee noted that participation in group meetings reinforced her understanding that "each person alone wasn't going to achieve anything" and that to effectively protect herself, she would benefit from being part of an organization. She further told me that "a person begins to grow, to learn empathy, solidarity, affection. These are ties that bind us, one to the other." [14] This solidarity is an emotional benefit that women value.

Actively banishing loneliness through the generation of social capital is another strategy for moving forward in feminist action. This organizational strengthening facilitated an incremental sense of change among the women. They began to notice that being part of the Liga lessened the burden of daily struggles, even if it did not bring an end to overall violence.

Once this solidarity was developed, Guerrero began to encourage women to legally register themselves with state institutions, making a *denuncia* of the crimes they had suffered during the conflict. The social capital they developed allowed the women to overcome their fears of making claims on the state, particularly as they saw their *compañeras* denounce. For example, one interviewee highlighted that after joining the Liga she was finally able to make her declaration of displacement: "[When I arrived to El Pozón] I didn't make my declaration of displacement because I was afraid. I didn't dare declare. There was a rumor that if you made a declaration, [the paramilitaries] would kill you. [After joining the Liga] I made my declaration. I knew that there would be benefits."[15] During this interview, she attributed her ability to declare, despite threats from armed groups, to her participation in the Liga. Another woman told me, "Denouncing is what makes us strong."[16]

When asked why women continue to mobilize despite the dangers this incurs, an employee of the regional *Defensoría del Pueblo* (ombudsman's office) reflected on her experience with women who denounced conflict-related violence: "They're not denouncing as individuals, they're denouncing as part of an organization, and this makes them feel safer. 'If you do something to me, you're going to have to do something to the whole group, too.' That brings a level of security that outweighs any insecurity that denouncing might bring."[17] Again, this ability to denounce is underpinned by leaders who frame mobilization in terms of the benefits to be gained within a high-risk context, and participants who incorporate this identity of resistance into their daily lives. The shared activity of denouncing as individuals, but in the name of a collective, means that the women of the Liga feel the strength in numbers of their *compañeras*. Despite the potential for a negative outcome, participation leads to a sense of collective risk management and collective burden-sharing that makes joining the group worthwhile.

As mentioned in chapter 3, social capital comes in two forms: bonding and bridging. Through Guerrero's efforts, the Liga was also able to generate bridging social capital. It was through her contact with Senator Leahy that she was able to generate the funds for the City of Women. She is a lawyer and was thus also able to use her knowledge of the legal environment to link women to various institutions of the state, such as the national Victims' Unit and the local Mesa de Víctimas. Making alliances with these purveyors of resources is another example of how the Liga works to create bridging social capital.

In another example of social capital as a high-risk feminism strategy, the Liga decided to undertake an internal census of its members' households.[18] The women used this data as a strategic way to engage in negotiations with national and international stakeholders, including the municipal government, the Constitutional Court, and the United Nations World Food Programme (Sandvik and Lemaitre 2013, 37).

Legal Framing

Members of the Liga told me that before joining the organization, they had no idea that they had special rights, both as women and as victims. As one interviewee said, "[Guerrero] began to meet with the women. . . . She began a process of training, where she gave workshops about human rights, about the rights that we have as victims. For us, this was totally new, because we did not know that as victims, we have certain rights. Truthfully, we also didn't know where we should go to find help. And this is how *la Doctora* helped us—she explained to us about the different state entities, and where displaced people could go."[19] Another woman said that when she first heard Guerrero speak, "it gave me goosebumps. . . . I wanted to know . . . what my rights as a woman were. I wanted to learn to express myself" (in Thomas Davis and Zulver 2015). Women told me that when they first began to meet with the Liga they were shy or scared to speak publicly. During the time I spent with them, however, I was always impressed by the clear and concise way that they drew on legal language to tell me about their experiences of conflict, and also about the rights to which they are entitled.

This was a deliberate strategy, consistent with high-risk feminism; as Sandvik and Lemaitre (2013, 41) note, "through consciousness-raising activities, members have been trained to 'speak up' and to use a human-rights and gender-conscious discourse." In doing so, the collective is able to communally fight for the implementation of legal measures and protections, social programs, and security details. Indeed, one of the organization's key strategies is to actively engage with national and international human rights courts (Sandvik and Lemaitre 2013). This was a strategy of resistance against their situations of insecurity and marginalization.

For example, the Liga actively petitioned the Constitutional Court to pass Award 092 of 2008, a landmark decision that draws on UN Security Council Resolution 1325 (on Women, Peace and Security) to recognize the disproportionate impact of conflict on women. Once it had passed, 150 Liga members were listed as special beneficiaries of the award. From 2006 to 2009, the women documented and compiled 144 testimonies of their members' experiences of displacement and violence and filed these with the Colombia attorney general's office, as part of a strategy they called the Gender Justice agenda (La Liga de Mujeres Desplazadas 2009, 17).

Furthermore, the Liga filed a complaint of impunity with the Inter-American Court of Human Rights against the Colombian state. Given the manner in which this established the organization as a legitimate entity before the agency and the Colombian state, it constituted an act of certification. With that said, it is important to note that this action also falls within the realm of legal framing, as it involved using legal mechanisms to underscore the injustice of the Liga's situation before the courts. According to Arango Olaya (2010, 4), these legal actions are consistent with the concept of "grassroots constitutionalism," a process which "through a participatory scheme has mobilized a movement towards the restitution of their rights, but moreover has served as a tool and space of empowerment by shifting power relations between sufferers and the state."[20] Later in her research, Arango Olaya notes that the Liga's experience "evidences how the human rights education activities and the creation of a physical space as the City of Women within the context of the legal intervention of the Decree (Auto 092) attempt to bridge the divide between legally and materially disempowered citizens to conscious citizens with tools to activate and participate in political spaces, but primarily claim and exercise their rights" (19).

Acts of Certification

The final "how" of the Liga's mobilizational strategies falls into the category of certification. This strategy provides the women of the Liga with a call to action, to draw attention to their situation and redefine themselves not simply as passive victims but rather as active protagonists in the process of reconstructing their lives. Certification is one of the ways that the Liga "demands recognition, respect, and services from local and national authorities" (Sandvik and Lemaitre 2013, S41).

In terms of outward actions, the building of the City of Women is the ultimate act of certification. Constructing a physical space to meet the safety, economic, and social needs of the Liga members is a sign of resistance against the violent status quo. It is a further demonstration of the way the women of the Liga conceptualize dignity. One member spoke about the lead-up to building the City: "There was a moment where the *Doctora* asked us, "What is the thing that you [women] need the most?" Almost everyone said that they needed a house. But she decided to add the word "dignified." More than just a house, we needed a dignified house, with water, with electricity. This way, our dream of a dignified life was born."[21]

Building the City of Women was an assertion of reclaiming the dignity that the women of the Liga felt they lost during their experiences with displacement and subsequent revictimization. Furthermore, the continuation of the project after the death of Don Julio shows the determination of the women; despite violent threats and acts, they did not stop their project. This was a sign to their victimizers—those who originally displaced them, those who continued to threaten and harm them, and the agencies and institutions that failed to protect them—that they would not be deterred from their project of rebuilding a dignified life.

While the City of Women is the most obvious act of certification, the Liga has also taken part in other actions that fall under this pillar of the high-risk feminism framework. Legal framing and action has been one of the Liga's most successful strategies. Certification is about claiming collective worthiness before authorities; and when the Liga continued to be subject to ongoing violence, they made their claims international.

In March 2009, a woman was killed 150 meters from a military checkpoint located near the entrance to the City of Women. This event was of particular importance because the state was under legal obligation, under Award 092, to provide security for displaced people generally and for the Liga specifically. Moreover, this came at a time when they were receiving threats from the paramilitary group Aguilas Negras (Sandvik et al. 2014, 39).[22] The Liga presented a case to the Inter-American Court of Human Rights against the Colombian state for not complying with its obligation to protect the women of the organization (Organization of American States 2009). In doing so, "it obtained protective measures from the Court by successfully arguing that members were subject to frequent and credible death threats" (Sandvik and Lemaitre Ripoll 2013, 41).

On 18 November 2009, the Commission ordered the Colombian state to implement security measures, as any existing measures were obviously insufficient. After granting precautionary measures for the Liga in 2009, it expanded these measures, in both 2010 and 2011, to the benefit of "all members of the Liga and 16 members of the organization's Youth League" (Organization of American States 2009). According to a Commission press release, the Liga informed them on multiple occasions that the Colombian authorities "have not responded in a timely manner to their situation of risk" and also reported "experiencing problems and delays in the implementation of the precautionary measures" (Organization of American States 2009). During a 2011 visit to Colombia by Rapporteur on the Rights of Women, the Commission "emphasized the need to establish a distinct approach to the measures of protection that seek to benefit women, in response to the causes and effects related to the situation of risk they face in light of their gender" (Organization of American States 2011). The Commission further publicly reminded the Colombian government of its obligation to investigate acts of violence and to punish perpetrators.

These examples demonstrate how the Liga used acts of certification to establish legitimacy, including before the Constitutional Court, municipal authorities, and the Inter-American Court of Human Rights.[23] Guerrero and other leaders of the Liga also told me about the *plantones* (sit-ins) they arranged and undertook when the Victims' Unit did not answer their petitions within a certain period of time. They also took part in a *toma* (takeover) of the Victims' Unit buildings in Cartagena. Such strategies are consistent with high-risk feminism, whereby the women of the Liga refused to be ignored.

Conclusion

The Liga de Mujeres Desplazadas is made up of a group of women who came together to make demands for gender justice, despite the horrific violence taking place around them. The risks associated with publicly engaging in acts of collective resistance cannot be taken for granted, nor can it be assumed that women automatically or naturally come together in groups to develop a feminist consciousness. Throughout this chapter, I have detailed the dynamics of how and why the women of the Liga were able to overcome barriers to mobilization to build the City of Women and, ultimately, develop a unique expression of high-risk feminism. Indeed, the National Center for Historical Memory (Centro Nacional de Memoria Histórica 2011, 21) notes that women from around the Caribbean coast engaged in social struggles, making themselves visible as promotors of memory and resistance, builders of peace, and actors demanding justice and reparation. This applies to the women of the Liga: "challenging the victimizations they suffered and the constant threats for participating in the public sphere, many women have taken on leadership roles in their communities, breaking the bounds of the domestic world with which they have been exclusively associated."

In *Sueño de Vida Digna,* Patricia Guerrero says, "We cannot desist in our hope that things can get better. . . . Because . . . we have achieved projects that at the beginning seemed unimaginable" (Sandvik et al. 2014, 73). When I interviewed her in 2015 in Bogotá, her narrative remained firm: "The most important right that these women have is the right to resist. This right to fight will be passed on to their children. They have a right to rights. They have a right to fight for these rights. The City of Women is a space where they can re-dignify themselves. They can't stop resisting—there is nothing else. . . . There are no other options, no other realities."[24]

Beyond ongoing threats, and despite a history grounded in feminist mobilization, in good faith I must note the growing feelings of mobilizational fatigue that I sensed during my time spent with the Liga in 2016. Leaders and rank-and-file members alike expressed frustrations that stemmed from stagnation. Many of these frustrations were related to a lack of success receiving individual and collective reparations, as part of the Victims' Law of 2011. Furthermore, I sometimes observed tensions between Liga leaders and Guerrero. In an interview in late 2016, Guerrero told me that since 2010, the women's *fuerza* (power, strength) is decreasing and that they need to find a way to be self-sustainable. What I take from this is that recent stagnation (in terms of a perceived lack of success related to reparations) has had a demoralizing effect on both Guerrero and the members of the Liga.

One of the other leaders told me, "sometimes I feel like I'm being pulled up and down and to the side and the other side. I feel like I'm being pulled and stretched too far."[25] She and other members are frustrated with the lack of incremental successes of the organization since the building of the City of Women in 2006. Although the collective reparations process has been initiated, at the time of my research, no one had received any benefits from this program yet.[26]

Despite the mobilization fatigue, however, it is important to mention that, their frustrations aside, I have not interviewed a single person who expressed any desire to abandon the project of creating a dignified life. As one leader said, "This train is moving, and you can stay aboard, or you can get off now. I've been on this train for so long now. There's no way I'm getting off until I reach my destination."[27]

Under the charismatic leadership of Patricia Guerrero, the Liga engaged in high-risk feminism as a strategy of resistance in the midst of a conflict zone. From collective identity building in El Pozón, to capitalizing on the individual and collective benefits of social capital, to learning to frame their conditions of marginality as illegal, to building an actual city (the ultimate act of certification), the women of the Liga have resisted and rejected their condition of being victims of gendered violence. They are protagonists in their own lives, and they rely on one another to overcome the daily struggles associated with forced displacement.

Moreover, the Liga's mobilization is a feminist rejection of strategic gendered violence, both in conflict and allegedly postconflict contexts. The strategy of coming together to demand gender justice is a form of resistance—a concerted effort to build a shield of social capital. As the charismatic bond strengthens and women adopt a feminist identity, they begin to encourage others to organize as a function of being women living in high-risk conditions who want to change societal gender relations. Such organization catalyzes more women into adopting the same identity and fortifies the protective functions of bonding social capital by adding strength in numbers. Forming a community group and giving value to collective identity can be seen as an insurgent act—an act that makes a demand for physical security and for gender justice. In turn, groups like the Liga can engage in certification techniques, acts that involve assuming risks, given the violent context, but that also have the potential to establish a certain level of legitimacy as actors on a public stage, further encouraging even more women to join.

Despite the manifold setbacks and obstacles they have experienced, the women of the Liga maintain that it is better to use their collective voice than to remain quiet. High-risk feminism has become a way of life, a strategy to create pockets of safe places for women in the midst of a conflict zone. A few weeks after the victory of the No vote in the national plebiscite, I asked one woman what she thought about the future of the Liga and her involvement with it. Despite her frustrations, her disappointments, and her ongoing fears of violence, her dedication was clear: "Look, now we women have a voice. What we built has a weight . . . and the union that we have, the alliances that we have as an organization of women, these have weight, too. It gives us power. A woman working by herself can't achieve the same result as women working in a group—a group of feminists. . . . This gives us force."[28]

5

Afromupaz

• • • • • • • • • • • • • • • • • • • •

Intersectional High-Risk
Feminism in *Cuerpo y Cara
de Mujer*

The day I decided not to be the victim,
  I looked at myself in the mirror,
I undressed, I saw myself with a woman's
  body and face, and I stopped blaming
  myself.

The day I decided not to be the victim,
I stopped crying for myself and cried for
  other people instead

The day I decided not to be the victim,
  I lifted my voice
And publicly denounced my malaise

The day I decided not to be the victim,
  I didn't forget
It is impossible to forget what is in your
  brain,
But with my whole soul I learned to
  forgive

When I decided not to be the victim,
I stood up, I loved myself, I made myself
    beautiful, I put on high heels,
I put on my best dress.
Again, I stood in front of the mirror
    with a woman's body and face . . .
I think I have healed,
Finally, I forgave myself.

When I decided not to be the victim,
We united our voices with others who
    thought the same.
So the fire will not put out fire,
And those who violated us with the goal
    of destroying us,
For our different ways of building and
    thinking,
We have converted this into an offering
    of peace

When I decided not to be the victim,
I stood up with others,
And today we are Afromupaz.
Association of Afro Women for Peace,
    together.
We are all the women of Colombia who
    are betting on peace,
And because of this today I simply
    want to say thank you, thank you,
    thank you.
I decided not to be the victim.
The best reparation that can be given to
    the victims is peace.
If we paid so much for war, why not pay
    for peace?
—María Eugenia Urrutia

Bogotá is the capital of Colombia, and with more than 11 million inhabitants in the metropolitan area, it has served as a hub of internal migration owing to displacement during the country's fifty-two year conflict with the FARC. Victims of leftist guerrillas, paramilitary organizations, state forces, and other armed groups fled to the city from all parts of the country. Arriving with their remaining family members and whatever belongings they could carry, victims had to reestablish themselves and their lives in an unknown and often hostile environment. This was no easy feat; they arrived with few economic resources and with no social network to welcome them. Usme, in the south of the city, has historically been a hub for displaced Afro-Colombians from the Pacific coast.[1]

Afromupaz—Asociación de Mujeres Afro por la Paz (Association of Afro Women for Peace) was founded in Usme in 2000. In the midst of a hostile environment, María Eugenia Urrutia—herself a victim of displacement, kidnapping, and sexual violence—established an organization for women who, like her, had fled from their homes in Colombia's Pacific Coast region and arrived in Bogotá with no personal ties or social links. She framed her experience of collective action around a shared understanding of racialized gender justice and resistance to the gendered dynamics of violence that have characterized Colombia's armed conflict. A charismatic leader, she was able to show displaced women that it was worth their while to act collectively, despite the risks this implied. The organization now represents the central community, support network, and employment opportunity for dozens of displaced Afro-Colombian women and their families in Bogotá.

For many victims of displacement—who have often also suffered physical, sexual, and psychological abuse—Afromupaz is the only safe space they have. It offers a welcoming community, the ability to heal the emotional scars of past abuses, protection against ongoing revictimization, and a source of fair employment. The high-risk feminism framework explains Afromupaz's mobilizational strategies. Indeed, as Kreft (2019) suggests, the women of this organization were able to collectively frame conflict-related violence as a threat to all women, thus catalyzing their own mobilization.

Usme represented a domain of losses for displaced women. Violence was commonplace, and inaction does not guarantee safety or protection. In this context, Urrutia was able to use a language of women's rights, victims' rights, and Afro-Colombian rights to bring women together in a coordinated gender-justice project. She showed these women, new and alone in a big city, the nonmaterial benefits of community and belonging. Moreover, she was able to facilitate material benefits for participants, including employment, healing, childcare, and reparations. In concert, these benefits complement an identity-building exercise whereby participants become ever more dedicated to the leader and to the movement, ensuring continued action over time.

Afromupaz serves as a uniting organization for women who live under high-risk conditions. From their displacement, to their settlement in Bogotá, to their daily strategies of resistance to violence, Urrutia created a charismatic bond with displaced women looking for leadership in a violent context. This mobilization can best be understood through the lens of the four pillars of the high-risk feminism framework. Afromupaz's actions of strategic feminist resistance met with success, though membership in the organization has not come without risks. María Eugenia and her cousin survived retributive violence because of the public roles they took in opposition to gendered violence. Such evidence problematizes agendas that promote women as peacebuilders in conflict and postconflict contexts without necessarily engaging with the localized and gendered threats to these women's security.

Particularities of the Case Study and Methodology

I spent ten months in 2017 doing fieldwork with Afromupaz. The organization is located in Usme, a locality in the south of Colombia's capital city. It is made up of about seventy families. These households are primarily headed by women, though some of them have husbands or partners with whom they live. The large majority of these women have multiple children. Socioeconomically, they struggle; although they work for the organization, they do not get paid wages. On their days off, the women work informally; some talked about selling plastic garbage bags at traffic lights to make enough money to pay their monthly rent.

As an organization, the women of Afromupaz engage in three primary activities: psychosocial healing programs based in traditional practices, providing economic security to displaced Afro-Colombian women through a series of small-business ventures, and legally denouncing past and present acts of violence committed against members of the organization. At the time of research, Afromupaz had its headquarters in a rented house that served as a meeting place,[2] a source of employment, an NGO headquarters, a daycare center, and a space for psychosocial healing.

Usme is far from a safe neighborhood, but the office's central location is easy for many displaced women to access on a daily basis. The neighborhood is home to criminal gangs engaged in the trafficking of drugs, weapons, and people. While my research in Usme took place in 2017, the label "high-risk" applies to the moment when Urrutia began her mobilization, in the early 2000s and into the 2010s. These dynamics of risk were ongoing, to a degree, during fieldwork. My fieldnotes highlight that the women were often concerned with my safety in the neighborhood. They used to ask their government-provided bodyguards to drive me to the bus stop, a short four minutes' walk away, instead of letting me go alone. Sometimes, if I arrived early for a meeting, they would tell me to wait for them to come and fetch me from the local Olímpica supermarket. This heightened concern for safety was not just about me; they did not want a foreigner walking around their neighborhood, drawing unnecessary attention to their meeting house. They told me on a number of occasions that they knew they were being watched by various armed groups operating in the neighborhood.

In February 2017, I contacted María Eugenia Urrutia, the founder and legal representative of Afromupaz, after meeting her at a conference. Over the following months, I spent time in the organization's headquarters in Usme. I interviewed Urrutia and her assistant, Victoria, multiple times. They often invited me to meetings with various state institutions, including the Alcaldía (mayor's office), the Victims' Unit, and the Defensoría del Pueblo (ombudsman's office). After these meetings, I was always invited to stay for lunch, which was a time when I was able to chat with the other members of the organization and their children. Over time, we developed a closeness that allowed the women to open up to me about their life stories, their past experiences with violence, and their day-to-day struggles of revictimization in Bogotá.

In terms of Afromupaz's engagement with the term *feminism,* members discuss feminism *en cuerpo y cara de mujer* (with a woman's body and face). When I once asked if she considers the organization to be feminist, María Eugenia Urrutia said, "Yes, but a differential feminism. We defend ourselves with the body and face of a woman—from our breasts to our vaginas! [Nosotras nos defendemos en cuerpo y en cara de mujer—de las tetas hasta la vagina!] We will defend ourselves as women—from our makeup to our high heels. . . . I don't want to hide my body. I don't hide my bottom or my breasts."[3]

There was a tense feeling when I asked this question, and Urrutia became slightly defensive when answering. She continued: "Afromupaz doesn't subscribe to the kinds of feminism where you wear suits. Sometimes we have disagreements with suit-wearing feminists. These women judge me for wearing colorful dresses or braids or makeup and looking sexy. But I am free—if I want to be a queen with a beautiful body, I will be."[4]

This illustrates a tension between Urrutia's feminism *en cuerpo y cara de mujer* and what she perhaps views as a more traditional or Western liberal definition of the term, or indeed what definition of feminism was implicit in the question itself. When she refers to "suit-wearing feminists," Urrutia seems to be talking about a formalized or institutionalized feminist project within which she does not categorize herself or the organization. Indeed, she might have been referencing her skepticism of conventional understandings of feminism associated since the 1990s with professionalization (that is, she might have thought of me as the kind of feminist who might wear a suit).[5] I also felt that Urrutia was referencing a class distinction, given her positionality vis-à-vis me as the researcher.

While it is clear that Urrutia is distinguishing Afromupaz feminism from what she considers more "traditional" feminism, what is also apparent is that her brand of feminism is tied up with racial identity. While at first glance, talk of colorful dresses, braids, and makeup might imply an ethnicized femininity or sexuality (perhaps consistent with body politics),[6] ongoing research with the organization reveals that she is referring to a specifically race-based identity that she is not willing to compromise. Waylen et al. (2013, 232) discuss body politics and "the way that gender intersects with race and ethnicity, sexuality . . . class . . . [and] other categories or axes of difference to illustrate that bodies are at intersections of different identity markers and powers."

Women have been the differentially impacted by the conflict in Colombia (see, for example, Centro Nacional de Memoria Histórica 2017). Marciales Montenegro (2015, 72, 86) puts forward the argument that Black women have been further targeted for both their sex and their race, an idea that this chapter continues to unpack. She notes that the intersection of the categories of sex, gender, and race results in a "differentiated impact" of past and present violence on Black women. For her, then, the violence suffered by the women of Afromupaz should be analyzed as part of a colonial discourse about "race," "women," and "black women" and the ways in which these are part of a social, sexual, and racial hierarchy in Colombia. Her overall argument is that sexual violence against the women of this particular organization (both in Chocó, where they had lived, and then again when they arrived in Bogotá) is not only an expression of gender-based violence but also one of structural racism. This intersectional experience of violence is recognized by some Afro-Colombian women's organizations themselves. For example, Laó-Montes (2016, 11) relates that at a high-level forum, Afro-Colombian feminists employed a "critical radical decolonial feminist analysis of the problem of femicide [in the conflict] as the product of regimes of domination founded on the entanglement of modes of accumulation of capital by dispossessing people from their territories, with a racist culture that denies importance to Black lives, combined with forms of patriarchal violence aggressively executed over bodies of Afrodescendent and Indigenous women."

Indeed, the National Center for Historical Memory (Centro Nacional de Memoria Histórica 2017, 297) notes that social hegemonic discourses about Afro-Colombian women's bodies (from the colonial era onward) hypersexualized them in a way that permitted and perpetuated sexual violence during the conflict. Reclaiming femininity and sexuality, then, can be seen as a way to reclaim physical integrity and personal agency. Afromupaz's feminism, then, is acted and represented with a woman's body and face.

Afromupaz: Narrating Experiences of Terror and Resistance

Social Context and Neighborhood: Violent Dynamics

The women of Afromupaz come from the Pacific region of Colombia. Oslender (2007b, 754; 2008, 86) describes the 1990s as a "time of hope" in this region, particularly following the recognition of Afro-Colombians as an ethnic minority group in the country's 1991 constitution. In late 1996, however, the Colombian army, in conjunction with paramilitary groups, began an offensive against guerrilla forces in the region, leaving in its wake civilian causalities.[7] Local communities were caught in the crossfire, "sandwiched between fighting groups" (Oslender 2008, 89). Thus began the phenomenon of mass forced displacements of hundreds of thousands of civilians. At the same time as the region experienced the violence of armed groups, powerful economic groups began to expand industries such as mining and palm plantations, often on land collectively held by local populations.[8] Community leaders who spoke out against this were disappeared and killed by paramilitary forces.[9] Scholars suggest that there were strategic economic interests in forced displacement (Escobar 2003; Oslender 2007b, 2008; Marciales Montenegro 2015).

The women of Afromupaz often spent interview time fondly remembering their homes in the Pacific. Most of them lived in small towns along the San Juan River, where they owned their own houses with gardens and farm animals. Their narratives always focus on how safe and peaceful their towns were before the guerrillas arrived.[10] When they arrived, everything changed: "The day [they] arrived, they destroyed all the lamp posts. They threatened all the men. People had to send their children away. . . . You couldn't have a daughter in town or the guerrilla would take her away. If you had a store, they came and ate everything. If you had a nice house, they would come and take it. They took my pigs, my hens, my eggs. Everyone had to leave."[11]

Interviewees spoke about the overwhelming fear they experienced. The guerrillas tried to forcibly recruit their sons and rape their daughters; "I had to *sacar mi gente* [get my people out of there] as quickly as possible. We had no time to take anything, just our clothes," one woman told me.[12] Some of the women interviewed sent their children away and stayed in the town to tie up loose ends. They remember hearing bombs and seeing the guerrilla soldiers kill and dismember people before throwing their corpses in the river. Then the army arrived and implemented a curfew: "We didn't have the right to leave our houses. It got to the point where we couldn't go out, night or day. People were starving to death in their houses."[13]

The experience of arriving in Bogotá as a displaced person was overwhelming, stressful, and threatening. Meertens (2001, 140) suggests that for women, the "rupture of social fabric at the family and neighborhood level has produced the sensation of being adrift: like a boat with no harbor." Victims of displacement recount that they would often call distant relatives, or people from their hometown who had already set up a new life in Bogotá, in hopes of staying with them until they could find their own housing. Despite this, victims reflected on how difficult it was to arrive in a new city with few relatives, far away from home, with no job prospects.

The women of Afromupaz are the victims of multiple and continuing acts of violence. After leaving the Pacific Coast, many of them moved to different parts of the country and experienced secondary and tertiary acts of displacement before arriving in Usme. One member of Afromupaz told me about being displaced from Chocó in 2001 with her children.[14] She went to Apartadó, Antioquia, but was displaced again, after suffering further acts of violence, in 2008. Because she had been given a small amount of money by the government when she arrived in Antioquia, she did not qualify for any further aid when she arrived in Bogotá.

The definition of feminism particular to Afromupaz is contingent on understanding lived experiences of structural racism, as well as sexism. Members of the organization talk about the racism they encountered in the city: as Afro women, they were often unable to find work or even rent a house owing to stigmatizing and racist attitudes: "Bogotá is a very racist city, it is hard to find employment. People might say you don't have the right skills for the job. You have to start denying your heritage. You have to straighten your hair. Your integrity suffers. But what can you do? You can't let your children starve."[15] Because of this vulnerability, Urrutia saw the need to establish an organization that offered a welcoming community, the ability to heal the emotional scars of past abuses, protection against ongoing revictimization, and a source of fair employment.

Arriving in Bogotá did not represent an end to violence. Usme is home to criminal gangs who engage in illegal economies and use violence to gain and maintain social control. Members of Afromupaz often spoke to me about revictimization. The experience of living in Usme exposes them to further dangers, related directly to the conflict and also as a function of living in a socioeconomically marginalized neighborhood. In a group interview, one woman noted that her "neighborhood is very dangerous for us, every day more so. The guerrillas aren't here, but there are other groups . . . *bandas* [gangs]. We feel revictimized here. We have suffered displacement even here in Bogotá, because of the danger."[16]

When they first arrived in Bogotá in the early 2000s, these women were threatened by unknown groups with paramilitary ties, who would come to their houses. The landlords thought that they were involved in criminal activity and accordingly threw them out. Although this is not the same violence as the forced displacement they experienced in the Pacific coast it represents another episode of homelessness that left them feeling isolated and vulnerable.

Moreover, as with the Liga, being part of the organization puts a further target on women's heads. As Marciales Montenegro (2013, 49) notes, beginning in the early 2000s, the group began to be the object of persecution and violent acts because of its community work and its demands that displaced peoples' rights be honored. This violence is ongoing, she notes; Afromupaz members have suffered threats, stalking, kidnapping, physical aggression, murders of family members, and sexual violence. Women's empowerment disrupts social norms around gender: when women dare to transgress violent power dynamics imposed by armed groups, they put themselves at risk for ongoing and retributive violence. In another group interview, a woman told me, "We have been threatened for being part of Afromupaz. We leave the building and they threaten us. They swear at us. We don't know what is going to happen. . . . We are afraid, but this also gives us strength. It makes us stronger."[17] Despite this, the organization continues to mobilize, with the goals of rebuilding the links destroyed by violence, creating community, and demanding that the state take adequate measures to protect Afromupaz members and their families.

Building a Charismatic Bond: María Eugenia Urrutia and Afromupaz

As noted in chapter 2, charismatic leadership can be attributed, in part, to a leader's ability to transform frames of fear into frames of resistance. In this way, the leader is able to effectively convince women to overcome barriers to mobilization by showing them the material and nonmaterial benefits of participation. In the case of Afromupaz, this role is filled by María Eugenia Urrutia.

Urrutia is herself a survivor of displacement and multiple incidents of sexual violence. Originally from San Juan in the Chocó department, in 1998 paramilitary soldiers raped her while her former partner and child were forced to watch. With only a suitcase, she brought her family to Bogotá and established Afromupaz as a way to help women in similar situations.

She also has a history of leadership.[18] Victoria told me that Urrutia's grandmother and aunts were prominent community members in Chocó and were involved in mobilizing women even before the conflict began. McAdam's (1982) resource-based explanation sees leaders with previous experiences of leadership as crucial for the ability of a new organization to effectively strategize. For him, the organizing skills and prestige that a leader gains through previous experiences are key resources that can be drawn on in the context of the new movement. He notes that unless there is someone with prior experience to guide the collective action, the population in question will lack the capacity to act collectively.

Urrutia was one of the organizers and participants in the *toma* (invasion) of the Red Cross buildings in Bogotá by displaced families.[19] When assembled together with other displaced people, the Afro-Colombian women present expressed their dissatisfaction with being represented by male leaders. They wanted differential representation. Victoria told me that "they said, no, we don't want to be lumped in with all the other women or with all the Afro-Colombian people."[20]

With her history of leadership and organizing, as well as her charismatic personality, Urrutia was the obvious choice, and was asked by those women present at the *toma* to become their leader. When she left the Red Cross building, she began to organize with other women, and they started to work together for women's rights. This group went on to become Afromupaz. According to Urrutia,

"The State made minimal [efforts in terms of meeting its obligations] . . . so we decided to organize ourselves . . . with the idea that we could guide those women who would arrive, so that they did not have to live what we were living."[21]

From this point onward, a group of fifty-three women began to act as an autonomous collective, amalgamating their collective knowledge, wisdoms, and ideas. There were no economic or technical resources for these women, but the organization began to take shape. Afromupaz started to work in Usme, where there was a high concentration of displaced women in need of help. Urrutia saw the need to develop a policy platform within the organization. She settled on creating initiatives within Afromupaz that would allow women to be productive and commercialize their labor. In this way, they would not have to rely on handouts or wait for the state, and they could also regain their dignity in their new communities.

Her leadership did not come without risk. In 2010 Urrutia and Victoria were kidnapped by paramilitaries from the Afromupaz office in Usme and taken to the town of Mosquera. Over the following days, they were repeatedly sexually abused. Urrutia was told that she had been kidnapped and treated this way as punishment for encouraging other women to denounce the crimes they had suffered (Moloney 2014; Gómez Carvajal 2015). This sexual violence is likely also tied up in "gendered hierarchies embedded in authority vested in race and class" (Boesten 2014, 57, 59), whereby "racialized sexuality" creates a violent social order around women who have transgressed gender norms and are therefore not deserving of respect.[22]

As a charismatic leader, however, Urrutia led by example. This is a case in which mobilization did indeed lead to violent reprisals. In the wake of her assault, she did not stop serving as the organization's leader. Instead, she used the experience to illustrate that despite increased risks for violence, the continued nonmaterial and material benefits of mobilization were worth ongoing action. After being released from Mosquera, she came home and locked herself in the house with her three children. She fell into a depression but then began to sing songs from her childhood in Chocó. "I remembered I had a life," she says, "and I realized that I was healing myself with these songs."[23] This experience strengthened her resolve to create a strategy within Afromupaz to help other women overcome their pain.

Rank-and-file members refer to Urrutia as their "mother hen." Her leadership role was fundamental in recruiting displaced women to join Afromupaz. Interviewees overwhelmingly concurred that Urrutia's personal style of leadership is to be credited for the organization's successes. An one Afromupaz member said, "María Eugenia has a very human quality, she is charismatic and intelligent. She treats other people well. She brings us into the organization because of her love, and because she values us. She understands what happened to us. When we have meetings she makes sure that we participate. She teaches us how to meet [as a group], how to resist, how to dialogue."[24] Another interviewee noted that Urrutia "loves the women and is very committed to helping us."[25]

This narrative was repeated time and time again: Urrutia's style of leadership—in terms of both personal charisma and networking abilities—permitted displaced women to create a community in their new city. Through her initiatives, socially isolated women came together and began to act collectively in the knowledge that this act of mobilization itself would bring certain benefits that merited assuming the extra risks of violence that came with such mobilization. In the terms of prospect theory, Urrutia has framed women's mobilization as a risk worth taking, given that everyone was operating in the same domain of losses. The risks of further violence become secondary to the benefits accrued through participation in collective action.

Material and Nonmaterial Benefits of Collective Action

These experiences of historical and ongoing violence give Afromupaz its reason for being. The organization sees a need to overcome the pain of the past while also protecting women from contemporary dangers and risks. The principal action strategies reflect the organization's mission:

- Develop actions that make demands and influence policy in favor of the rights of the displaced population, especially of female Afro-Colombian victims of sexual violence in the context of the armed conflict;
- Denounce and resist violent actions directed toward the organization;
- Reconstruct life projects that have been affected by violence, through the realization of collective healing exercises . . . using Afro-Colombian wisdom and customs
- Create and strengthen productive initiatives and develop strategies to promote and commercialize these initiatives (based in community wisdom);
- Empower political formation of the community;
- Increase awareness about violence against women in order to prevent it;
- Rescue and disclose the culture of black and Afro-Colombian communities, as a crosscutting strategy for all the above points. (Afropumaz 2014, 7)

One of Urrutia's primary focuses within Afromupaz is the creation of an identity of survivorship. She vocally speaks out against calling women victims and instead encourages a celebration of the experience of having survived

FIG. 5.1 This quilt hangs in the main meeting room of the Afromupaz house. Created over time by members of the organization, it represents the Huerta al Perejil model, and features phrases such as "we build peace," "cultural diversity," "healing," and "the town of the survivors." (Credit: author.)

violent acts.[26] Figure 5.1 shows a quilt that hangs in the downstairs meeting room at the Afromupaz house.

The quilt is a product of the Huerta al Perejil [Parsley Garden] fourteen-step program, developed by Urrutia and the women of Afromupaz. The program is named after a traditional song from the Chocó department. The introduction to the related book, written by Urrutia and published by the Defensoría del Pueblo (Afromupaz 2014, 5), states that "Afromupaz . . . began a community process to heal the damages caused by the armed conflict, particularly in terms of sexual violence. This process was born of an initiative thought up by María Eugenia Urrutia . . . who, from her personal healing process, and through the use of traditions of the black community, and after having lived various situations of sexual violence, designed a proposal of collective work to overcome her pain, and thus initiative a new life project through an understanding of the strengths of each of the women of Afromupaz."

Another part of Urrutia's vision for Afromupaz involved creating an economic safety net for displaced Afro-Colombian women. The experience of arriving in Bogotá, often widowed and with children, was socially isolating for victims of displacement (see Meertens 2001). Moreover, the social dynamics of racism made it hard for these women to gain employment or even rent a place to live. Seeing these dynamics, and having experienced them herself, Urrutia decided to create a space—both physical and emotional—for women to come together and gain the benefits of community solidarity.

Given the situation of unemployment, Urrutia realized that Afromupaz needed to create not only a space for women to share their emotional burdens but also a safe place, free from racism, where women could be productive and earn a living. As such, Afromupaz is not only an organization but also a business. She elaborates: "Women have to generate their own resources—this actually serves to prevent violence! Women are then going to be less willing to accept violence. We do not allow for a narrative of inequality in Afromupaz. . . . We can't cry all the time, we have to protest in front of the things we don't like. We do not talk about victims, we talk about survivors."[27]

The Afromupaz house is home to an industrial kitchen that women use to bake coconut biscuits, *chontaduro* cake, and other sweets. They import the ingredients from Chocó and use traditional recipes. They are trained in catering and hire themselves out to cook for and serve food at events. When the kitchen is not being used for cooking, they use traditional recipes to make beauty products such as soaps and creams that they sell at markets. Upstairs, they have sewing machines, and they design and produce clothing and jewelry. All of the women of Afromupaz are expected to participate in these activities (according to their skills)—this becomes their day job. Interviewees express their satisfaction at being able to work in an environment with their friends, away from racism and discrimination. Every day, the women prepare a hot lunch for themselves and their children. When I was visiting, I was always invited to eat with them, and invariably the women would tell me about the way that the food had been prepared and how it reminded them of their homes in the Pacific. Moreover, the attic of the building has been converted into a daycare room, so the women do not have to worry about childcare while they are at work.

Success of Incremental Gains

Beyond internal benefits, Afromupaz also calls on the government and state institutions to help displaced Afro-Colombian women. Since 2015, the organization has been receiving the benefits of their collective reparations. In terms of framing, Urrutia shows pragmatism in her understanding of formulating the organization's demands. She highlights that any campaign the Victims' Unit or the mayor's office devise with Afromupaz needs to bring about change. She is cognizant of the importance of maintaining a balance between the scope of the reparations program and the needs of the organization. In this way she builds bridging social capital in a manner consistent with Afromupaz's values.

FIG. 5.2 Women in Usme, including some members of Afromupaz, prepare a *sancocho* during a community mural painting activity. (Credit: author.)

The women of Afromupaz are outspoken in denouncing violence and demanding action from the state. They recognize that by continuing to denounce ongoing, gendered violence, however, they make themselves targets for even more violence, as Urrutia notes: "It's clear why we receive so many threats. . . . We have filed reports [to the state institutions], we have done sit-ins until the [institutions] listen to us. We go to the Fiscalía (attorney general). . . . We have to keep denouncing this behavior, so that it doesn't happen to us again. . . . [We] go to the Defensoría del Pueblo, to the Fiscalía, we send letters to the Procuraduría. We have to sit down at the table and tell them everything that is happening, and obviously this makes us targets."[28]

Members of the organization say that despite the risks they run, denouncing violence "is our strength, our resistance."[29] As with the Liga, a shared idea of community and togetherness is seen as a nonmaterial benefit that encourages continued participation, despite the risks associated with membership. Moreover, successes over time reinforce continued behavior. For example, one day while I was at the Afromupaz house, Urrutia introduced me to a teenage boy (the son of a member) who had been recruited into a local gang. His mother and the other women of Afromupaz had protested at state institutions until he was brought back to them. Small successes, despite the risks they incur (especially in terms of gang retaliation, in this case) emphasize to women why they should continue to act collectively.

Finally, Afromupaz engages in a series of public strategies that are based in educating and showcasing Afro-Colombian culture to the Colombian public. It does so in two ways, through cultural fairs and through organization open days. In concert, these activities comprise the day-to-day functions of Afromupaz.

Like the Liga, Afromupaz operates in a social context dominated by gendered and generalized violence. Urrutia—a charismatic leader—was able to catalyze women's mobilization: she communicated to potential participants that within this domain, engaging in collective action would bring about material and nonmaterial benefits. Moreover, this mobilization is grounded in an understanding and pursuit of gender justice that renders it an interesting example of high-risk feminism.

Discussion

Collective Identity

Afromupaz tries to foster a sense of collective identity by drawing on a shared racial-ethnic culture and the way that this shapes women's experiences of displacement.[30] This is especially pertinent when it comes to the intersections of gender and race (Hooker 2005; Marciales Montenegro 2013, 2015). In doing so, collective identity "reconstructs the social and communal fabric" of the Afro-Colombian community in their new city (Afromupaz 2014, 7). Using a narrative of cultural wisdom and ancestral traditions, Afromupaz invites women displaced by the conflict to reassociate themselves with their roots. This way, they become consciously united by a shared heritage. They are further united by their shared experiences of pain suffered during the armed conflict. Afromupaz (2014, 7) intends to carry out activities that "[allow] for a path of healing for the women, in which the feeling of estrangement and isolation generated by displacement is transformed thanks to the recovery of ancestral roots that contain shared memories previously silenced by the violence."

Afromupaz's process of collective identity creation can be understood as a form of resistance against gendered and racialized violences. For example, the Huerta al Perejil program employs dance, song, theater, and relaxation exercises to allow participants to go through an "individual and collective comprehensive healing process" (Afromupaz 2014, 10). It is important to emphasize the collective element of this process. In completing the steps of the program, the survivor is engaging in an exercise that dispels the idea that she is alone in her pain and, rather, stresses that she is part of a community of other women who have also suffered.

For example, step nine of the program, "before dawn," encourages participants to reflect on the sort of society that they want to build. This step is written from a first person plural perspective: "What society are we going to build for a new tomorrow?" "As survivors of violence, we consider ourselves to have an important role." "We will share our ideas about . . . our personal motivations" (Afromupaz 2014, 31). This language is deliberate—the healing process for survivors of violence is purposefully collective. In creating a shared identity of survivorship, Afromupaz builds a solid base from which to execute its other goals of resistance, reconstruction, and political training. In an interview, a member of the organization, noted, "What gives a person the strength to erase all of this is the knowledge that it's not just one person, but many together. I lived an ugly situation in my village. I was almost mute. And now I am a little parrot! In the meetings, in the dialogues, I talk."[31]

Urrutia's successful use of collective identity creation is also noted by state officials. Carmen Marciales Montenegro, of the Defensoría del Pueblo, has worked with Afromupaz since 2011. In an interview, she told me, "The true *fuerza* (power, strength) of Afromupaz is its ability to provide a space where people can participate in collective community action. They have created an identity that is not just about being a woman, or an Afro-woman, but about being an integral part of Afromupaz itself. They have all lived and experienced discrimination . . . but, importantly, they have an organizational structure which creates a sense of shared identity and community bond. And this is continuous, it is reinforced every day."[32]

Indeed, the question of strength is a daily topic of conversation in the Afromupaz house. A participant in a group interview said that "being in Afromupaz gives us the strength to continue in our lives. This is what saves us. We have lived harsh things."[33] Another interviewee reiterated, "remember, we are not victims, . . . we are survivors now."[34] All of this serves to highlight the collective identity developed by Urrutia and the women of Afromupaz—an identity that binds them together as strong women who actively choose to resist the violences to which they are exposed, and to do so using an intersectional and feminist lens. This identity gives organization members a sense of importance and a sense of belonging. As one woman told me in an interview, "Above all, we have been united. *Somos guerreras, somos resistentes* [We are warriors, we are resilient]."[35] This language goes beyond mere survivorship—the women of Afromupaz actively struggle for justice.

Social Capital

In an environment where women are victimized and revictimized, taking a stand against gendered violence is a form of resistance. In a climate where this violence is both gendered and racialized, Afromupaz builds bonds of social capital that form part of a feminist strategy of resistance. There are benefits—both emotional and material—that come with belonging to Afromupaz. This is part of the strategy the organization employs to protect its members against violence. Beyond just a shared identity of survivorship, however, the women speak of community bonds, as outlined in an organizational publication (Afromupaz 2014, 19):

> "I feel [that Afromupaz] is our own space where we can build our lives."
> "I don't feel like a stranger, rather, I feel like I am part of a family, like I am in my home."
> "I feel happy, liberated, and supported—I feel companionship."
> "Many women have been raped and violated, but there is trust between us to talk about sexual violence."

One of the factors implicated in building social capital in the case of Afromupaz is related to nonmaterial, emotional elements. For example, a long-time Afromupaz member said in an interview that when she first arrived in Bogotá after being displaced three times, she felt isolated and desperate. After only a short time in the city, her youngest daughter died. "This was incredibly hard for me. I didn't know anyone. I suffered alone," she related.[36] She has now been involved with the organization for nine years. In January 2017, her son-in-law was murdered in his house in Usme. Tears filled her eyes when she told me about this, but she was quick to highlight how much support she had to carry her through her grief. The women of Afromupaz grieved together (her widowed daughter is also part of the organization), sharing the emotional burden. Afromupaz provides an emotional safe space for its members. This space does not necessarily guarantee physical safety; as mentioned, Urrutia and her cousin were kidnapped from the office itself.[37] The other aspects of the organization—its provision of emotional safety, for example—makes up for the unsafe environment in which it is situated. Such benefits ("feeling safe," as opposed to actually and objectively ensuring physical safety) are accrued through—and not as an outcome of—mobilization.

Building social capital through bonding, therefore, serves to promote membership and collective action by offering benefits only to those who participate actively. The nonmaterial benefits of mobilization persuade those who may not have mobilized before to participate in collective action, as the risk of exposure to further violence is eclipsed by the perceived benefits of emotional support and feeling safe. Highlighting the potential for benefits (despite a high-risk environment) is a strategy initially employed by leaders (like Urrutia) and then continued by members as they begin to experientially rationalize their reasons for mobilizing.

The Huerta al Perejil program has now been mentioned a number of times, including as a form of collective identity building. Its most important contribution, however, is generating social capital for members of Afromupaz. The program guides victims of violence through acceptance, grief, anger, and forgiveness. For many women, this is the first time that they have been able to speak about their experiences of displacement. One member of the organization related, "The Huerta al Perejil is one of the best parts of Afromupaz. It has been the best psychosocial attention I have received. [Before I came to Afromupaz] I was raped, I was afraid. . . . This is the sort of trauma we were left with. But through the process of the Huerta I am much better. We all talked about our experiences of rape. And then afterwards I had the courage to report what had happened to me [at the Victims' Unit]."[38] Simpson (2007, 95) explains that violence is so personal because it affects the mind, body, self-identity, and personhood. Accordingly, "the role of public story-telling after such violence thus is significant. It can allow for victims to 'take back' their self-pride, their self-worth, and assume their place as an intrinsic part of the new post-conflict political order."

Many of the women who suffered abuses were subsequently threatened by their perpetrators. They were told that if they reported their attacks, they would be killed. As a result, before they joined Afromupaz, organization members had not felt safe relating their stories, often leading to symptoms of posttraumatic stress. An interviewee told me, "joining Afromupaz was the first time I was able to talk about what had happened to me. Things happen to you, and you have to live with them. I was afraid. They said that if I told anyone what they had done to me, that they would kill me. I was so afraid that they would kill me. I lived that nightmare and I lost trust in everyone. Here, I regained that trust."[39]

The bonding social capital generated through participation in Afromupaz and the Huerta al Perejil program helps these women—many of whom have lost their families in the act of displacement—regain a community that brings them material, psychological, and emotional benefits. As one woman noted, "Afromupaz is the organization that has helped us the most. We are part of it.

Our *compañeras* are our family now."[40] The women gain further strength in the knowledge that they have a community that supports them. Whereas before they were silenced by the fear of retribution, the knowledge that they are part of an organization that protects them inspires them to denounce their perpetrators. When I asked about fear of revictimization, one woman told me, "Yes, we are all afraid, but we can count on the organization. Here, we feel safe inside. . . . I am in my house, I am not afraid."[41]

Not all social capital is of the bonding variety, however. The organization has strong ties to, and has received financial and programmatic support, from the mayor's office, the Victims' Unit, the ombudsman's office, and a number of foreign embassies. This way, Urrutia has been able to create strategic connections that have led to material benefits over time, including, for example, money to rent a house, to buy machinery for the kitchen, and to design and publish the Huerta program. Moreover, she has the ability to take advantage of political opportunities at specific moments in time. McAdam (1982, 47) might attribute this to her previous experiences of leadership, but others would say that she has a natural ability to create linkages through her strong interpersonal skills and her ability to think critically. Having worked with Urrutia for many years, Marciales, of the ombudsman's office, said, "Why has Afromupaz been so successful? Honestly, it's mainly based in the leadership of Maria Eugenia. She has a way of connecting things that others don't imagine connecting. She knows how to connect with the various institutions and to propose things at the right moment to the right people."[42]

In the case of Afromupaz, then, the leader of the organization creates connections that play an important role in the organization's ability to obtain material benefits. At the same time, however, she creates a narrative that highlights to members that the nonmaterial benefits of membership (belonging and solidarity) are equally important to their sustained participation over time.

Legal Framing

In other cases of organizations that employ the high-risk feminism framework, legal framing has taken the form of highlighting the illegality of the situations in which many victims find themselves. For example, women in El Salvador refer to the Special Law (Ley Especial de 2011) that explicitly outlines the various forms of violence against women that exist and establishes that these acts are illegal and punishable by law (Zulver 2016). In the case of the Liga, participants organized collectively to denounce before the state the crimes they had suffered over the years. Moreover, when these demands were not met, the Liga filed a case before the Inter-American Court of Human Rights to highlight the illegal nature of the Colombian state's refusal to deal with the claims.

These examples highlight that part of a strategy of resistance, within the high-risk feminism framework, involves using legal mechanisms and a strong rights frame to establish the legitimacy of the members' claims. In the case of Afromupaz, legal framing has been twofold. First, the organization has worked closely with state institutions to successfully establish themselves as eligible for collective reparations. Second, on an ongoing basis, the organization helps its members to declare their situation of displacement, as well as denounce present-day crimes.

In 2011 the Colombian government passed the Victims' and Land Restitution Law (Ley de Víctimas y Restitución de Tierras). As part of this law, the government included collective reparations in the form of special compensations for collective victims. These are supposed to be integral—comprehensive. An umbrella term, comprehensive reparations are intended to include social, economic, cultural, and environmental provisions (Unidad para las Víctimas 2017). Since 2015, Afromupaz has been receiving the benefits of their collective reparations. In March 2017, I attended a meeting with the Victims' Unit, the Alta Consejería de Paz, Víctimas, y Reconciliación (High Council of Peace, Victims, and Reconciliation), and Afromupaz. At the end of the meeting, one of the government employees informed María Eugenia and the rest of the leaders present that the Alta Consejería had approved a budget that would allow Afromupaz to buy its own headquarters. This news was met with cheers and embraces. As the official told the women, "The idea is that we get moving." Her words refer to both the physical act of moving into new premises and the symbolic act of moving forward with collective reparations.

Afromupaz's focus on reparations is centered on healing the scars left by the conflict. The organization frames its collective reparations in terms of psychosocial healing—redressing the violence members suffered during the conflict. In an interview with Urrutia, it became clear that Afromupaz was cognizant of the need to maintain a balance between the scope of the reparations program and the necessities of the organization. She noted that the women were acutely aware of the moment in time when it was possible for their demands to be realized in practice: "we were able to take advantage of the willingness of the government to negotiate and advance."[43] Within this discourse, however, Urrutia discussed a flexibility: in outlining their holistic collective reparations plan, the women accepted that there would be specific issues that would not be negotiable at that moment. "In what we could not [negotiate], we said, let's put it to the side and wait and see. In what we can [negotiate], let's advance!"[44] Urrutia was able to successfully and strategically navigate the legal and political opportunities that become available.

Collective reparations are not the only way Afromupaz frames its mobilization. The organization also makes an effort to systematically declare instances of violence—both past and contemporary—before the institutions of the state. In an interview, Urrutia described this work: "We have to denounce this network [of criminals]. Afromupaz is very clear that we are not going to allow [more violence] to happen to us. And more than anything, we won't let it happen to the victims of the conflict. These are the most vulnerable women that exist. They are so vulnerable that no one pays attention to the situation. We have to denounce."[45]

These sorts of actions, however, do not go unnoticed by perpetrators. Urrutia and Afromupaz continue to receive threats. Referring to documenting displacement and other crimes, she noted, "As [women] human rights defenders, we are still victims [of violence]. It is going to be very difficult to get to a place where we are not persecuted. The theme of the Peace Process is polarizing in society, and we have become a target for [criminal groups]. The situation has improved—it's not like the paramilitarism of the 80s and 90s.... But we are still in a conflict zone. There are Bacrim groups [living up the street] in the neighborhood."[46]

The emotional benefits of participating are seen as worth the risks of retributive violence when operating in a high-risk context (that is, where nonaction does not guarantee safety). Afromupaz resists acts of violence by involving the institutions of the state that have the duty and the responsibility to act to protect citizen security. By strategically couching their complaints within the existing legal structures of the Colombian state, these women exercise a form of feminist agency (based in their positions as women, victims, and survivors) that serves to resist ongoing violence in the hope of reducing future acts of victimization. They use the same language of rights used by the state to validate and legitimize their experiences and to make demands for protection and redress.[47]

Acts of Certification

The Huerta al Perejil strategy brings together survivors, who develop a collective identity and learn that the pain of one is the pain of all. In terms of the high-risk feminism framework, however, this psychosocial program can further be understood as an act of certification. By creating an alternative psychosocial healing program to the limited options made available by the state, Afromupaz highlights that the government programs are not tailored to the specific needs of Afro-Colombian women. The program further makes clear that without a differential (that is, feminist and racialized) understanding of the violences they have suffered, existing state programs will not be successful in terms of emotional healing.

Other acts of certification involve further exposing Afro-Colombian culture to the community to reduce racist stigma. This takes the form of open days and cultural fairs. Previous events have used music, dance, and song, as well as a culinary fair to showcase Afromupaz to the wider public. Usually held in public spaces such as the Plaza de Bolívar (in the center of Bogotá), the fair looks to use cultural diversity to promote healing. Afromupaz is founded on the belief that the revindication of cultural traditions can bring about healing, and the cultural fairs are an example of how the organization shares this with the public (Secretaría Distrital de la Mujer 2015).

The open days are a new strategy in the Afromupaz repertoire. In June 2017, the organization advertised one particular open day to the various state institutions with which they work so that their employees could come and learn more about the group's cultural heritage. The garage doors of the house were opened, and the main meeting room was cleared to display all of the different products and food items created by the organization. Other open days are designed for the neighbors. An interviewee explained that to create further social cohesion in the neighborhood, it is imperative that the neighbors understand what the women of Afromupaz do in their headquarters. The group further hopes to create bonds of trust between the organization and the neighbors to prevent further violence and victimization of organization members.

The act of opening the organization's doors to the public not only allows the community to get to know its strategies, but also establishes Afromupaz as a legitimate social actor within the neighborhood. Especially given the sentiment of being targeted both for being women and for being Afro-Colombian, outwardly celebrating the intersection of these two identities in a public space is an act of resistance. Certification is the act of making one's organization legitimate in the eyes of the state and the public via action. Afromupaz's primary strategies directed at community outreach are consistent with this definition, further highlighting the utility of the high-risk feminism framework in describing the organization's mobilization.

Successful Mobilization: High-Risk Feminism as a Harbinger of Change

High-risk feminism is a way to frame and understand how and why women living in precarious settings choose to expose themselves to the ongoing risks of mobilizing for gender justice. The experiences of Afromupaz highlight the ways in which members of this organization choose to engage in feminist collective resistance, despite the dangers of doing so.

Indeed, Afromupaz's mobilization attracts a continuation of threats against organization members. One day, while sitting in her office, I asked Urrutia if she is afraid of the threats she and other members of Afromupaz receive. "Of course", she replied. "Every day I wake up afraid to die. . . . But eventually I realize that I am not afraid of death. . . . I am not going to stop doing what I'm doing, I will not stop doing my work. . . . I'm not going to stop standing up to say, 'this is wrong.'"[48]

Urrutia's statement echoes her understanding—promulgated to organization members—that when the risk of violence or death becomes unexceptional, the perceived benefits of participating in something that gives life meaning become relatively more important than abstaining from participation. This demonstrates her use of prospect theory to encourage participation. The rank-and-file members of Afromupaz share Urrutia's bravery: "The war . . . was fought against the civilians, who didn't have anything to do with it. . . . It has been cruel to us. But now, in Afromupaz, we are no longer victims, but rather, survivors. The victims are behind. We are survivors now. For all that they have tried to push our heads down, we haven't [let them]."[49]

Feminist collective action has sprung forward from experiences of gendered and racialized violence and risk. Afromupaz uses high-risk feminism as a strategy for protection amid ongoing sources of victimization. Acting as an Afro-Colombian feminist organization in a high-risk context exposes the women of the organization to danger by making them targets of further violence. Despite this, the nonmaterial and material benefits accrued by being part of Afromupaz outweigh the fears of further victimization.

6

La Soledad

• •

When Women Do Not Mobilize

The previous two chapters discuss instances of high-risk feminist mobilization in Colombia, with an eye to describing how and why women mobilize in high-risk contexts. In the case of the Liga de Mujeres Desplazadas and Afromupaz, we saw how, under the guidance of a charismatic leader, groups of women came together to engage in high-risk collective action in the pursuit of gender justice. Despite personal histories of destructive and gendered violence, they mobilized for a more equitable future. In La Soledad, however, women did not mobilize for gender justice, despite similar scope conditions to those women organizing in Turbaco and Usme.

Riohacha, the departmental capital of La Guajira, is home to a significant population of displaced people, victims of Colombia's conflict. It is also the site of historical and ongoing violence and insecurity at the hands of paramilitaries and their successors. I conducted research in the La Soledad land invasion neighborhood, interviewing and hanging out with displaced women, who are also survivors of displacement and sexual, physical, and psychological violence.[1] The majority of these women are single mothers, and none of them are involved in formal or stable employment. Furthermore, despite having declared their victim status with the institutions of the state, none of them have received their individual reparation payments. Ethnically, religiously, and socioeconomically, these women are demographically similar to their displaced counterparts in other parts of the country.[2] What makes La Soledad different from Turbaco and Usme, however, is that despite a similar domain of losses, there is no high-risk collective action.

What this negative case illustrates is the finding that without a charismatic leader, high-risk feminist mobilization will not take place. This is the case even if the potential participants and the social context closely resemble those where we do see mobilization. Without a leader who is able to convince women that there are material and nonmaterial benefits to mobilizing within a domain of losses, those who might otherwise participate are not able to overcome barriers of fear, which we know prevents risk-taking behavior (Lerner and Keltner 2001). In her study on leadership, Robnett (2013, 5) notes that "as scholars of social movements, we must be as concerned about who becomes a leader as by who does not." This chapter engages in that task, and in doing so provides further evidence to support the mechanisms that do or do not facilitate gendered high-risk collective action.

The selection of a negative case follows Mahoney and Goertz's (2004) possibility principle (2004). La Soledad and its inhabitants fall within this principle, in that they have the characteristics of a group that could engage in mobilization, but does not. In the case of La Soledad, one of the mechanisms that catalyzes high-risk mobilization is missing: the presence of a charismatic leader.

By referring to these women's experience as a negative case, I do not mean to ascribe normative judgement. Their case is negative only insofar as these women do not fit within the definition of a high-risk feminist organization. Such categorization is not to negate or diminish their survival and agency, despite adverse conditions—including histories of violence and contemporary struggles. Indeed, I include this case to highlight the importance of a charismatic leader, not to present its failed mobilizational potential. La Soledad demonstrates the strength of the barriers to mobilization. It cannot be assumed that women automatically or naturally come to engage in collective action for justice or peace; rather, the nuanced dynamics of both why and how they are able to overcome barriers to mobilization need to be explored, particularly those represented by historical and contemporary violence.

Selecting a Negative Case

To find a negative case, I set out to find scope conditions similar to those of the Liga and Afromupaz: populations of displaced women who are victims of violence, in situations of conflict and of postconflict, who are considered victims under Colombia's 2011 Victims' Law, and who continue to live in contexts of high-risk, including the risk of revictimization by armed groups for the transgression of gendered social orders. Crucially, however, I wanted to find a case where women were not able to overcome the barriers to high-risk collective action to engage in high-risk feminist mobilization.

This task came to fruition in 2017, when a colleague put me in touch with an official at the regional Victims' Unit in Riohacha. The same colleague also introduced me to Estefania, who was the departmental representative for victims of sexual violence in the Mesa de Víctimas at the time.[3] We spoke over the phone, and I explained my research project. She was interested in meeting me and invited me to her neighborhood, where, over time, she introduced me to other women in the community. Through initial contact with these two interlocutors, I used snowball sampling techniques to meet other interviewees. Estefania facilitated my ability to work in La Soledad, and also put me in touch with other social leaders in the area. She shared contact information for her point people at various institutions of the state, and through meeting them I was able to interview other officials who work with victims. During my time in Riohacha, I interviewed and spent time hanging out with more than thirty community members, as well as people at the Victims' Unit, the ombudsman's office, the mayor's office, and the governor's office. I conducted the bulk of my research in May and June 2017, with follow-up fieldwork taking place in January and February 2018.

A Similar Domain of Losses: La Soledad in Comparative Perspective

Dynamics of Violence

La Soledad is a neighborhood on the outskirts of Riohacha, the capital city of La Guajira. According to residents, the neighborhood was founded about seventeen years ago and is primarily inhabited by displaced people. As in the cases of El Pozón, Turbaco, and Usme, residents were displaced owing to Colombia's armed conflict. Originating from departments along the Caribbean coast and along the northern part of the border with Venezuela, they eventually made their way to Riohacha, a hub for displaced people. An institutional employee told me in an interview that of the city's 150,000 inhabitants, approximately 62,000 are registered as displaced.[4]

The borders of La Soledad are unclear, and it blends into adjoining informal neighborhoods. The ad hoc approach to naming streets often made getting to Estefania's house a challenge, as local taxi drivers did not know how to navigate its warren of unpaved avenues. As is the case with many land invasion neighborhoods, access to services such as light, sewage, and water is not guaranteed. Estefania and her neighbors have small wells at the back of their patios. They pay private companies to fill these wells every few weeks, and they use the water for drinking, bathing, and cleaning. Residents should, in theory, have access to public electricity, but the crisscrossed wires that precariously hang at eye level suggest that they pirate their power. The style of house varies; while some are built of cinderblocks and concrete, others are tin and wood shacks.

There is little foliage, and the sun beats down on the hot, dusty neighborhood. Children play in the streets, and teenagers drive motorcycles, hoping to make extra money by ferrying residents into the center of town. I was told on a number of occasions that these *mototaxistas* moonlight as small-scale drug dealers. They also allegedly provide security, intelligence, and messenger services for armed groups (Idler 2019).

Like the other case studies in this book, La Soledad is a site of ongoing violence. Indeed, I decided to conduct fieldwork here in part because of the similar dynamics of violence it shares with these positive cases. The very fact that it is in an invasion neighborhood puts it at odds with local authorities. In 2001, around the time it was established, the local police organized operations to remove more than 200 families who had invaded land that had been sold by private companies to build a housing project. Despite having been forced off the land, the mainly displaced population returned and began squatting again. In an interview, a representative from the departmental governor's office told me that there are ongoing struggles between those who squat on the land and the landowners. She talked about the conflict between the "competing visions" the two groups have for the use of the territory and said that the relationship is not respectful.[5]

In the early 2000s, La Soledad was a site of concentrated paramilitary activity, which continues in new iterations. The department's proximity to the Venezuelan border makes it a center of smuggling and contraband activity, which continues to present violent dynamics. Conversations with interviewees reveal their understanding that contemporary armed groups are merely modern configurations of the same paramilitary actors from years past.

The combination of criminal gangs and an unemployed, disaffected youth makes La Soledad a hotbed for trafficking and contraband. The district victims liaison told me that the socioeconomic vulnerability of the residents makes them an apt target for armed groups to recruit new members.[6] Interviewees talked to me about their worries of violence in their neighborhood: this usually takes the form of armed robbery but has historically included physical violence and murder.[7] I have a distinct memory of sitting in Estefania's patio while she desperately sent out group text messages trying to find a neighbor's disappeared son. When I was back in Bogotá a few days later, she forwarded me a Whatsapp voice note detailing that the teen had been found dead in a nearby swamp.

Moreover, as in Usme, El Pozón, and Turbaco, a climate of criminality means that armed actors look for total social control. Leaders who dare to contest armed groups' claims of social and territorial control receive threats, pamphlets, and messages sent via Whatsapp or Facebook. Estefania shared a photo of a pamphlet she received. It read, "The only way to end these plagues and rats is by exterminating them." Signed by the Autodefensas Gaitanistas, a paramilitary

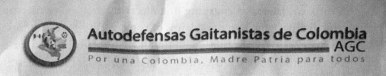

COMUNICADO A LA OPINION PUBLICA

LA ÚNICA FORMA DE ACABAR CON TODAS ESA PLAGAS Y RATAS ES EXTERMINANDOLAS

Les vamos a demostrar que si existimos, les prometemos perros hijueputas Tortura y muerte, se les hará saber quién manda en este país.
Declaramos objetivo militar a todas las organizaciones de Derechos humanos, Sindicalistas, reclamantes de tierras, defensores de presos de las FARC y ELN, los que hacen informes de derechos humanos, miembros de las organizaciones políticas de las FARC, congreso de los pueblos, unión patriótica, marcha patriótica.
Muerte a todas esas gonorreas sapos hijueputas que están fomentando y apoyando el crecimiento de la violencia.
Les informamos que a partir de la fecha son declarados objetivo militar

MUERTE A TODOS ESTOS HIJUEPUTAS

**¡¡AGC PRESENTE!!
MAYO 2017**

**Por una COLOMBIA

Madre patria, para todos**

FIG. 6.1 A pamphlet delivered to Estefania by a criminal group. The note threatens torture and death to human rights defenders. (Credit: photo received via Whatsapp Messenger, 25 May 2017.)

successor group, it puts a target on the back of human rights organizations, unions, and people making land claims. Estefania told me on multiple occasions that she received these pamphlets because of her work with the Mesa de Víctimas, through which she was exposing gendered violence of the past, thus speaking out against a social order that crosscuts past and present contexts.

The violent dynamics in La Soledad are comparable to those in Usme, El Pozón, and Turbaco insofar as engaging in collective action is a dangerous activity, given ongoing armed groups' claims of control. The context of insecurity indeed presents risks for those who mobilize, but this is also true in the other two case studies; in Turbaco and Usme, women mobilized despite and because of the violence to which they continue to be exposed. Put in comparative perspective, I did not identify factors that made La Soledad any more or less conducive to mobilization. The reason for the absence of this particular mobilization, then, must be based on something other than a high-risk context.

Displacement and Arrival in La Soledad

As with the women in Turbaco and Usme, the women living in La Soledad fled violence and terror in their home territories in the late 1990s and early 2000s. Their stories are similar, involving displacement, sexual violence, murder, disappearances, and torture. Estefania and her family have been displaced multiple times. On various occasions, she has had to send her children to live with relatives in other parts of the country, as she could not afford to move the entire family. Her personal story is also marked by extreme and gendered violence at the hands of various armed groups. Her story is not unique in the neighborhood: other women I spoke with also had to flee, but not before enduring conflict-related sexual violence.

When I met the women living in La Soledad in 2017 and 2018, they were all single mothers, with children between two and six. They lived close to one another in informal housing, and most did not own the deeds to the land. The quality of their housing varied; the more rudimentary houses are vulnerable to damage from flash floods and are usually insufferably hot, especially when the roofs are made of zinc sheeting. None of the women I interviewed had any formal employment, and many were unable to generate income from the informal economy as well. The latter relied on remittances sent by family members in other parts of the country, on stolen electricity, and on the charity of their neighbors. One interviewee showed me how she made commissions from selling clothes from a magazine. Another ran a makeshift bar out of her house, selling cheap beer to the local men. Estefania sometimes made extra money by allowing Venezuelan migrant men to string up their hammocks in her back patio. Their stories are not dissimilar to those of the women of Afromupaz or the Liga. Their situations are precarious. On multiple occasions they shared with me their worries about the ongoing violence in the neighborhood, and they particularly expressed being afraid for the safety of their children.

The newly displaced women in Turbaco and Usme, facing similar situations of vulnerability, began to come together to meet with other women. For the Liga, this took the shape of women uniting to create an *olla común* to feed

FIG. 6.2 The makeshift house where Estefania and her children lived in La Soledad before they were violently displaced to Medellín. (Credit: author.)

their children and then to raise money for a coffin for a deceased neighbor. These actions helped reveal their shared experiences of conflict and began the process of developing a collective identity. For Afromupaz, this took the form of women gathering to specifically address Afro-Colombian women's issues, including experiences of suffering racism, unemployment, and the need for differential psychosocial healing.

Women in La Soledad, however, do not mobilize. It would be disingenuous to say that there is no solidarity in the neighborhood, however, so this distinction requires explanation. Immediately apparent to me when I first visited the barrio was that all of the mothers watch over one another's children. Estefania's children played in the patio with the other women's children. Each mother treated the children as her own, in terms of praise and of discipline. They referred to one another as "comadre." One interviewee explained, "The *comadres* are . . . like godmothers. If I need something, I go to Estefania, and ask her, and if she has it, she'll help."[8]

I spent many hot afternoons sitting under the mango tree in Estefania's patio with groups of women. They came to chat, to ask for advice, or to beat the boredom of unemployment. They let me sit with them, have a glass of juice, and participate in their conversations. They often talked about issues of violence in the neighborhood, sharing information about an unknown car they saw driving by or a neighbor who had been robbed. They universally worried about the safety of their children and discussed this often. During one conversation, a woman recounted that the previous Sunday a strange car pulled up outside her house and a man asked her son a question. "Thank God I went outside! I grabbed [my son] and took him inside. You can't talk to strangers in this neighborhood!"[9] Estefania privately explained to me afterwards: "The majority of [the women who we had been chatting with earlier] are victims of sexual violence, and they are the heads of their household. We don't have the support of a partner, and not even the state helps us."[10] Daily life, she explained, is characterized by ongoing fear of violence. She described the women as living lives full of "terror."

The difference between collective action and neighborhood solidarity, however, took time for me to understand. When I first met Estefania, she told me that she heads an organization which she claims has 190 members and offers support to victims of sexual violence. In an interview, another woman told me that she too had started an organization that allegedly addresses issues of abuse against children. A third woman discussed her own organization for victims of physical violence. Initially, these interviews confused me and led me to believe that the neighborhood women were engaging in some sort of high-risk collective action.

Deeper questioning, however, revealed that these organizations exist only nominally, and they do not engage in collective action in practice. Apart from Estefania's organization, they are not legally registered with the chamber of commerce, do not have any formal structure (indeed, some do not even have any members), do not have defined strategies or goals, and do not participate in shared activities. Estefania explained: "In other places in Colombia there are organizations, but not here. We don't have offices, we don't have money for that."[11] While it is true that legal registration, offices, and resources may represent a barrier to some types of action for these women, the women of the Liga and Afromupaz did not begin their collective action with these resources either. Estefania's explanation that the neighborhood does not have active women's organizations because of the cost does not seem convincing.

Wanting to find out more about Estefania's organization and what role it played in the neighborhood, I asked other women if they were part of any local organizations or community groups. I was intrigued by one interviewee's response: "I am not part of any women's organization. . . . If there were a women's organization in the neighborhood, however, I would like to take part."[12] Another neighbor noted "there isn't much organization. . . . [La Soledad] is a forgotten place."[13] A third neighbor said: "I am not part of any organization. If Estefania invites me to an event or a meeting, I'll go, but I don't really like organizations."[14] These responses were particularly interesting to me, given that I met these interlocutors through Estefania, who introduced them to me as members of her organization for victims and vulnerable people. The lack of cohesive collection action was confirmed in interviews with officials at the Victims' Unit and the offices of the ombudsman, the mayor, and the governor, all of whom reported they did not know about any women's organizations in La Soledad. One of these officials told me, "The interests of these groups are a political question. . . . What you see, then, is that whenever there is a call by the government for 'women's representatives' there is a surge of 'women's organizations,' but they exist on paper only. As soon as you look at their work, you see that there is nothing backing it up. There are very few women who actually work for women's rights."[15]

Explaining Inaction: Why Did These Women Not Engage in High-Risk Feminist Mobilization?

To better grasp why women in La Soledad do not mobilize in practice, I spent time speaking with officials at state institutions in an attempt to ascertain whether other dynamics were preventing mobilization. A gender specialist at the ombudsman's office told me, "There is no clear feminism. . . . Here, women know that as women they have different and unequal conditions within the displaced population, but they don't necessarily know how to organize themselves accordingly. The knowledge that there is a clear need for an organization based around being a woman—this is barely starting here."[16] The official attributed women's inaction to a lack of consciousness that they could mobilize around a shared condition of gendered inequality. On an earlier occasion, when I asked her about a lack of women's mobilization, she replied, "There is no culture of that here."[17] Her words reminded me of Patricia Guerrero's reflections about arriving in El Pozón and finding that while women could express sadness about their suffering, they did not necessarily have the tools to reframe their fear as anger or resistance. This is why she needed to "ignite a fire in their hearts" (Nobel Women's Initiative 2016). The women in La Soledad, then, were lacking a leader who could catalyze action.

I later saw the dynamics described by the gender specialist in action. In May 2017, I attended a meeting hosted by the Victims' Unit in Riohacha. Invitees were contacted by the agency to attend a ceremony at the Casa de la Cultura at the end of the city's tourist boardwalk. Government employees sat on a dais with a white tablecloth, and local women and their families sat in rows of chairs. A woman with a microphone called up certain members of the audience to present them with a formal letter of apology from the Colombian state. A saxophonist played loud songs to the audience. Then the event was over. A full page spread in the next day's local newspaper read, "Women victims of sexual violence dignified."[18]

After the event finished and the government officials had gone home, I sat down with about fifteen women, all of whom had been recognized in the ceremony. Some, but not all, were from La Soledad. They were visibly pleased to see one another, and as they chatted and gossiped, I realized that many of them were catching up after not having seen one another for some time.

When I asked if they spent time together outside events such as this, they replied that no, they did not. They said that they enjoy coming together and chatting, and even went so far as to say that it was important for them to know other women who openly discuss their experiences of displacement and sexual violence, but that they have not formed any sort of group or organization. When I asked if they had any plans to continue meeting up (this was the third of three events organized by the Victims' Unit), there was unified agreement that they would like to continue meeting. "We would like to (*quisiéramos*), but if [the Unit] invites us."[19] I was surprised that there was no independent will or desire to arrange something outside of the context of the Victims' Unit meetings. When I asked if there was anyone among them who took charge of organizing activities or who might be a natural leader, they replied that no one had ever shown a desire to take charge.

I was struck by how enthusiastic they were to spend time together, yet only met up when they were invited by an external organizer like the Victims' Unit. The stories and struggles they shared with one another were similar to those that I heard many times with I was with the Liga or Afromupaz. Yet the next step—to develop a collective identity and begin building social capital—eluded the group I met in Riohacha, including those women from La Soledad. Why did these women not mobilize? More specifically, why did they not engage in high-risk feminist mobilization?

Departing from the assertions of the gender official about a lack of vision of gender justice, and then the women's own assertions about a lack of leadership, the rest of this chapter holds up the case of La Soledad to the mechanisms of high-risk feminism illustrated in the previous two case studies. Even when there are groups of women who could potentially participate in collective action, they will remain inactive unless there is a leader who can frame the benefits of doing so—shifting from frames of fear to resistance in the domain of losses.

Neighborhood and Social Context

The neighborhood characteristics in La Soledad seem to lend themselves to mobilization, insofar as they are similar to the social contexts described in earlier chapters. For the sake of thoroughness, though, my research also needed to assess whether La Soledad experiences a lack of high-risk feminist mobilization or a lack of all mobilization. In El Pozón (and then Turbaco) and Usme we saw that the neighborhoods are home to a variety of instances of social action, not just mobilization particular to women. For example, in El Pozón, aid groups did not pay specific attention to the differential needs of women, resulting in a context ripe for Patricia Guerrero to mobilize a specifically women's organization that would deal with women's needs. In Usme, it was during the sit-in at the Red Cross building that participating women decided they wanted an organization that purposely dealt with their needs as Afro-Colombian women. Women's organizations in these two neighborhoods emerged tactically from an environment in which a variety of other organizations already operated. They had the option to join existing mixed organizations but chose to mobilize as women instead. That they came together specifically with feminism as a mobilizing strategy was not an accident but rather a strategy.

The question then arises in La Soledad: Are women not engaged in high-risk feminism because no one is engaged in any sort of mobilization in the context of La Guajira, or even Riohacha? If this is the case, it would imply that the social context does not permit mobilization, owing to additional limiting factors, and therefore that a lack of high-risk feminist mobilization is a reflection of this wider context.

To answer this question, it was necessary to look at the larger mobilizational landscape in Riohacha, including other invasion neighborhoods with the same dynamics of risk as La Soledad. Quite quickly, I made contact with an organization of Indigenous women that engages in high-risk collective action around the department: Fuerza de Mujeres Wayuu (Force of Wayuu Women). The Fuerza was founded in 2006, when various leaders in different towns in the department realized that they were engaged in similar processes of trying to protect Wayuu women from violence. The department was the site of extreme levels of paramilitary violence, which disproportionately impacted Indigenous communities (Ramírez Boscán 2007; Centro Nacional de Memoria Histórica 2010, 2013, 2017). The leaders decided to unite under the banner of making visible the human rights violations suffered by Wayuu women and their families, as well as supporting them to declare these violences. Together, they realized that community members did not know about their rights, "and you can't fight to defend what you don't even recognize you have, can you?"[20] The local coordinator for the Barrancas chapter of the Fuerza explained in an interview that the organization is a collective and that each town or city has its own group. The leadership structure is horizontal, meaning that local leaders all have a say in organization-wide decisions. With that said, Karmen Ramírez Boscán, now in exile in Switzerland owing to the many threats on her life, is often referred to as the "mother" of the project (Guerrero 2017).

More often than not, these groups work locally, but sometimes they come together to achieve broader, more general goals. At the local level, the organization teaches classes on human rights and victims' rights, so that women within the communities can develop their leadership skills and learn to defend themselves. They also help women declare their displacement and experiences of other violences before the relevant institutions of the state. More generally, they try to find ways to dialogue with the government on behalf of Wayuu women's rights. As part of their strategy, they also make links with international aid agencies and embassies.

The Fuerza has had successes over time. For example, they were recently awarded the National Prize for the Defense of Human Rights, a recognition supported by the Swedish government. They also managed to have their communities included as subjects of collective reparations. During an interview in January 2018, an interlocutor told me that they were in the process of registering the Fuerza—and not only their local Indigenous clans—as subjects of collective reparations with the Victims' Unit. It has been documented, she said, that because the Fuerza was considered a military target by the paramilitaries, it qualifies as a collective subject for reparations (Verdad Abierta 2015). Members have been recognized as recipients for protection measures by the Inter-American Court of Human Rights, and the group has collaborated on projects with the European Union, the United Nations, the Swedish Forum for Women and Development (FOKUS), and the Global Fund for Women (IPES 2015).

To be clear, my research with the Fuerza was not developed enough for me to feel comfortable making assertions about whether it has a defined pursuit of gender justice that would classify it as an example of a high-risk feminist organization. Indeed, within Wayuu culture, social norms around gender roles are well established and interwoven with ideas of family, nation, and environment. Like my interactions with Afromupaz, the conversations I had with various women in the Fuerza about feminism were sometimes held in tension with their Indigenous identities (Gargallo Celentani 2012; Rodriguez Castro 2020).

Yet when I asked one interviewee about why she continues to mobilize despite her high-risk surroundings, she told me, "Right now, we are in such a critical moment, they are killing social leaders almost every day, and no one is doing anything. I am motivated because I see people suffering and I see the situation getting worse. And this pushes me to continue—I have to keep moving forward. After everything we've suffered internally with the organizations of men who have attacked us, and externally with the threats and the stigmas and the violations, I don't have any option but to continue my work. I have to keep going."[21]

Her words echo comments from members of the Liga and Afromupaz and reveal that the collective identity she helped create has become fundamental to her individual identity, as Calhoun (1991) might suggest. And indeed, she and other women in the organization engage in high-risk collective action with a focus on women's experiences of conflict. Within a context of insecurity, where participating in the organization attracts threats and acts of violence from various armed groups, the women continue to make demands for localized and gendered justice.

This goes to show that there are organizations that mobilize within the social context of Riohacha. Even more substantially, we can see some level of mobilization around women's rights. This leads me to believe that there is nothing in particular about La Soledad that prevents mobilization, when compared with other invasion neighborhoods in the area. That women in the neighborhood do not mobilize, despite their shared condition as victims of the armed conflict, therefore, is a reflection of something other than a favorable social context. The government gender specialist's assertion that there is no culture of mobilization in Riohacha and in La Soledad is incorrect. In all, this case shows that a propitious social context or neighborhood is a necessary but not sufficient condition for high-risk feminist mobilization.

Charismatic Leadership

The main finding from this case study, however, is that in La Soledad, the lack of high-risk feminist mobilization can be primarily attributed to the lack of a charismatic leader. As a result, a group of potential participants operating in the same domain of losses is not encouraged to value the nonmaterial benefits of group membership, nor are there incremental successes over time that promote continued participation. The shift from fear to resistance remained elusive, as highlighted when Estefania talks about the "terror" she and the other women continue to feel in their neighborhood. When violence is high and participating adds an extra layer of risk to daily life, it is not surprising that in the absence of someone who can strategically frame the benefits of mobilizing, women do not mobilize. If there is no shared understanding that the "tomorrows of violence" can be modified, there is no justification for exposing oneself to heightened risk. There is no charismatic bond, and therefore there is no high-risk feminist mobilization.

What was originally confusing about this finding, however, is that there is a leader who has an organization and is recognized by others in the neighborhood as an organizer. What is it, then, about Estefania, that has prevented her from heading a high-risk feminist mobilization effort? It comes down to the fact that Estefania is not a charismatic leader and is therefore unable to create a charismatic bond with potential participants.

Personal relationships facilitated through ethnographic research initially made it difficult to gain critical perspective of her leadership tactics. I spent a lot of time not only interviewing Estefania but also playing with her children, cooking meals together, sharing bus rides to meetings, and chatting with neighbors in her patio. Her dedication as a community organizer is immediately evident. She says about herself—and I have witnessed on multiple occasions—that when people have questions about a victims' issue, they come to her. Moreover, when I interviewed other neighbors and asked about their organizational behavior, many related that although they are not part of a formal organization, they go to Estefania if they are in trouble. She is a member of the Mesa de Víc-timas and was previously the president of the neighborhood Community Action Committee (Junta de Acción Comunal). She evidently has experience in leadership positions, and through these she has met other leaders, has observed leadership practices, and has connections to certain institutions such as the Victims' Unit. She is a leader in the neighborhood but not a charismatic figure in the way that high-risk feminism requires, particularly in terms of mobilizing a group of women in the pursuit of gender justice.

As noted, Estefania is the founder of an organization for women victims. When compared with the Liga or Afromupaz, however, there are notable dif-ferences. First, no one seemed to know much about Estefania's organization. Neighbors talked about "Estefania's women" or "Estefania's meetings" but did not include themselves as part of this narrative nor refer to the proper name of the organization. One interlocutor, who lives two blocks up the road, says that if Estefania invites her to an event she will go. Another says that if a woman needs something in the neighborhood, she will go to Estefania, but there is nothing formal in terms of organization. Another neighbor told me she did not know about any women's organizations in the neighborhood, despite the fact that Estefania had introduced us by telling her that I was going to be asking questions about her organization.

Second, during the many discussions I witnessed and participated in, even in informal spaces like Estefania's patio, there was never any dialogue about shared identity (and no marketing of the potential for "psychic income," or nonmaterial benefits). Estefania talks about working with female victims of the conflict and with victims of sexual violence, in particular. Despite this, I never saw her engage in any work relating to identity creation. Her organ-ization does not host meetings for members, and even in the informal gather-ings that took place, there was never any constructive discussion of women's rights, much less about using women's rights as a point of departure for any collective action.

Third, apart from hearing Estefania discuss her organization, I never saw any evidence of collective strategies or action undertaken by the group. As a leader, Estefania has been unsuccessful in rallying any sort of collective exer-cises on behalf of the organization. The question emerges: If Estefania self-identifies as a leader, and indeed is named by institutional officials as a leader, what is it about her leadership style that is not compatible with high-risk feminist mobilization?

Compared with the positive case studies, what is missing in La Soledad is a specific style of leadership, one that facilitates a charismatic bond. Without a dynamic leader who mobilizes around an identity of gender justice or even fem-inism, there is no way to highlight the nonmaterial benefits of mobilization in a domain of losses. If potential participants do not see that there are benefits to participation—such as feelings of unity and belonging—it is not apparent why they should risk their security and mobilize. Furthermore, without a base of collective identity, it is hard to convince people to take part in collective actions that also put them at further risk. Risk-taking becomes "worth it" when your identity is tied up in group membership and you feel a responsibility for others' well-being as well as your own.

Prospect theory posits that if women perceive themselves to be in a domain of losses (a losing situation), they are more inclined to engage in risk-taking than if they perceive a safe situation. To frame this domain of losses, however, a leader has to highlight the potential benefits of mobilization, that these benefits are only available to participants (not free riders) and that shying away from risk does not guarantee safety. A charismatic leader is able to frame this in a way that makes it justifiable—and even logical—for an individual to engage in collective action.

In La Soledad, women see that Estefania receives direct threats from armed groups for her work with the departmental Mesa de Víctimas. In an interview, a woman told me that she has never received a specific targeted threat from anyone but is aware that Estefania has. "She had to go to Bogotá one time, she had to leave in the middle of the night," she recounted.[22] Although this woman also lives in a domain of losses, where she is threatened by daily violences such as robbery, attacks, and physical and sexual violence, it is understandable that she would not want to label herself as a social leader—especially one making gendered demands that transgress social norms—and thus attract personalized threats. This is where a charismatic leader could potentially change her way of assessing risk and encourage her to join a group of like-minded women in the same domain of losses, as was done in the positive cases. Without a charismatic leader to create a charismatic bond, however, this action is not personally justifiable.

To further contrast Estefania with Patricia Guerrero or María Eugenia Urrutia, what we see is the absence of a concerted gender-justice project based in the pursuit of women's rights and victims' rights, both in the context of the armed conflict and ongoing insecurity, and the everyday gender violence perpetuated in a patriarchal society. While Estefania has clearly learned some of the basics of a rights discourse while on the job, she has not connected this to creating a bond that overcomes the barriers to mobilization.

What is missing is her ability to recognize why women choose not to mobilize (fear of increased violence) and accordingly reframe their understandings so that ideas of nonmaterial benefits and incremental successes become more attractive. People can get on board with a gender-justice project that promises to improve their daily lives. It takes a charismatic leader to identify and activate this potential, forming a charismatic bond and transforming fear into resistance.

While it is clear that a charismatic leader is a necessary condition of high-risk feminist mobilization, what exactly constitutes or gives rise to a charismatic leader is less obvious. For example, Patricia Guerrero was able to draw on her own educational resources and successful organizational skills to facilitate action and procure houses for the City of Women. María Eugenia Urrutia had very little formal education (most likely a similar level to that of Estefania, in fact) but did have a history of community organizing. As well as being a leader within the Afro-Colombian community, she grew up with a mother and grandmother who were seen as community leaders in the Chocó department. She was able to draw on her experiences of previous mobilization to effectively direct the strategies of Afromupaz.

What becomes clear is that neither a certain educational background nor previous experiences of mobilization are requirements for the charismatic leaders of high-risk feminist organizations. Ganz's (2009) study on leadership suggest it might have to do with a leader's biography. It could be Estefania's lack of educational attainment or her lack of a certain type of experience with community organizing that precludes her from recognizing the specific ways in which women can be convinced to mobilize. McAdam's (1982) studies of leadership suggest that leaders are recycled from previous movements and that their experience and organizing skills can be applied to an incipient movement (1982). As mentioned earlier, when it comes to what makes a leader charismatic, Madsen and Snow (1991, 145) note that "psychological readiness for a savior plainly does not lead a public to seize upon the first available candidate for that role. Something—very probably a mixture of style and substance, of promise and performance—must be seen in the would-be leader which persuades the public that this is the one to turn to."

At the time of writing, I am beginning in a three-year research project that sets out to identify and compare a larger set of women leaders of high-risk collective action to better ascertain where they come from and what about them makes them able to develop a charismatic bond in a high-risk context. In sum, and when taken in comparison with examples of other high-risk feminist leaders, however, the case of La Soledad demonstrates that Estefania's style of leadership is incompatible with mobilizing a high-risk feminist organization. She lacks the correct mix of style, substance, promise, and performance. Crucially, then, charismatic leadership is a necessary condition for high-risk feminist mobilization.

Nonmaterial Benefits

Given Estefania's lack of charismatic leadership, it is not surprising that she does not try to leverage the value of nonmaterial benefits to potential participants. In La Soledad, each woman operates like an atom. For example, people go individually to the Victims' Unit to present a case. There are no *plantones* or collective actions undertaken by the group, as is the case with the Liga and Afromupaz.

The mantra within the Liga that the pain of one is the pain of all is not materialized in La Soledad. There is no shared notion that coming together as a collective group of victims could bring about solidarity, belonging, and camaraderie. As noted in chapter 2, part of the charismatic bond involves creating connections not only with the leader but also with the group, which leads to the restoration of a sense of security, competency, and renewed autonomy (Madsen and Snow 1991, 15).

In fact, a woman in La Soledad told me that she does not always like to ally herself with other women victims of the conflict. "There is a lot of stigma," she says. "People see you in the group and say, 'Oh look, there go the raped girls.'"[23] Paradoxically, in Turbaco and Usme, these understandings of shared pain and violence, rather than stigmatizing women, are what gave the organizations their strength and what convinced individuals to continue to identify with the collective. Kreft's (2019) assertion that women engage in collective framing in response to threats against all women, and that more mobilization is likely where there is more conflict-related sexual violence, may require additional interrogation here. The micro-dynamics of mobilization in the case of La Soledad show that experiences of conflict-related sexual violence may actually serve as a barrier to mobilization.

Stigma around sexual violence is not unique to La Soledad. Women in all of my fieldwork sites have discussed the psychological and emotional trauma of declaring themselves as victims before the institutions of the state. In these cases, it was the ability of the leaders not only to persuade these women to declare but also to convince them that doing so is a collective good: the more women declared, the more the state would have to act. Again, it is clear that a leader's ability to frame women's understanding of their situation as part of the same domain of losses is key to mobilization.

The promise and materialization of psychic and emotional benefits allows women to overcome the barriers of mobilizing; even if the only benefit is a sense of solidarity, this can mean a lot when a person feels isolated and fearful. This is partly about the framing on behalf of the leadership (that is, that such benefits exist) but is also partly experiential. This is the effect of the inherent feedback: over time, participants reap the benefits of being part of the collective, thus encouraging continued participation. In La Soledad, however, it is evident that the women were uncomfortable talking about their experiences of violence, both with one another and, certainly, with an outsider.[24] This was in stark contrast to the women in Turbaco and Usme: although it was clear that talking about these experiences was painful, they overcame their fear and shame. Indeed, they often did so even after I asked a neutral question about their pasts, or about where they were from originally.

It is not enough for a leader to encourage an individual victim to declare her experiences of violence; the leader needs to frame this declaration in a way that highlights the nonmaterial benefits of being part of a larger group who have suffered similar stories and are prepared to mobilize in the name of gender justice. Sharing suffering, knowing that the pain of one is the pain of all, must be encouraged by a leader who knows that creating collective identity is one way to encourage women living in a domain of losses to take collective action, despite the further risks this may involve.

Success of Incremental Gains

Also in contrast to the Liga and Afromupaz, Estefania's organization has not had any incremental successes over time. Accordingly, there is no shared vision of how collective action can modify the tomorrows of violence. Seemingly, Estefania's only foray into organized collective action was trying to build a soccer pitch for neighborhood children in 2015.[25] First, the project had nothing to do with gender justice or women's rights. While the idea of building a safe space for children is appealing (especially to single mothers), as a leader there was no way that Estefania could use this project to show women why participating under high-risk conditions had the possibility to produce incremental successes that would in some way ameliorate their situation as women victims. There was no strategy behind the project and what it meant for the collective. It is unclear what long-term tactical planning was behind the soccer pitch project; rather, there was a lack of the strategic forethought required from a charismatic leader.

Second, the project was never finished. Links with donors were evidently not strong, and the majority of the promised money never appeared. Therefore, not only did the project not bring any shared sense that gains are possible if women mobilize, but the opposite was also true. The lesson that women in the neighborhood could draw was that even if they do mobilize, things do not get finished, and hopes are crushed.[26] The narrative around this project—and around its failure—is that there is no point in actively working together.

Estefania and another interlocutor blame the failure of the project on a lack of commitment from the mayor's office and other state institutions. This sentiment is not unique to them; text messages exchanged with members of Liga since I finished fieldwork highlight similar frustrations with the institutions of the state. One woman wrote that one of their projects "is not advancing at all, there is no willingness on behalf of the state administrations."[27] Despite frustration with the state, however, she and the other members of the Liga continue to mobilize around this particular project. They have a history of success, and of overcoming hardships and barriers. In part, however, this determination is dictated by Patricia Guerrero, who over time has refused to let organization members accept defeat. This is part of her overall architecture of mobilization, whereby certain projects are not just about the material gains they bring but also about creating and sustaining morale over time. As such, perhaps what was missing in the case of Estefania is an ability to create bridging social capital, to create networks between institutions of the state, and to effectively take advantage of political opportunities.

The soccer pitch project represents more than just a lack of strategic forethought: rather, it indicates that Estefania herself is motivated by the fear or cautiousness in the face of violence that prevents other women from participating in collective action. Without strategic vision as to how collective action could facilitate engagement in projects that make assuming risk justifiable, it is not possible to generate solidarity among potential participants. A cautious project is unable to convince others that mobilizing is worthwhile. Again, Madsen and Snow's (1991) mix of style and substance, of promise and performance, is not reached.

Estefania says that there have not been any meetings of her organization since the attempted construction of the soccer pitch in 2015. Moreover, she does not appear to have any current or ongoing projects. In our last meeting in early 2018, Estefania talked about presenting a project on behalf of a rural women's collective to the mayor's office. It was unclear what this project has to do with the victims of sexual violence in her own neighborhood, who allegedly make up the rank and file of her organization.

Conclusion: What This Means for High-Risk Feminism: Why Do Some Women Mobilize?

There is no gendered high-risk collective action in La Soledad, a neighborhood that suffers ongoing and gendered violence, and also is home to a population of women who are similar to their mobilized counterparts in other parts of the country. Despite bearing similarities to the other cases presented in this book— and even to other neighborhoods in Riohacha and other parts of La Guajira— there is no leader able to form the charismatic bond necessary for collective action. It is this lack of charismatic leadership—and, subsequently, a charismatic bond—that has prevented women who operate in the same domain of losses from coming together in their shared identity to work together in the pursuit of gender justice.

Earlier chapters discuss mobilization strategies within the context of the pillars of high-risk feminism (collective identity, social capital, legal framing, and acts of certification). There is no such mobilization in La Soledad; consequently, there are no collective strategies in the pursuit of gender justice. Within the context of the possibility principle, though, the lack of a charismatic leader gives us an inverse reinforcement of the relationship between the mechanisms that prompt gendered high-risk collective action and the pillars of high-risk feminism. That is, without a charismatic leader in a high-risk social context, potential participants are unable to overcome the barriers to mobilization, which automatically limits collective identity creation and social capital building. Without a unified group, there is no one to undertake legal framing or acts of certification.

As outlined in chapter 2, within a specific social context, a particular type of leader is able to convince women that they should group together and act collectively, based on their shared identities as victims and their shared location in the domain of losses. When leaders highlight the potential benefits that come from mobilization, as opposed to the potential exposure to further and targeted violence, women decide to act collectively. The shared identity and the bonds of social capital that this creates over time become integral to that woman's individual identity. As the remarks of various interviewees over the course of this book document, the women are unwilling to desist in their *lucha*, their struggle, even when they are under particular moments of threat.

These bonds of collective identity generate nonmaterial benefits that justify continued participation. For victims of extreme violence, feelings of belonging and understanding make it worthwhile to expose themselves to ongoing risk. Especially when inaction is not necessarily safer than action, the bonus of nonmaterial benefits is enough to tip the scale toward mobilization.

Once these bonds are solidified, and participants are convinced of the utility of nonmaterial benefits, projects that show that there are also material benefits to be generated through collective action further compound continued participation. For example, the women of the Liga saw that by working together they were able to generate dignified housing for themselves and their families. The women of Afromupaz saw that sustained collective effort brought them jobs and the ability to feed their children. Even smaller successes contribute to this dynamic: getting a meeting with the National Protection Unit after years of sustained pressure (as was the case with Fuerza de Mujeres Wayuu), or being recognized for an international prize contributes to group morale, which justifies why continued action is necessary. Without a leader to make the connection between mobilization and outcomes, however, there will be no high-risk feminist mobilization.

7

Conclusion

●●●●●●●●●●●●●●●●●●●●●●

Why Understanding Women's
Grassroots Mobilization
Matters

Since I began research for this book in 2015, Colombia has undergone enormous shifts in its security situation. The signing of the peace accords between the FARC and the Government of Colombia was supposed to usher in a new era of optimism, closing the chapter on five decades of armed conflict. Indeed, the final agreement included comprehensive provisions "with the potential for structural change to reduce gender inequalities and make progress in women's rights" (Kroc Institute 2020, 1). The gender perspective crosscuts the different chapters of the accords, including issues related to rural development, political participation, security and protection, reincorporation, and victims' rights. Yet the most recent Kroc Institute monitoring report notes that as of July 2020, 32 percent of the gender stipulations had not yet been initiated, and 40 percent had only been implemented to a minimum level (6). These numbers reveal that the implementation of the gender approach is lagging behind the Final Accord's general implementation (9).

Yet, as Merry (2016, 1) notes, "quantification is seductive" and "the process of translating the buzzing confusion of social life into neat categories that can be tabulated risks distorting the complexity of social phenomena." Fuentes and Cookson (2019, 2–3) expand: "quantitative data alone is highly vulnerable to *dislocating* women's experiences from their spatial and temporal contexts." Writing about the context of Colombia's transition to peace, Krystalli (2019, 69) also draws on the work of Merry to underscore that "one effect of power is what gets measured" (2016, 29).

Accordingly, this book has aimed to move beyond the swelling statistics of displacement, sexual violence, and homicide featured on the Registro Único de Víctimas (Victims' Registry) website, to overlay names, faces, and experiences on the gendered continuum of violence. Over the past five years I have managed to engage in ethnographic fieldwork during a moment in time that illustrates what the continuum looks like in practice. Throughout the preceding chapters, I have spoken about the importance of centering women's voices and local experiences at the heart of the narrative, to build arguments about inclusive peace and security from the grass roots up.

Indeed, the bulk of my research with the Liga de Mujeres Desplazadas took place in the latter half of 2016, when the country was at a crossroads in its history.[1] Its citizens had the chance to vote to approve a peace deal that would end fifty-two years of armed conflict between the government and the FARC. I attended peace rallies with members of the Liga, where we wore white bandanas and waved flags with other women's organizations in a plaza in Barranquilla, as part of the One Million Women for Peace (Un Millón de Mujeres por la Paz). Referring to the upcoming plebiscite, brightly colored banners around us proclaimed, "Women Choose 'Yes'"!

On 2 October 2016, I served as an international election monitor at a polling station in Cartagena. Hurricane Matthew was in full force, and I had to wade through knee-deep water to reach the school where the votes were being cast. A fellow observer gave me a ride home after the polls closed, and we were both shocked to hear the announcement over the radio that the No had won. We sat in silence for the remainder of the drive. This silence continued into the next morning when I went to visit one of the Liga members. We sat on the concrete porch outside her small home, drinking *tinto* and speaking very little.

By the time I began work with Afromupaz in 2017, the Santos government had pushed through an amended version of the peace accords, and Colombia was officially moving into a postconflict moment. When I met with the women at the Afromupaz house in Usme, there was a feeling of hope that things were finally going to change for the better. This was largely linked to optimism related to collective reparations: I often attended meetings held between Afromupaz and various state institutions in charge of organizing and distributing the comprehensive measures the women were due to receive. As we sat around the long table in the converted garage that served as a meeting room, I saw the women's faces light up as they discussed a new house for the organization, ongoing resources for their psychosocial healing program, and

FIG. 7.1 Women wearing white bandanas at the One Million Women for Peace event in Barranquilla, shortly before the October 2016 plebiscite. (Credit: author.)

resources for their *proyectos de vida* (life projects). Although my one-on-one interactions with the women often revealed ongoing fears and experiences of trauma in Usme, the first half of 2017 brought with it excitement that things were finally going to change for the better.

Yet by late 2017 and early 2018 when I was in La Guajira, some of that optimism had begun to fade. Gendered insecurity and violence were returning to the neighborhood, and women often expressed their fears of living in La Soledad. Interlocutors talked to me about how they feared for their children, particularly as they had begun to notice strange cars with tinted windows driving around the neighborhood. During moments spent together, Estefania told me about the times that she had been threatened; she had even had unknown men break into her home. It was months after fieldwork ended, when I sent her a Facebook message, that I found out she had suffered another violent break-in; this time, the threat was serious enough that she took her children and fled to Medellín, where they were living in a shelter. Over the years we have lost touch, but I often find myself wondering where she and her children have ended up, and whether they have finally found somewhere safer and more stable to call home.

Later that year, I found myself in Putumayo, a department in the south of the country, nestled against the river that forms the border between Colombia and Ecuador. The department is of strategic value for armed groups, given a geography and climate that facilitate the cultivation and transport of coca (Tate 2015). Historically, this part of the country was a FARC stronghold, but in the late 1990s, the AUC paramilitaries—with the complicity of the armed forces—initiated a bloody incursion that exposed citizens to the terrors of conflict (Cancimance López 2014; Tate 2017). Rape, torture, disappearances, and murder were widely used by paramilitaries. Women suspected of being FARC sympathizers were subject to public acts of sexual violence. They were also violated to punish and humiliate their male relatives (Centro Nacional de Memoria Histórica 2012, 168). Moreover, women engaging in community leadership were systematically disappeared by paramilitaries when they became "an obstacle for armed groups to act" (Alianza de Mujeres Tejedoras de Vida del Putumayo 2009, 96).

During this first trip to Putumayo, I had the great fortune to meet the Alianza de Mujeres Tejedoras de Vida, based in the capital, Mocoa, but with associations of women distributed throughout the province (see Zulver 2021). The case of the Alianza illustrates what women's high-risk collective action looks like over time and during different iterations of conflict-related violence. It is a scenario where women who actively mobilized for women's empowerment during the conflict are once again being targeted both for their collective action in an area where armed groups want territorial and social control, and for transgressing gender norms that do not look favorably on women's empowerment. Indeed, this fits with Enloe's (1993) findings from the post–Cold War period that the patriarchal structures that color wartime live on in postwar societies (see also Cockburn 2013a; Wibben 2020).

The Alianza is an umbrella coalition of women's associations that formed in the late 1990s and early 2000s, during the aforementioned paramilitary incursion into the region. In the midst of extreme risk, these women decided to come together in small groups. Many of these groups were focused on creating emotional support networks and visiting one another's houses to unite women suffering under paramilitary rule. Doing so was a high-risk activity: multiple interviewees told me that the paramilitaries closely monitored these meetings, as well as women's movements around town. Over time, these small associations were united under the umbrella of the Alianza, which focused on human rights and armed conflict, women's political participation, and women's social and economic empowerment (see Tate 2017). They openly supported the country's peace process and engaged in national and international advocacy to discuss women's experiences of conflict in Putumayo (Tate 2013).

Supporting the peace process for the Alianza meant promoting women's rights in the region. This involved, for example, denouncing crimes that took place during the conflict to the authorities, creating economic empowerment programs, facilitating anti–gender violence campaigns, making memorial walls

FIG. 7.2 This Alianza mural in La Dorada, Putumayo, pays tribute to María Quintero Gualpaz, who was murdered by paramilitaries in 2001. (Credit: author.)

for women who had been killed or disappeared during the conflict, and lobbying local authorities for access to justice.

In November 2018, Sandra—a community leader for the Alianza—led me through the central park in La Dorada, a bustling town about half an hour's drive north of the border with Ecuador. We had already finished eating lunch, and although it was still early in the afternoon, our time was limited, as I needed to catch a bus back to Mocoa before evening fell and travel would be dangerous. Sandra was adamant that she wanted to show me a few more important sites in the town before I left. She took me to a small plaque under one of the park's many shady trees that pays "homage to the dignity of the Galarraga girls," four sisters who were disappeared and murdered by paramilitaries in 2001. She then took me to a mural of María Quintero Gualpaz, a young Awa Indigenous girl, holding a small doll and told me the horrific story of sexual abuse and murder that she had suffered. The sign next to the mural reads, "This homage is for all of the women who suffered unspeakable violences in this community. We will always demand justice, truth, and reparation."[2] Sandra took me to these sites to impress upon me the ways that, for her and other members of the Alianza, the conflict lives on in their daily lives. The empowerment activities that they undertake are grounded in historical and ongoing violences.

Indeed, even in late 2018, things were not safe for women like Sandra. After the signing of the peace accords in 2016, the women of the Alianza experienced a "beautiful peace" (Voge and Zulver 2019), but this quickly disappeared. As Sandra said, "peace has a lot of enemies here."[3] Fátima Muriel, the president of the Alianza told me, "Things are going back to how they were before" (Zulver 2019b). In this iteration of violent conflict, women are again directly targeted for engaging in activities promoting women's rights. This violence included threats against women and their children, stalking, and disappearances of members of the Alianza. According to local government employees, the Alianza is seen by armed actors as a strong example of community organization; these actors target the Alianza to suppress their collective action and to serve as a warning to other organizations not to mobilize.[4]

I returned to Putumayo in September 2019 to film a short documentary about women social leaders in Colombia's postconflict context, with my video-journalist friend (Voge and Zulver 2019). I was surprised to find that Sandra was no longer engaging in community organizing in La Dorada; after a series of threats from both FARC dissidents and paramilitary successors—including an attempted kidnapping of her eldest daughter from her place of work—Sandra decided that she needed to move to the (relatively) safer departmental capital of Mocoa. Nonetheless, she continues to work with the Alianza to promote gender justice.[5]

Elsewhere (Zulver 2021), I have documented how this new wave of gender violence could be considered a type of patriarchal backlash, one that is rooted in the same dynamics of militarized masculinity that guided armed actors in years gone by (see Meger and Sachseder 2020). Yet in these ongoing high-risk contexts, women continue to mobilize and make demands for gender justice. Indeed, despite the threats and violence in recent years, members of the Alianza—like Sandra—continue to engage in economic empowerment activities, hold workshops with lawyers to denounce crimes, and impart political empowerment trainings. Over time, they have compounded the successes of incremental gains, both material and nonmaterial. Walking around their office in Mocoa, posters, photographs, and awards highlight the multiple funders with whom they have worked over the year, including the Swedish-Norwegian Cooperation Fund, Mercy Corps, the United Nations Refugee Agency, and the U.S. Agency for International Development. They draw on the repertoires of action developed in earlier iterations of conflict to shape the strategies they once again adopt to protect themselves when living in a domain of losses (Zulver 2021). The resulting mobilization continues to pursue a vision of gender justice consistent with high-risk feminism.

This situation of gendered backlash is not unique to the Alianza or to Putumayo. When I returned to visit the Liga again in the summer of 2018, former interlocutors told me about ongoing risks to their safety. They had recently been granted government protection—in the form of bodyguards and a four-by-four vehicle—through the National Protection Unit. Members of the Liga in Montes de María had been threatened—and some had been stalked—for their community activism (see also Arredondo 2019). Still later, by the time the global pandemic began in 2020 and the Duque government declared a national public health crisis, including a shelter-in-place order, violence against social leaders reached new heights (International Crisis Group 2020; Parkin Daniels 2020; Zulver and Janetsky 2020). This violence included gendered risks for women social leaders, who were punished by armed groups for engaging in community mobilizing (Zulver 2020).

The experience of the Alianza as well as the transforming security situations of the Liga and other social leaders in areas experiencing conflict highlights that the gendered continuum of violence continues in Colombia. In this so-called postconflict country, machismo has a way of seeping into all corners of society: the public, the political, and the private. This was also highlighted in Rodriguez Castro's (2020, 13) research: one of her interlocutors in Buenaventura, on the Pacific coast, noted that her organization is witnessing "how men start to perpetrate violent practices like torture that they learned in the context of the armed conflict against women."

Yet beyond permeating all "ambits of life and relationships" (Castro 2020, 13), my own research takes the issue of ongoing violence in peace time a step further. When women dare to raise their voices to call out sexual and gender-based violence, to decry longstanding impunity, or to demand reparation for their suffering and loss, they are acting in a doubly transgressive manner. They are not only challenging the status quo of violence and conflict; they are also challenging deeply entrenched patterns of gender norms. This exposes them to ongoing, targeted violence in the form of patriarchal backlash (Berry 2017; Zulver 2021). This is, in part, what makes their feminism high risk.

In this book I have drawn on grounded research from different corners, coasts, and contexts within Colombia. I have centered the research in empirical examples of what it looks like to be a woman mobilizing for gender justice amid an armed conflict: how they make the decisions to do so, and what this collective action looks like in practice. Throughout, I have applied a gender lens to these findings to explore how the gendered power dynamics that govern these communities, as well as the armed groups who infiltrate them, impact women's experiences of conflict and resistance.

What Can We Learn from High-Risk Feminism?

I write these pages from my apartment in Bogotá, as 2020 draws to an end. I clearly remember this time exactly a year ago, when I read Ford's (2019) piece in the Guardian hailing 2020 as the year when "women's rights" would "take

FIG. 7.3 A street art campaign in Bogotá in January 2020 that reads "being a woman social leader is high risk." (Credit: author.)

centre stage." Clearly, the global pandemic has compromised this aspirational statement. Yet Ford's optimism was based in reasonable hope: 2020 represents the twenty-fifth anniversary of the Beijing Platform for Action and the twentieth anniversary of the UN's Women, Peace and Security agenda.

When it comes to advocating for women's rights to take center stage—and what "strong actions" should look like—it is important to remember whose voices and whose experiences count. As feminists, we must value situated knowledge and learn from those whose everyday lives are shaped by violence and by resistance to this violence. In keeping with Merry's (2016) warnings about the seduction of quantification, it is important to listen to what women want rather than assume that we—as academics, policymakers, lawmakers, or humanitarian workers—know what their needs are.

The research presented in this book therefore adds to a larger conversation about how to include these marginalized, silenced, or forgotten voices into debates about what feminism looks like in contexts of conflict and its aftermath. As discussed in chapter 1, this feminism may not be self-defined as such, but it shares a commitment to dismantling oppressive gendered power structures that are concentrated by armed conflict and its aftermath. In doing so, the research also serves as a call to think about gender justice from the grass roots up. It offers rich, qualitative gender data that uses "women's accounts of their own lives" (Cookson 2018, 159) to narrate cases where women's experiences with violence catalyzed feminist mobilization, even when this might not be expected.

This book adds to understandings of leadership and high-risk collective action in social movement studies, applying a gender lens to studies of civilian agency and providing rich local context and nuance to notions of gendered security. It has furthered employed an intersectional lens, looking at the roles that race, ethnicity, and class, among other identities, play in these feminist mobilizations. The case studies have overlaid a gender lens on women's high-risk collective action: how it stems from gendered conditions of oppression and how it takes form with gendered strategies and actions. Throughout the chapters, I have reflected on the questions of why and how women mobilize in high-risk contexts. This question implies that there is a puzzle to be solved: Why would women knowingly and willingly expose themselves to potential lethal and nonlethal violence in the pursuit of a more equal future?

To answer these questions, I have used empirical evidence to paint a picture of three case studies in different parts of the country: in El Pozón and then Turbaco (Bolívar), in Usme (Bogotá), and in La Soledad (La Guajira). Two of these cases were positive insofar as they involved working with groups that I identify as engaging in high-risk feminist mobilization. The third case was negative in the sense that, notwithstanding its apparent similarity to the other two cases, there was no high-risk feminist mobilization present among the local population of displaced women, despite similar contextual factors.

Drawing on ethnographic research to shine a light on these three case sites, it became obvious that leadership is critical when it comes to convincing a specific population to mobilize, in spite of the risks this entails. Charismatic leaders are able to frame the benefits—both material and nonmaterial—of mobilization to those who operate in a domain of losses. That is, when not mobilizing does not necessarily guarantee any further protections, and the benefits of mobilization can only be accrued through participation, the risks of mobilizing become palatable to potential participants. Women form a bond with the leader and then with one another and the movement's goals. This charismatic bond is a good in itself—part of Silver's (1974, 64) "psychic income"—contributing to a dynamic of protracted mobilization.

High-risk feminism is the framework that builds from this charismatic bond. It answers the "how" element of the research question. Directed by a charismatic leader, women operating in conditions of violence strategically engage with four pillars of action. By building collective identity, creating bonding and bridging social capital, employing legal framing techniques, and participating in acts of certification, they contest their violent surroundings and demand a more gender-just society. In this way, women are able to modify their tomorrows of violence—the ways in which they will experience and perceive violence in the future. They turn their fear into anger and resistance, which shifts their perspectives on risk-taking.

In El Pozón, displaced women came together under the leadership of Patricia Guerrero. Members of the resulting group—the Liga de Mujeres Desplazadas—were able to generate a collective identity that paved the way to building the City of Women, a symbol of gendered peaceful resistance in a zone of conflict. Meanwhile, in Usme, María Eugenia Urrutia was able to show a group of women that by working collectively they would not only reap the psychosocial benefits of solidarity and friendship but could also direct their strategies in a way that led to material benefits such as collective reparations. Finally, in the La Soledad neighborhood in Riohacha, we saw that the lack of a charismatic leader precluded the possibility for high-risk feminist mobilization. Despite a similar context of violence and similar profiles of potential participants, Estefania did not have the ability to frame mobilization in a domain of losses as worthwhile. Instead, we see displaced women who act in isolation and consequently do not reap any benefits of collective action.

Yet, as noted in chapter 2, the charismatic bond in itself is not sufficient for sustained mobilization. While the presence of a charismatic leader is a necessary but not sufficient condition for overcoming barriers to mobilization, Madsen and Snow (1991, 15) also hint that over time, the bond between the leader and the participant facilitates the development of a group identification with others. In this way, the participant is connected to the struggle itself, restoring a sense of "security and competency." Indeed, this book is not simply a study of leadership; rather, it portrays everyday women, most of whom had never engaged in collective action before joining the groups discussed in previous chapters, who have dedicated themselves to a risky project that held promise to improve the material and nonmaterial conditions that shape their lives. These conditions are molded by the gendered power dynamics that govern the territories in which live, both during and after wartime.

When I first began my research in El Salvador, and later in Colombia, I realized that the people I was spending time with did not fit neatly into existing categories of how women mobilize during conflict. As I documented in the preceding chapters, their collective action was shaped around building a more gender-just world for themselves and their communities. This book has shown that there is room to discuss alternative narratives about women who mobilize for themselves and for gender equality more generally, despite the risks they incur by doing so. High-risk feminism is a way of resisting gendered acts of violence along the continuum of violence. It allows women to express agency, voice, and identity. Instead of viewing women solely as victims of the conflict, or through their capacity to act as mothers (or on behalf of others), the framework allows for a nuanced reading of women as survivors, activists, and *luchadoras* (fighters) in contexts of risk. The value of this book, then, is that it considers not only that mobilization can actually take place in high-risk contexts, but also why and how such mobilization takes shape.

Finally, this last chapter poses some preliminary questions about the long-term implications of women's high-risk collective action—notably, what does it look like over time? Although answering questions related to the durability of high-risk feminism was not the primary focus of this book, the experience of the Alianza in Putumayo and the Liga in different parts of Bolívar illustrates that mobilization has a certain level of durability, particularly during different iterations of conflict and postconflict related violence. Just as Fátima told me in late 2018 that "things are going back to how they were before," so too are women seemingly prepared to continue to expose themselves to violence in the pursuit of gender justice over time, and in the face of new and threatening actors.[6]

Gender Justice from the Grass Roots Up

"At the core of solidarity is mutual aid: the idea that we give our platforms, resources, legitimacy, voices, skills to one another to try to defeat oppressive conditions" (Olufemi 2020, 136). Beyond academic inputs, this book offers important, bottom-up insights to policymakers, international organizations, and civil society actors engaging in Women, Peace and Security spaces in conflict and postconflict settings around the world. The research—stories, narratives, memories, dreams, fears, and struggles—presented here illustrates that women's high-risk actions cannot be taken for granted. Women's mobilization for gender justice is not an immutable characteristic, it is a political phenomenon that needs explaining. This mobilization is further complicated when collective action takes place in a context of gendered violence—one that gives rise to the mobilization in the first place, but also makes the resistance particularly vulnerable to retributive and even backlash violence.

This project also underlines that women are not inherently peaceful; their mobilization is not always premised on the pursuit of peace or launched in the interest of the greater good, whether that be at the familial, community, or broader level. While these goals are often implicit in the actions, the women introduced in this book mobilized for themselves and for gender justice. Women have political interests as individuals, not just as conduits for the interests of others. Indeed, Goetz and Jenkins (2016, 215) remind us that a "pacifist/ maternalist—as opposed to equality-based—justification for participation depoliticizes women's agency." They suggest limiting the focus on women to their capacity as peacebuilders (or mobilizing on behalf of others) does not allow the necessary space to understand where women's agency fits within this narrative. "To the extent that women have organized to resist violence and claim their right to a political voice, they have been spurred on to do this by their context-specific experiences rather than through an innately peace-loving nature" (El-Bushra 2007, 144).

Additionally, that their mobilization simply takes shape cannot be assumed. As outlined in chapters 2 and 3, there are specific factors that come together to allow women, many of whom have never participated publicly before, to run the risks of high-risk feminist mobilization. After overcoming barriers to mobilizing, they engage in repertoires of action that reflect their strategic and political interests. Yet high-risk feminism is not solely confined to conflict contexts, and peacetime is not always a time of peace for women. Women adapt and modulate their repertoires of action to the varying conditions of risk that appear at different moments on the gendered continuum of violence.

In accepting that women's high-risk collective action is shaped by gendered power dynamics present in the logics of militarized masculinities governing conflict and postconflict moments, it becomes clear that such mobilization cannot be taken for granted or expected to materialize as a given. Rather, as this book has outlined, women make considered calculations when they are deciding to expose themselves and their families to potentially fatal violence. Moreover, the strategies they use are context specific and change to accommodate fluctuating patterns of violence in their communities. This only becomes visible, though, when viewed from a grassroots perspective of women's pursuit of gender justice. The broader implications of situating our understanding of gender justice from the grass roots up are multiple. Women's voices and experiences need to be centered at the heart of what gendered security looks like in conflict and post-conflict contexts.[7]

The Women, Peace and Security agenda (UN Women 2020) offers an "essential analytical lens to understand and respond to conflict and instability." Comprised of ten United Nations Security Council resolutions, it places women's differentiated experiences of conflict at the forefront of efforts to prevent conflict or bring about its end, or both. Indeed, the first resolution on that agenda—1325—specifically calls for women's participation in peace processes and at all levels of decisionmaking, as included in four pillars: participation, protection, prevention, and relief and recovery. Subsequent research has shown that when women are involved in peace processes, durable peace is more likely (Krause, Krause, and Bränfors 2018).

Yet some have accused the Women, Peace and Security agenda of perpetuating a "protectionist narrative" by failing to better enable or support "women's participation in peace and security processes" (Goetz and Jenkins, 2018, online abstract).[8] Otto (2018) goes one step further, arguing that the Security Council continues to rely on the "gendered paradigm that men fight wars in order to protect women (and children), and that women are naturally predisposed to peace." El-Bushra (2007, 142) notes that a view of "womenandpeace" finds its "most potent expression in Resolution 1325."

The case studies presented in this book further demonstrate that peacebuilding in fragile communities can be dangerous work. This is particularly the case when women's peace work is linked to the promotion of gender justice, which actively transgresses locally entrenched gender norms. Across these case studies, women who mobilized in their communities during the conflict were directly targeted for their actions; for example, María Eugenia Urrutia was kidnapped and raped as a direct result of the work that she was undertaking in Usme. Similarly, in the current post–peace accord context, women engaging in community mobilization can face lethal violence for doing so; for example, women from the Alianza have been disappeared in recent years for their involvement in the organization.

Even the most recent Kroc Institute (2020, 2) report recognizes that four years after the official end to the conflict, "attacks against women leaders and human rights defenders, especially Afro-Colombian, indigenous, and rural communities, continue." Of the security guarantees including in the Final Agreement, 41 percent of those that include a gender approach have still not been initiated, and 35 percent have be implemented only to a minimal degree (Kroc Institute 2020, 20). The UN Special Rapporteur on the situation of human rights defenders wrote about Colombia, "Women defenders face differentiated risks and disproportionate effects that are exacerbated according to the rights they defend . . . and, in a common way to all of them, their belonging to a population victimized by the war" (Forst 2018, 21). His report continues: "the attacks [against women] have also taken the form of stigmatization, in which degrading stereotypes are used . . . [including] questions about noncompliance with traditionally assigned gender roles, and devaluations of their contributions to social change" (22). Women engaging in high-risk collective action at the grassroots level require guarantees of security and protection with a gender perspective that reflects that gendered security needs.

Accordingly, this book illustrates the need to critically engage in context-specific analysis when encouraging women's participation in conflict and postconflict moments. In doing so, it adds evidence to growing calls for the localization of the Women, Peace and Security agenda. Such localization takes a bottom-up rather than a top-down approach and is favorable insofar as it "emboldens local agency . . . but also because it is likely to produce outcomes that are meaningful and sustainable for the communities most affected" (Lynch 2019, 83).[9] Kirby and Shepherd (2016, 385) further note that localization programs create a local ownership that "enhances their efficacy as a WPS [Woman, Peace and Security] implementation tool." The Global Network of Women Peacebuilders (2020) is an inspiring example: a civil society organization that engages directly with local authorities, leaders, and local women to ensure that Woman, Peace and Security resolutions and National Action Plans are being implemented at the local level, in several conflict and postconflict societies around the world.

Practically speaking, creating context-specific policies and programs that center women's lived experiences at the heart of post-conflict reconstruction involves changing our understanding of who is an expert.[10] Many of the women I spent time with during research did not complete primary school. They are poor and do not necessarily fit within the definition of professionalized or NGO-ized organizations (Alvarez 1999), or the "suit-wearing feminists" against whom María Eugenia contrasts herself and her organization. They are Indigenous and Afro, in a country where racism is deeply entrenched yet inadequately acknowledged in spaces of power (see Marciales Montenegro 2015; Centro Nacional de Memoria Histórica 2015; Acosta et al. 2018) and where places that are considered "black and Indian" are associated with "disorder, backwardness, and danger" (Appelbaum 2003). They are *campesinas*, which paints them as guerrilla sympathizers and isolates them from state institutions and access to justice (FIP 2017).

Yet their lived experiences of violence—and of resistance—are of value and have much to teach international and national "experts" in terms of how best to create programs and policies that support women's right to a life free from violence in the post–peace accord context. As Olufemi (2020, 135) notes in *Feminism, Interrupted*, "Solidarity has to come from understanding, and understanding comes from listening to those who are in a position to know that they're talking about." Indeed, as Berry and Rana (2019, 324) observe, "While formal peacebuilding interventions play an important role as scaffolding for grassroots peacebuilding work, these efforts will be insufficient insofar as they fail to center the informal, emotional, embodied, and creative ways that women pursue peace in their daily lives."

To put this finding into action, policymakers and international donors can design and fund polices and projects that reflect this expanded view of who is an expert. This will necessarily involve earmarking sustainable funds for grassroots leaders and organizations that might not necessarily conform to the professionalized and formal organizational structures that Alvarez (see 1999, 2009) problematizes as consistent with the "NGO-ization" of feminist organizations in the 1990s and beyond. It will mean that donors adopt a more holistic understanding of how to measure and evaluate progress and outputs over time, with an expanded understanding of what counts as gender data. It will require flexibility and adaptability when working with grassroots organizations, based on the technical capabilities of the organization in question. As Fuentes and Cookson (2019) note, this type of programming requires starting with the principle of including the voices of those who are the object of research or intervention to avoid relying on statistical accounts of women's experiences that are dislocated from space and time (see also Hay 2012; Rooney 2017).

Localizing the implementation of the Women, Peace and Security agenda further involves expanding our understanding of gendered security, to ask women what they need to feel safe and able to participate in collective action.

This will require that policymakers and lawmakers engage in both intersectional and gendered conflict analyses. In fact, many of the organizations already undertake these *caracterizaciones* (analyses) of the situations of women in their territories and make recommendations for how municipal, departmental, and national authorities, as well as members of the international community, can best support women's mobilization. By way of example, a gendered analysis of the situation of women in Putumayo notes the need for the creation not only of short-, medium- and long-term projects for women's economic and educational empowerment but also of an enabling environment in which authorities prioritize women's access to justice, local institutional employees are trained in how to apply a gender perspective to their work, and impunity is eliminated, particularly in the case of gender violence that is imparted by authorities themselves (Alianza de Mujeres Tejedoras de Vida del Putumayo 2009, 133–135). The report notes, "The scandalous gravity of the situation of women contrasts with their capacity for resilience, which is exemplified in their 'life projects' and their defense of community interests, despite the violences against them that they endure and have endured, both in the public and private domain" (133).

Paarlberg-Kvam (2019, 196) writes of Colombia that "feminists and women activists have argued tirelessly for a *paz integral* (a comprehensive peace) that would address the foundations, not simply the expressions, of conflict"[11] (see also Berry and Lake 2021). As Lemaitre (2016, 533) documents in the case of displaced women in different parts of Colombia, violence takes multiple forms: violent displacement and arrival in slums controlled by armed groups but also the structural violence of hunger, a lack of shelter, and witnessing their children's suffering. For example, for the women of the Liga, being unable to pay their water and electricity bills—despite owning their houses—was a theme that came up multiple times during discussions of security in their neighborhood. One of Afromupaz's main goals was to create jobs and establish economic security for members. And the Alianza is clear that economic empowerment forms the basis of a key set of activities that it will continue to pursue into the post–Peace Accord era. While it is clearly important to include women at peace talks and in all levels of decisionmaking, this must be accompanied by an "enabling environment" that allows them to enter, remain, and contribute effectively to peace processes (UN Women 2018). This enabling environment requires financial support, logistics support, social services, and security and protection from violence, as well as inclusivity as a social and cultural norm (UN Women 2018).[12] As noted above, an enabling environment further requires that different levels of government consciously work to eliminate impunity related to issues of gender-based violence, particularly in contexts where violence has historically been used by state forces as well as armed groups.

Finally, the findings of this book have implications for how the international community can and should support women's grassroots efforts for gender justice along the continuum of violence. Particularly given the uncertainty and instability around women's exposure to gendered violence in conflict and postconflict settings, it is critical that support be flexible and easily adaptable to exogenous shocks. For example, gendered targeting of social leaders increased with the onset of the Covid-19 pandemic in Colombia (Zulver 2020). These programs must also be premised on an understanding that sexual and gender-based violence do not end when war ends—nor do the risks for those mobilizing for gender justice—but rather extend into peacetime in both the public and private spheres.

Some international donors are already aware of the importance of putting a feminist lens front and center in both their development assistance and their foreign policy, including in so-called postconflict settings.[13] For example, in 2017, the government of Justin Trudeau announced Canada's Feminist International Assistance Policy. This policy states that "Canadians are safer and more prosperous when more of the world shares our values. Those values include feminism and the promotion of the rights of women and girls" (Government of Canada 2017). Canada's feminist approach to international assistance "has committed to support that which is human-rights based, strategic and focused, transformative and activist, and evidence-based and accountable" (Starr and Mitchell 2018, 107). Starr and Mitchell (2018, 115), themselves Canadian researchers of sexual violence in Ethiopia, conclude their assessment of the policy with a hopeful outlook: "[Canada's] feminist assistance policy has an excellent chance of doing something right . . . if the idea of advocacy for the local through participatory approaches with women (rather than about women) is supported financially and in spirit."[14]

As a feminist Canadian researcher, I share their enthusiasm. As a note of caution, though, adding women's voices, or "listening to women," should not be considered policy panaceas. When an organization seeks to simply "add women," often any woman will do, and this has the potential to reinforce discriminatory structures. Instead, funders need to find ways to shift their notions of what an expert looks like and therefore what types of organizations are prioritized and offered funding. Cookson (2018, 153) further cautions against using women as a means to an end rather than an end in themselves and hopes that the Feminist International Assistance Policy will not replicate these dynamics. Her concerns are echoed by other scholars, who question how transformative the policy really is, given its embodiment of a "neoliberal feminism and feminist neoliberalism" (Parisi 2020, 164) that fails to incorporate an intersectional approach to policy (Morton, Muchiri, and Swiss 2020). Despite these real and legitimate concerns, I maintain hope that there is reason to be optimistic about a future in which women's grassroots and local approaches to gender justice are adequately bolstered and supported by international allies, particularly if donors are willing to adapt the ways and modalities through which they support postconflict communities based on the realities they encounter.

The lessons of high-risk feminism travel beyond the borders of a single Andean nation. Women do not mobilize under violent circumstances only in Colombia. There are plenty of other conflict situations around the world that could benefit from research that identifies local, feminist responses to gendered expressions of violence. These spaces offer reprieve from contexts where gendered violence is pervasive and ubiquitous. Since beginning this project in 2015, I have identified countless potential expressions of high-risk feminism around the world. Consider, for example, a women-only village in Kenya, founded by a woman who was beaten after attempting to teach women about their rights (Bindel 2015); a tent that serves to teach women about feminism in the context of "conflict and upheaval" in the Philippines (Redfern 2017); and a city of joy "turning pain into power" for survivors of sexual violence in Democratic Republic of the Congo (City of Joy Congo 2020). I have read about women in Kashmir who are protesting for gender justice, despite the pressures of the conflict context in which they live. As one interviewee revealed, "In the male-dominated societies like ours, women usually give [up] their dreams and suffer in silence. . . . But I chose not to do so" (Zahra and Sheikh Muzamil 2020). These women are breaking with expectations about their submissive roles in society. They are resisting—turning their frames of fear into frames of anger—to fight for a better future for themselves. This vision of the future is grounded in equality, and in justice. Feminism—high-risk though it may be—offers a reprieve from the tomorrows of violence.

Clearly, high-risk feminism and visions of gender justice will take different forms in different cultural contexts.[15] For example, research by the United States Institute of Peace about women's leadership in peacebuilding in Afghanistan highlights the ongoing tensions between "the increasing number of liberal initiatives and the long-standing conservativism in Afghan society, which has traditionally restricted women's activities to the domestic sphere" (Humayoon and Basij-Rasikh 2020, 2). After the Taliban take-over of the country in August 2021, women's roles in public life have been severely restricted, and activism has become even more contentious. Yet I have also read reports of women resisting Taliban segregation and the imposed restrictions on women's rights; one woman interviewed by the *Financial Times* (Qazizai and Kazmin 2021) said: "We are going against people who only know the language of arms and nothing else. It is a huge risk, but we have no choice." Another said: "When we have lost everything, there is nothing left for us to lose."

Moreover, we need to bring a critical eye to policies that ostensibly should serve women's interests—even the best-intentioned policies can have hidden costs (Cookson 2018). For example, when writing about the impact of the UN Security Council's Resolution 2242—which called on member states to include in the Women, Peace and Security agenda efforts to counter terrorism and violent extremism—in Kenya, Aroussi (2020, 24) shows that "without contesting the power hierarchies on the ground or addressing the structural factors that constrain women's agency, attempts to increase women's participation will only reinforce existing inequalities." Centering women's understandings and experiences of conflict at the heart of international and national responses and support will result in more meaningful engagement in acts of solidarity that underpin what it means to practice feminist action.

Concluding Remarks

On 3 September 2020, still stuck inside owing to the global pandemic, I logged on to a virtual event held by the Rodeemos el Diálogo transnational civil society organization. Francia Márquez's face flashed across my screen. Only shortly before this event, this winner of the 2018 Goldman Environmental Prize and the 2015 Diakonia Human Rights Defender of the Year had publicly expressed her intentions to run for president of Colombia in the next national elections. When questioned about this step, she replied, "It is hard for me—a woman, a poor woman, a racialized woman—to dare to consider this. They have taught us to not even think about this, let alone announce it. But I think we have to dare to think about it. Opening this possibility is the way to build a more just society and heal ourselves as a nation, a country, and build a path toward the peace." Almost as an afterthought, she added words that I have heard—in slightly different formulations—so many times before: "If we're silent, they kill us. If we speak out, they'll kill us. So, we may as well speak out."[16]

Her sentiments further echo those of the interlocutors in Rodriguez Castro's (2020) work, which is titled, "We Are Not Poor Things" (see also Rodriguez Castro 2021). In this article, she outlines Colombian women's understandings of their own agency and their own ability to fight systems of oppression. The women I spent time with over the course of research for this book would similarly reject the label "poor things"—they have spent decades consciously and strategically engaging in collective action for gender justice in contexts of high risk. Like Francia Márquez, over years of struggle they are convinced that they must continue to "speak out."

Colombia continues to represent a vulnerable context, especially for women, and particularly for poor, displaced, single, unemployed, and ethnic and racial minority women. Despite the peace accords, violence—including gendered violence—remains rife and presents ongoing challenges to women's security. This violence is, in some cases, a direct result of women's mobilization for their own rights, a type of exaggerated patriarchal backlash that follows the same logics of the militarized masculinities that crosscut moments of conflict and postconflict. Their feminism is high risk. Yet throughout these different iterations of violence, women choose—time and time again—to continue to pursue gender justice.

Acknowledgments

Unexpectedly, I have found myself living, working, and traveling around Colombia for the better part of seven years. This book is the product of years of ongoing support, friendship, and camaraderie developed in this beautiful Andean country. It only became possible because of people's intellectual generosity and willingness to share with me their time, their homes, their stories, their insights, and their memories.

The line between professional and personal connection is often blurred. So too has been the case of the research I have undertaken in Colombia. My ability to reach some of the country's far-flung corners has only been made possible through the generosity of people like A, A, J, Y, D, S, D, J, A, J, I, and particularly, M. On our many car, taxi, and bus rides, they have explained to me how Colombia works in practice. They have listened to my questions, and patiently helped me shape better ones. Although it brings me sadness not to be able to recognize them as they deserve, I do not include their full names because their commitment to making this country more peaceful means that they face ongoing risks of violence as they continue in their *lucha*.

Leigh Payne supervised both my master's and doctoral degree projects and is now a mentor for my early career research fellowship. Despite such a longstanding relationship, I still have more to learn from her. Over the years, she has guided me and helped me to identify the puzzles that are worth untangling. She has lent me her books, her guest bedroom, and her wisdom. One of the most precious things that has developed over the course of the years is our friendship, one that I am sure will last for many years to come.

During my time at Oxford, I have been lucky enough to make dear and lasting friends. They have listened to me present research, read over my drafts, and encouraged me personally and academically. Thanks to Jonas von Hoffmann, who read multiple theory chapters, and Simón Escoffier, who sat with me at the Royal Oak to hash out the finer details of social movement theory. I owe a special thanks to Francesca Lessa, who, in encouraging me to turn my thesis into a book during Covid-19 lockdown, unwittingly became my mentor in all things publishing, not to mention all things European Commission. To Anna O'Kelly, for telling me when it's time for a Power 10, and Graeme Thompson, for feeding Anna and me during an entire academic term. To 3CW: Rafa Gude, Diego Scardone, Marcos Todeschini, Alejandro Espinosa, Pauline Ravillard, and Nicolás Robinson Andrade. To Maryhen Jiménez, Nancy Tapias, Laura Bernal, Juan Masullo, Carl Drott, Clara Voyvodic, Marcel Dirsus, Dáire McGill, Annette Idler, and Felipe Roa. Further thanks to those teachers and colleagues who offered insights into earlier drafts of my doctoral thesis, the articles and papers that developed from it, and this book itself: David Kirk, David Doyle, Federico Varese, Diego Sánchez Ancochea, Julieta Lemaitre, Mara Loveman, Caroline Moser, Maxine Molyneux, Erin Baines, Andrew Woolford, Alex Hinton, Brooke Ackerly, Elisabeth Friedman, Nathalie Lebon, Janet Conway, Juan Masullo, Jana Krause, Emily Paddon Rhoads, Jennifer Welsh, and a host of anonymous reviewers and editors.

Then there are those colleagues who evade geographic pinpointing: we stay in touch via Zoom calls, Twitter posts, and Whatsapp audio messages. We make deliberate time to see each other at international conferences, at university events, or at our favorite Italian restaurant in Chapinero. Although our meetings are often fleeting—before a flight, in between panels—the connections are no less important to me. For inspiring me to be a more thoughtful scholar, my thanks to Gwen Burnyeat, Sanne Weber, Tatiana Sánchez, Adriana Rudling, Marie Berry, Adam Baird, and Devin Finn. Thank you to Hilary Matfess for extracting me from last-minute spirals. And to Roxani Krystalli, who gifted me an evergreen guiding question: By whom do you want to be taken seriously?

I have long grappled with how to turn ideas into practice and beliefs into action. I never could have guessed that a meeting at a conference in 2014 would eventually transform into a connection that has enriched my career so profoundly. Working with Tara Cookson, Lorena Fuentes, and Alex Berryhill at Ladysmith has challenged me, inspired me, and supported me beyond measure. I hope that in publishing this book, I am contributing to our shared goal of creating a more just and caring world.

Lizzie and the entire Dorrell family have adopted me, made me innumerable gin-and-tonics, and made it clear that I have a home with them—the halcyon summer sabbaticals that I have imposed on you all make up some of my happiest memories. Joshua and David have been a feature in my life as long as memory extends, and their doors have been open to me whenever I needed respite. In Colombia, my life has been forever enriched by having friends like Julia Symmes Cobb, Steven Grattan, Tom Newton, Dylan Baddour, Pu Huang,

Anastasia Moloney, Luis Castillo, Antonia Eklund, Marc Robinson, Cady Voge, Paola Sabogal, Shauna Gillooly, Jennifer Bitterly, Juan Sebastian Perdomo, Mónica Arango, and Jorge Delgado. In keeping with the blurred boundaries between friends and colleagues, I thank Kiran Stallone, with whom I share adventures and *locuras*, and Samuel Ritholtz, with whom I share stream-of-consciousness phone calls. Also, thanks for helping me with the hyphens. In Canada, I count on limitless encouragement from my real family—Margaret and Peter, Cath and Dave—and those who are as good as family—Elizabeth, Laura, Bronwyn, and their parents. Thank you to Dani for being a constant source of balance, and of love.

Research like this takes time. I am grateful to have been funded by the Commonwealth Scholarship Commission and the Social Sciences and Humanities Research Council of Canada throughout my doctoral research. Additional funding from St. Antony's College and the Santander Bank further supported my extensive fieldwork over the years. I have been fortunate enough to receive support to attend conferences from the Latin American Studies Association, the Society for Latin American Studies, the International Feminist Journal of Politics, the Europaeum, the John Fell Fund, the Malcolm Deas Fund, and the Latin American Centre at the University of Oxford. Thanks also to colleagues at the Universidad de los Andes, Universidad del Rosario, the Instituto Pensar at the Pontificia Universidad Javeriana, the Instituto Chileno de Estudios Municipales at the Universidad Autónoma de Chile, the Latin American Centre at Oxford, McGill University, the Geneva Graduate Institute, the Pontifícia Universidade Católica de São Paulo, and the University of Manitoba for facilitating opportunities to present my research and benefit from the comments and critiques of my peers.

Thank you to Rutgers University Press and the anonymous reviewers who facilitated the development of this manuscript, and especially to Kim Guinta for her editorial support.

I have somehow managed to convince my mother to spend a decades' worth of holidays in my field sites: she has endured taking minibuses through the winding roads of the Guatemalan highlands, eating questionable *pupusas* in Salvadoran beach towns, and sitting through hours of Spanish-language, un-air-conditioned town hall meetings on Colombia's Caribbean coast. Rather than complain, however, her deep sense of curiosity has always shone through. She has shown me that empathy and kindness transcend language barriers and are the building blocks of any work that is worth doing.

Catherine has always kept me grounded by reminding me that when it comes to being a doctor, I am the equivalent of Ross from *Friends*. Teasing aside, I have long admired her balanced view on how we can—and should—dedicate ourselves to those projects we are most passionate about, the ones make us more human.

Although my memories of my father are, by now, limited, I know two things for certain: he loved adventure, and he could find a way to relate to anyone. If these are the two traits of his that I have been fortunate enough to inherit, I consider myself eternally lucky.

As I finish writing these words, at the recommendation (another gift!) of a dear friend, I am reading *Feminism, Interrupted,* by Lola Olufemi. The following words jumped off the page:

"Solidarity refuses a narrow worldview and invites us to link our visions for the future to one another. . . . We break open the idea that feminism has a continental origin point; to recognize each other in struggle is to say, I *see* you, I understand that you have agency and because I cannot stand alongside you, I wish to bolster you from where I am. Solidarity, in an internationalist context, requires an emergent political practice. This means the ability to remain flexible in our responses and solutions; to listen to those on the ground and to redistribute resources" (Olufemi 2020, 137).

High-risk feminism is about solidarity through struggle. The real protagonists of this project are the women who have long worked to make Colombia a more fair and just society: the Liga de Mujeres Desplazadas, Afromupaz, the women of La Soledad, the Fuerza de Mujeres Wayuu, and the Alianza de Mujeres Tejedoras de Vida. I am keenly aware that their dedication, energy, and emotional candor are what has given shape, clarity, and color to this work. I hope that this project will in some way begin to repay their generosity, by shining a light on their ongoing *lucha* and saying "I *see* you . . . and I wish to bolster you from where I am."

The cover of this book features a photograph I took on the streets of Cartagena in 2016. The artwork is named *Las Tres Guerreras*—The Three Women Warriors. I wish to extend special thanks to the artist Fin DAC and the model Ana Luisa Muñoz Ortiz, who generously allowed me to use this photograph as my book cover.

Notes

Chapter 1   Introduction

1   Referring to a Yes vote in the national plebiscite; see Krystalli and Theidon (2016); Symmes Cobb and Casey (2016).

2   While the term *victim* can hold negative connotations (and many prefer to use the term *survivor*, particularly in relation to gender-based violence), in Colombia it can also be adopted as a form of political agency. For more, see Krystalli (2019).

3   The discussion of practical and strategic gender interests comes from Molyneux (1985). See also El-Bushra (2007, 135) for similar experiences of women's organizations in post–Cold War warfare in Africa

4   See Navarro (1989) and Elshtain (1996) for this definition of feminist mobilization.

5   A complete discussion of prospect theory is outlined in chapter 2 (based on Kahneman and Tversky 1979, 1992).

6   Menjívar's (2011) work dives deeply into these dynamics in postconflict Guatemala.

7   See Cockburn (2013b); Berry and Rana (2019).

8   Ruddick (1995) is clear, however, that she does not necessarily think women or mothers are inherently peaceful. See also Cohn (2013).

9   Of note, other work aiming to break the victim-perpetrator binary focuses on women as perpetrators of violence, including sexual violence, during war. See Sjoberg (2016) and Sjoberg and Gentry (2015), although this does not have a concentrated focus on Latin America.

10 As an example, in the process of demobilization in El Salvador, collected data showed that of the women in the Frente Farabundo Martí para la Liberación Nacional (FMLN) (rebel group)—about 30 percent of total forces—only 15 percent were armed combatants, while the rest filled logistical roles. See Luciak (2001).

11 The following are exceptions to this pattern: Villareal and Ríos (2006); Domingo, Rocha Menocal, and Hinestroza (2015); Lemaitre and Sandvik (2015); Kreft (2019)

12 Appelbaum's (2003, 4) work, for example, highlights the patterns of racial regionalization in Colombia that associate places traditionally defined as "black and Indian" with "disorder, backwardness, and danger."

13 Indeed, some feminist scholars suggest reconceptualizing the wave narrative as an "affective temporality," focusing on both feeling and a historically specific form of activism. See Chamberlain (2016, 458).

14 Even the word *gender* has become controversial in some settings; Corredor (2019) eloquently documents increasing resistance and countermovements to so-called gender ideology in Latin America; others (Krystalli and Theidon 2016; Tate 2016) have written about the role that "gender" played in the victory of the No vote during Colombia's 2016 plebiscite.

15 Interview by author, 11 September 2019, Mocoa.

16 For more on the professionalization or "NGO-ization" of feminist groups in Latin America, see Alvarez (1999, 2009) and Murdock (2008).

17 Interview by author, 16 October 2016, Turbaco.

18 The women of the Liga, Afromupaz, and the Alianza have a long history of media engagement, including coverage in national and international publications. When discussing informed consent, they were clear that previous media exposure had not led to backlash violence, and that they wanted increased international exposure and visibility of their experience, both in journalism and academia.

Chapter 2 Why Women Mobilize in High-Risk Contexts

1 Villareal and Ríos's (2006) report on women's nonviolent resistance in Chocó, Nariño, and Cauca is an important exception.

2 It is further important to remember that "men" is not a monolithic category. Men can also be the victims of conflict-related sexual violence, and their experiences in the aftermath are also shaped by social norms around masculinity and femininity (see Schulz 2020). Furthermore, women can also be the perpetrators of violence, including rape (see Sjoberg 2016).

3 Centro de Nacional Memoria Histórica (2011, 83–84).

4 Weber's other styles of authority—traditional and legal-rational—are not useful for an analysis of high-risk feminism, particularly given the high-risk context in which this type of mobilization takes place.

5 Interview by author, 12 October 2016, Turbaco.

6 Interviews by author, 12 October 2016 and 5 November 2016, Turbaco.

7 Interviews by author, 23 June 2017, 31 June 2017, Usme.

8 Indeed, at the time of writing I am engaged in a research project that aims to make claims about what a woman high-risk leader looks like in the Latin American context: What traits or characteristics does she possess? What is her mobilizational background? What can we learn about her ability to successfully convince participants to engage in high-risk collective action? See https://www.juliazulver.com/hrl.

9 I draw on Goodwin's work as it relates to affectual—rather than sexual—ties and solidarity.

10 Interview by author, 31 May 2017, Usme.

11 Indeed, Bandura (1973) notes that vicarious reinforcement (the perception of positive outcomes accruing to others) is a powerful source of motivation.

12 Interview by author, 19 October 2016, Turbaco.

Chapter 3   The High-Risk Feminism Framework

1 These loosely correspond to McAdam et al.'s (2001) ideas of brokerage, category formation, object shift, and certification as elements of the dynamics of contention.

2 For more on the legal construction of victimhood in Colombia, see Arango Olaya (2010); Lemaitre, et al. 2014; Krystalli (2019). Interestingly, women interviewed for this book highlighted on multiple occasions that they no longer consider themselves victims but rather survivors. The transformational element of collective identity is discussed in each of the empirical chapters.

3 McGarry and Jasper (2015) note that in recent years scholars have started to highlight the restrictive nature of collective identities in social movements. Their book, *The Identity Dilemma*, examines both the advantages and disadvantages of the concept. Collective identities, some scholars note, are "traps that distort complex realities, 'naturalize' labels and deceive individuals about their own goals and desires" (McGarry and Jasper 2015, 4). In my view, however, this dilemma is not pertinent to high-risk feminist mobilization. While there are problems with an essentializing identity that looks only at the lack of agency and victimhood, in the case of high-risk feminism, victims do not have the luxury of expanding beyond the immediacy of their identities as targets of ongoing acts of violence. These remain constant, and thus looking for an organization that fits better with one's identity extends too far beyond the lowest common denominator here—seeking protection from violence.

4 Additionally, for an excellent history of how Colombian groups have used human rights frameworks, and for what, and how they have developed over time, see Tate (2007). As she writes, "thought relatively powerless, these activities use human rights claims as a means to force state representatives to claim responsibility for abuses and thus enact an accountable state" (2007, 5).

5 As Sanford (2008) outlines in the case of feminicide, the crime of murdering a woman also has political implications; the murderer is guilty, but so are the state and judicial structures that normalize misogyny via impunity, silence, and indifference when it comes to prevention, investigation, and prosecution. Fuentes (2020) further queries the role of the media in reinforcing hierarchies between victims of femicide.

6 Interview with author, 31 January 2018, Riohacha.

Chapter 4   The Liga de Mujeres Desplazadas

1 Interview by author, 12 October 2016. All interviews in this chapter took place in Turbaco unless otherwise noted.

2 Interview by author, 12 October 2016.

3 Interview by author, 12 October 2016.

4 Interview by author, 12 October 2016.

5 Interview by author, 12 October 2016.

6 Interview by author, 12 October 2016.

7 Interview by author, 19 October 2016.

8 Interview by author, 12 October 2016.

9 Interview by author, 19 October 2016.

10 For a longer and more comprehensive discussion on feminist antimilitarism, see Cockburn (2007).

11 Jackeline Howard, Speech, 30 August 2016, Turbaco.
12 The same gendered social roles that gave rise to the militarized masculinity that characterized conflict in Colombia (see Theidon 2009; Cockburn 2013).
13 Interview by author, 19 October 2016.
14 Interview by author, 29 September 2016.
15 Interview by author, 5 November 2016.
16 Interview by author, 3 July 2015.
17 Interview by author, 13 October 2016.
18 This was part of a larger research project spearheaded by a group of academics from Bogotá.
19 Interview by author, 12 October 2016.
20 Arango Olaya adapted this concept from Skapska (1999), who writes about constitutionalism in Poland in the post–Cold War era.
21 Interview by author, 5 November 2016.
22 Moreover, on 31 August 2009, the son of one of the women in the Liga was killed in Cartagena. It is assumed he was murdered because of his role as the leader of the *Liga Joven* (the youth arm of the Liga).
23 For more examples of the Liga's use of acts of legal certification, see Arango Olaya (2010); Sandvik et al. (2014); Sandvik and Lemaitre (2013).
24 Patricia Guerrero, interview by author, 13 September 2015, Cartagena.
25 Interview by author, 7 September 2016, Cartagena.
26 After finishing this book manuscript, I received a Whatsapp message and series of photos (in September 2021) from a contact, documenting how the Liga has begun to build a restaurant-gallery with land provided by the mayor's office of Turbaco and funds from the United Nations Development Program, as part of their collective reparations program. It will be interesting to see, through further research, how this development has impacted organizational morale.
27 Group interview by author, 6 November 2016, Carmen de Bolívar.
28 Interview by author, 19 October 2016.

Chapter 5 Afromupaz

1 "La lucha cotidiana de los afros desplazados en Bogotá," *El Tiempo,* 16 May 2014.
2 Since I finished fieldwork, Afromupaz has moved to a permanent headquarters.
3 María Eugenia Urrutia, interview by author, 2 March 2017. All interviews in this chapter took place in Usme unless otherwise noted.
4 Urrutia, interview, 2 March 2017.
5 Conway (2018, 189) highlights that throughout the 1980s, "third world feminists' critique of the Western liberal project of global sisterhood problematized hegemonic Western feminism, . . . enabling the emergence of South-based feminist perspectives on the international scene." Indeed, Murdock's (2008) work in Medellín details the ways in which the professionalization of grassroots feminist movements within the context of "new development demands" created strained relations between middle- and working-class women.
6 These sentiments perhaps relate to some African American feminists' preference for use of the term *womanism*. See Monroe (2005).
7 For more on this campaign of violence, see Oslender (2007b, 754–756).

8   The constitution of 1991 was the first to offer Afro-Colombians collective land ownership rights. For more on this, see Oslender (2007a, 2008); Hooker (2005, 2008); Asher (2017).

9   For more on social movements in Colombia's Pacific coast, see Oslender (2004); Asher (2017).

10 It should be noted that it was not always guerrilla forces that forcibly displaced these women. The FARC, Ejército de Liberación Nacional (ELN), and Autodefensas Unidas de Colombia (AUC) groups all operated in these regions (with different levels of frequency over the years). Interviewees, however, were often vague or unclear about which actors had displaced them, and in keeping with the ethical protocols for the project, particularly around asking about traumatizing subjects, I never pushed for more information.

11 Interview by author, 23 June 2017.

12 Interview by author, 23 June 2017.

13 Interview by author, 23 June 2017.

14 She mentions that she had eight children but that only four are alive. She implied that some of the children died during the experiences of displacement.

15 Interview by author, 28 February 2017.

16 Interview by author, 28 February 2017.

17 Interview by author, 23 June 2017.

18 Part of the leadership explanation may reflect McAdam's (1982) notion of recycling.

19 This event involved more than 200 displaced people forcibly taking over the headquarters of the International Red Cross in Bogotá in an effort to force the Colombian government to find solutions to the problems of housing, food, and education that arose from displacement. See Pinilla (2000). Also see "Fin a toma de tres años en Zona Rosa," *El Tiempo*, 22 December 2002.

20 Interview by author, 25 September 2017.

21 María Eugenia Urrutia, interview, in Marciales Montenegro (2013, 47).

22 Fuentes (2020) expands on this idea of "disposability" of certain bodies through racialized and gendered imaginaries in Guatemala.

23 Urrutia, interview by author, 4 April 2017.

24 Interview by author, 23 July 2017.

25 Interview by author, 8 February 2017.

26 The transition from self-identification as survivor to victim is discussed in detail in Lemaitre, López, et al. (2014); Sandvik and Lemaitre (2015). For more on the hierarchies of victimhood in Colombia's transitional justice system, see Krystalli (2019).

27 Urrutia, interview by author, 2 March 2017.

28 Urrutia, interview by author, 11 May 2017.

29 Interview by author, 23 June 2017.

30 For more on the specificities of race and ethnicity as they pertain to Colombia's Afro-descendant population, see Ng'weno (2007).

31 Interview by author, 23 June 2017.

32 Carmen Marciales, interview by author, 23 June 2017, Bogotá.

33 Interview by author, 23 June 2017.

34 Interview by author, 23 June 2017.

35 Interview by author, 23 June 2017.

36 Interview by author, 31 May 2017.
37 Since this incident, however, the government (via the National Protection Unit) has provided Afromupaz with bodyguards for Urrutia.
38 Interview by author, 23 June 2017.
39 Interview by author, 23 June 2017.
40 Interview by author, 23 June 2017.
41 Interview by author, 23 June 2017.
42 Marciales, interview, 23 June 2017, Bogotá.
43 Urrutia, interview, 11 May 2017.
44 Urrutia, interview, 11 May 2017.
45 Urrutia, interview, 11 May 2017.
46 Urrutia, interview, 11 May 2017.
47 For more on how conflict victims navigate the transitional justice process and strategically frame their grievances, see Lemaitre and Sandvik (2015); Krystalli (2019).
48 Urrutia, interview, 11 May 2017.
49 Interview by author, 23 June 2017.

Chapter 6   La Soledad

1 *Land invasion* is the name given when people mobilize to invade land illegally and build informal shantytowns. For more, see Dosh (2009). La Soledad is a pseudonym.
2 As with the women of the Liga, while most of the women in La Soledad are of mixed racial and ethnic backgrounds, there is no concept of shared identity based on race or ethnicity.
3 The Mesas de Víctimas, which are run by the Victims' Unit, are spaces where people affected by the conflict can dialogue with the state and help create public policies for victims. See Unidad para las Víctimas (2018).
4 Interview by author, 1 February 2018, Riohacha.
5 Interview by author, 31 January 2018, Riohacha.
6 Interview by author, 1 February 2018, Riohacha.
7 As reported in newspaper articles I consulted but am not citing here, as they reveal the actual name and location of the neighborhood.
8 Interview by author, 13 June 2017, La Soledad.
9 Interview by author, 25 May 2017, La Soledad.
10 Interview by author, 25 May 2017, La Soledad.
11 Interview by author, 25 May 2017, La Soledad.
12 Interview by author, 14 June 2017, La Soledad.
13 Interview by author, 14 June 2017, La Soledad.
14 Interview by author, 14 June 2017, La Soledad.
15 Interview by author, 30 January 2018, Riohacha.
16 Interview by author, 30 January 2018, Riohacha.
17 Interview by author, 13 June 2017, Riohacha.
18 Gámez, Ingrid. "Dignifican a mujeres Víctimas de Violencia sexual," *al día,* 25 May 2017.
19 Interview by author, 24 May 2017, Riohacha.
20 Interview by author, 31 January 2018, Riohacha.
21 Interview by author, 31 January 2018, Riohacha.

22 Interview by author, 14 June 2017, La Soledad.
23 Interview by author, 13 June 2017, La Soledad.
24 Although questions around past experiences with conflict often came up over the course of interviews, I never pushed women to speak about potentially retraumatizing experiences. The semi-structured nature of my interviews allowed for flexibility when these circumstances presented themselves.
25 It is worth mentioning that Estefania told me that she founded her organization in 2004. It is unclear what actions, if any, were taken between 2004 and 2015.
26 Interview by author, 30 January 2018, La Soledad.
27 Whatsapp message, 9 February 2018.

Chapter 7   Conclusion

1 My initial research, however, began in 2015, while writing a newspaper story about the City of Women.
2 Photo on file with the author.
3 Interview by author, 10 September 2019, Mocoa.
4 Interviews by author, 11 September 2018, Mocoa.
5 Interestingly, the women of the Alianza do not necessarily identify their *lucha* as feminist, but rather as an issue of women's rights and empowerment with a focus on their roles as peacebuilders. To return to the conversation begun in chapter 1, however, despite not necessarily seeing themselves as feminists, I identify that their "narratives and actions [demonstrate] their deep commitment to [overthrowing] gender and ethno-racial [and class] inequalities" (Vergara Figueroa and Arboleda Hurtado 2016, 125).
6 Interview by author, 19 November 2018, Mocoa.
7 It is important to note that some scholars have flagged the pitfalls of romanticizing and homogenizing notions of "the local," particularly in the context of peacebuilding. See, for example, Mac Ginty and Richmond (2013); Mac Ginty (2015).
8 See also Kirby and Shepherd (2016); Castillo-Diaz and Cueva-Beteta (2017).
9 The 2019 Resolution 2493 includes the first mention of "context-specific approaches" for implementing the Women, Peace and Security agenda, acknowledging a need for nuance when applying a broad, global agenda to local settings and conflicts (see O'Rourke and Swaine 2019).
10 For an interesting discussion of who is considered an "expert" in the Colombian peace process, see Burnyeat (2020, 155). See also Franco Gamboa (2016) and Dávila Sáenz (2018).
11 Her work further notes that Colombian feminists' visions of peace include a deep-seated rejection of neoliberal and extractivist economic models and policies (Paarlberg-Kvam 2019).
12 For more on how to guarantee women's ability to meaningfully participate in grassroots peacebuilding in the context of the Covid-19 pandemic, see Global Network of Women Peacebuilders (2020).
13 For example, countries such as Sweden, Canada, Mexico, Luxembourg, and France have (or are in the process of adopting) specifically feminist foreign policies.
14 What's more, as Starr and Mitchell (2018) point out, Canada is not the only country that is taking steps toward including gender inequality more substantially within its international assistance programs. The United Kingdom has a new special envoy for gender equality; Sweden has a new policy framework for

development that includes global gender inequality; Norway has an Action Plan for Women's Rights and Gender Equality in Foreign and Development Policy, and Australia has a Gender Equality and Women's Empowerment Strategy. Other countries are increasingly developing feminist foreign policies; see, for example, the work of the Centre for Feminist Foreign Policy, https://centreforfeministfor-eignpolicy.org/feminist-foreign-policy.

15 Indeed, Hume and Wilding (2019, 15) note that our assessments of mobilization should move beyond a binary of agency versus passivity and that women's ability to resist violence should be assessed in relation to where they sit in the "violent landscape of agency—what is means to act within a violent world."

16 Rodeemos el Diálogo, #ReDDialogues—Afro-Colombian perspectives on Transitional Justice, 3 September 2020, https://www.youtube.com/watch?v =MnoBh6quobw&t=2283s. These words have become somewhat of a rallying cry among social leaders in Colombia. From what I have found, they were first spoken by Cristina Bautista, an Indigenous woman and leader, in her final speech before she was murdered in Cauca (Aquí 2019).

References

Acosta, M., et al. 2018. "The Colombian Transitional Process: Comparative Perspectives on Violence against Indigenous Women." *International Journal of Transitional Justice* 12 (1): 108–125.

AFROMUPAZ (Asociación de Mujeres Afro por la Paz). 2014. *Verdades ancestrales: La huerta al perejil*. Bogotá: Defensoría del Pueblo.

Alianza de Mujeres Tejedoras de Vida del Putumayo 2009. *Caracterización de la situación de las mujeres del Putumayo, 2007–2008*. Mocoa: Alianza Departamental de Mujeres del Putumayo.

Alimi, E. Y. 2009. "Mobilizing under the Gun: Applying Political Opportunities Structure in a Highly Repressive Setting." *Mobilization: An International Quarterly* 14 (2): 219–237.

Alvarez, S. 1999. "Advocating Feminism: The Latin American Feminist NGO "Boom.'" *International Feminist Journal of Politics* 1 (2): 181–209.

———. 2009. "Beyond NGO-ization? Reflections from Latin America." *Development* 52 (2): 175–184. doi: 10.1057/dev.2009.23.

Appelbaum, N. 2003. "Muddied Waters: Race, Region, and Local History in Colombia, 1846–1948." Duke University Press.

Aquí 2019. "*Si nos callamos nos matan, si hablamos también, entonces hablemos': Cristina Bautista Q.E.P.D.* Youtube video, posted 30 October 2019. https://www.youtube.com/watch?v=5e_mOab_wZo.

Arango Olaya, M. 2010. "Displ@ced." Paper prepared for Master of Laws degree. Harvard University. Cambridge, MA.

Arias, E., and D. Goldstein. 2010. "Violent Pluralism: Understanding the New Democracies of Latin America." In *Violent Democracies in Latin America*, edited by E. Arias and D. Goldstein, 1–35. Duke University Press.

Arjona, A. 2016. *Rebelocracy: Social Order in the Colombian Civil War*. Cambridge University Press.

Arostegui, J. 2013. "Gender, Conflict, and Peace-Building: How Conflict Can Catalyse Positive Change for Women." *Gender and Development* 21 (3): 533–549. doi: 10.1080/13552074.2013.846624.

Aroussi, S. 2009. "Women, Peace and Security: Moving beyond Feminist Pacifism." *PSA Annual Conference*. University College London.

———. 2020. "Strange Bedfellows: Interrogating the Unintended Consequences of Integrating Countering Violent Extremism with the UN's Women, Peace, and Security Agenda in Kenya." *Politics & Gender*, 1–31.

Arredondo, J. 2019. "The Slow Death of Colombia's Peace Movement." *The Atlantic*, December 2019. https://www.theatlantic.com/international/archive/2019/12/colombia-peace-farc/604078/.

Asher, K. 2017. "From Afro-Colombians to Afro-Descendants: The Trajectory of Black Social Movements." In *Beyond Civil Society*, edited by S. Alvarez et al., 199–218. Duke University Press.

Auyero, J. 2003. *Contentious Lives: Two Argentine Women, Two Protests, and the Quest for Recognition*. Duke University Press.

Baines, E. 2015. "'Today, I Want to Speak Out the Truth': Victim Agency, Responsibility, and Transitional Justice." *International Political Sociology* 9 (4): 1–17.

———. 2016. *Buried in the Heart: Women, Complex Victimhood, and the War in Northern Uganda*. Cambridge University Press.

Baines, E., and E. Paddon. 2012. "'This Is How We Survived': Civilian Agency and Humanitarian Protection." *Security Dialogue* 43 (3): 231–247.

Baker, A. 1982. "The Problem of Authority in Radical Movement Groups: A Case Study of a Lesbian-Feminist Organization." *Journal of Applied Behavioral Science*, 18: 323–341.

Ball, P. 2005. "On the Quantification of Horror: Notes from the Field." In *Repression and Mobilization*, edited by C. Davenport, H. Johnston, and C. Mueller, 189–208. University of Minnesota Press.

Bandura, A. 1973. *Aggressions: A Social Learning Analysis*. Eaglewood Cliffs, NJ: Prentice-Hall.

Bantjes, R. 2007. *Social Movements in a Global Context: Canadian Perspectives*. Toronto: Canadian Scholars Press.

Barrios Sabogal, L. C., and S. Richter. 2019. "Las Farianas: Reintegration of Former Female FARC Fighters as a Driver for Peace in Colombia." *Cuadernos de economía* 38 (78): 753–784.

Bastian Duarte, A. I. 2012. "From the Margins of Latin American Feminism: Indigenous and Lesbian Feminisms." *Signs* 38 (1): 153–178.

Benford, R. 1997. "An Insider's Critique of the Social Movement Framing Perspective." *Sociological Inquiry* 67 (4): 409–430.

Berry, M. E. 2017. "Barriers to Women's Progress after Atrocity: Evidence from Rwanda and Bosnia-Herzegovina." *Gender and Society* 31 (6): 830–853.

———. 2018. *War, Women, and Power: From Violence to Mobilization in Rwanda and Bosnia-Herzegovina*. Cambridge University Press.

Berry, M. E., and M. Lake. 2021. "Women's Rights After War: On Gender Interventions and Enduring Hierarchies." *Annual Review of Law and Social Science* 17: 459–481.

Berry, M. E., and T. R. Rana. 2019. "What Prevents Peace? Women and Peacebuilding in Bosnia and Nepal." *Peace and Change* 44 (3): 321–349.

Bindel, J. 2015. "The Village Where Men Are Banned." *The Guardian*, 16 August 2019. https://www.theguardian.com/global-development/2015/aug/16/village-where-men-are-banned-womens-rights-kenya.

Boesten, J. 2014. *Sexual Violence during War and Peace: Gender, Power, and Post-Conflict Justice in Peru*. New York: Palgrave Macmillan.

Bonkat, L. 2014. "Survival Strategies of Market Women and Violent Conflicts in Jos, Nigeria." *Journal of Asia Pacific Studies* 3 (3): 281–299.

Brockett, C. 1991. "The Structure of Political Opportunities and Peasant Mobilization in Central America." *Comparative Politics* 23 (3): 253–274.

Burnyeat, G. 2020. *The Face of Peace: Pedagogy and Politics among Government Officials in the Colombian Peace Process with the FARC-EP.* University College London.

Calhoun, C. 1991. "The Problem of Identity in Collective Action." In *Macro-Micro Linkages in Sociology*, edited by J. Huber, 51–75. Newbury Park, CA: SAGE.

Callen, M., et al. 2014. "Violence and Risk Preference: Experimental Evidence from Afghanistan." *American Economic Review* 104 (1): 123–148.

Cancimance López, A. 2014. *Echar raíces en medio del conflicto armado: Resistencias cotidianas de colonos en Putumayo.* Universidad Nacional de Colombia.

Carpenter, C. 2005. "'Women, Children, and Other Vulnerable Groups': Gender, Strategic Frames, and the Protection of Civilians as a Transnational Issue." *International Studies Quarterly* 49 (2): 295–334.

Castillo-Diaz, P., and H. Cueva-Beteta. 2017. "The Promise and Limits of Indicators of Women, Peace, and Security." In *The Oxford Handbook of Gender and Conflict*, edited by F. Ní Aoláin et al., 185–199. Oxford University Press.

Castro, C., et al. 2020. "Understanding the Killing of Social Leaders in Colombia during COVID-19." *LSE Latin America and Caribbean Blog*, 6 October 2019. https://blogs.lse.ac.uk/latamcaribbean/2020/10/06/understanding-the-killing-of-social-leaders-in-colombia-during-covid-19/.

Centro Nacional de Memoria Histórica 2010. *La masacre de Bahía Portete: Mujeres Wayuu en la mira.* Bogotá: Centro Nacional de Memoria Histórica.

———. 2011. *Mujeres y guerra: Víctimas y resistentes en el Caribe colombiano.* Bogotá.

———. 2012. *El Placer: Mujeres, coca, y guerra en el Bajo Putumayo.* Bogotá.

———. 2013. "¡Basta ya! Colombia: Memorias de guerra y dignidad." Bogotá.

———. 2015. *Aniquilar la diferencia: Lesbianas, gays, bisexuales, y transgeneristas en el marco del conflicto armado colombiano.* Bogotá.

———. 2017. *La guerra Inscrita en el cuerpo: Informe nacional de violencia sexual en el conflicto armado.* Bogotá.

———. 2019. *Ser marica en medio del conflicto armado: Memorias de sectores LGBT en el Magdalena Medio.* Bogotá.

Chamberlain, P. 2016. "Affective Temporality: Towards a Fourth Wave." *Gender and Education*, 28 (3): 458–464.

City of Joy Congo 2020. *Turning Pain into Power.* https://www.cityofjoycongo.org/splash/.

Cockburn, C. 2004. "The Continuum of Violence: A Gender Perspective on War and Peace." In *Sites of Violence: Gender and Conflict Zones*, edited by W. Giles and J. Hyndman, 24–44. University of California Press.

———. 2007. *From Where We Stand: War, Women's Activism and Feminist Analysis.* London: Zed Books.

———. 2012. "What Kind of Feminism Does War Provoke?" *OpenDemocracy*, 2 December 2012. https://www.opendemocracy.net/en/5050/what-kind-of-feminism-does-war-provoke/.

———. 2013a. "Against the Odds: Sustaining Feminist Momentum in Post-War Bosnia-Herzegovina." *Women's Studies International Forum* 36 (2): 26–35.

———. 2013b. "Sexual violence in Bosnia: how war lives on in everyday life." *Open-Democracy*, 28 November. https://www.opendemocracy.net/en/5050/sexual-violence-in-bosnia-how-war-lives-on-in-everyday-life/.

Cohn, C. 2013. "'Maternal Thinking" and the Concept of 'Vulnerability' in Security Paradigms, Policies, and Practices." *Journal of International Political Theory* 10 (1): 46–69.

Colletta, N., and M. Cullen. 2000. *Violent Conflict and the Transformation of Social Capital: Lessons from Cambodia, Rwanda, Guatemala, and Somalia*. Washington, DC: World Bank.

Collier, D., J. Mahoney, and J. Seawright, J. 2004. "Claiming Too Much: Warnings about Selection Bias." In *Rethinking Social Inquiry*, edited by D. Collier and H. Brady, 85–105. Lanham, MD: Rowman and Littlefield.

Conexión Putumayo. 2019. "Defensoría del pueblo rechazó casos de feminicidios en el Putumayo." *Conexión Putumayo,* 22 October 2019. https://conexionputumayo .com/defensoria-del-pueblo-rechazo-casos-de-feminicidios-en-el-putumayo/.

Conway, J. M. 2018. "When Food Becomes a Feminist Issue: Popular Feminism and Subaltern Agency in the World March of Women." *International Feminist Journal of Politics* 20 (2): 188–203.

Cookson, T. 2018. *Unjust Conditions: Women's Work and the Hidden Cost of Cash Transfer Programs*. University of California Press.

Corradi, J., P. W. Fagen, and M. Garretón Merino. 1992. *Fear at the Edge: State Terror and Resistance in Latin America*. University of California Press.

Corredor, E. S. 2019. "Unpacking "Gender Ideology" and the Global Right's Antigender Countermovement." *Signs: Journal of Women in Culture and Society* 44 (3): 613–638.

Crenshaw, K. 1991. "Mapping the Margins: Intersectionality, Identity Politics, and Violence against Women of Color." *Stanford Law Review* 43 (6): 1241–1299.

Davies, S., and J. True. 2015. "Reframing Conflict-Related Sexual and Gender-Based Violence: Bringing Gender Analysis Back In." *Security Dialogue* 46 (6): 495–512.

Dávila Sáenz, J. 2018. *A Land of Lawyers, Experts, and "Men Without Land": The Politics of Land Restitution and the Techno-Legal Production of "Dispossessed People" in Colombia*. Harvard University Press.

Domingo, P., A. Rocha Menocal, and V. Hinestroza. 2015. *Progress despite Adversity: Women's Empowerment and Conflict in Colombia*. London: Overseas Development Institute.

Dosh, P. 2009. "Tactical Innovation, Democratic Governance, and Mixed Motives: Popular Movement Resilience in Peru and Ecuador." *Latin American Politics and Society* 51 (1): 87–118.

Drysdale Walsh, S., and C. Menjívar. 2016. "Impunity and Multisided Violence in the Lives of Latin American Women: El Salvador in Comparative Perspective." *Current Sociology* 64 (4): 586–602.

Van Dyke, N. 2003. "Protest Cycles and Party Politics: The Effects of Elite Alliances and Antagonists on Student Protest in the United States, 1930–1990." In *States, Parties, and Social Movements*, edited by J. Goldstone, 226–245. Cambridge University Press.

Eatwell, R. 2006. "The Concept and Theory of Charismatic Leadership." *Totalitarian Movements and Political Religions* 7 (2): 141–156. doi: 10.1080/14690760600642156.

Eisinger, P. K. 1973. "The Conditions of Protest Behavior in American Cities." *American Political Science Review* 67 (1): 11–28.

El-Bushra, J. 2007. "Feminism, Gender, and Women's Peace Activism." *Development and Change* 38 (1): 131–147.

El-Bushra, J., and J. Gardner. 2016. "The Impact of War on Somali Men: Feminist Analysis of Masculinities and Gender Relations in a Fragile Context." *Gender and Development* 24 (3): 443–458. doi: 10.1080/13552074.2016.1233668.

Elcheroth, G., and S. Reicher. 2017. *Identity, Violence, and Power*. London: Palgrave Macmillan.

Elshtain, J. B. 1996. "The Mothers of the Disappeared: An Encounter with Antigone's Daughters." In *Finding a New Feminism: Rethinking The Woman Question for Liberal Democracy*, edited by P. G. Jensen, 129–147. Lanham, MD: Rowman and Littlefield.

Elster, J. 1987. "Solomonic Judgments: Against the Best Interest of the Child." *University of Chicago Law Review* 54 (1): 1–45.

Enloe, C. 1993. *The Morning After: Sexual Politics at the End of the Cold War*. University of California Press.

———. 2000. *Bananas, Beaches, and Bases: Making Feminist Sense of International Politics*. 2nd ed. University of California Press.

Ensalaco, M. 2006. "Murder in Ciudad Juarez: A Parable of Women's Struggle for Human Rights." *Violence against Women* 12 (5): 417–440. doi: 10.1177/1077801206287963.

Epstein, B. 2015. "The Decline of the Women's Movement." In Goodwin and Jasper, *Social Movements Reader: Cases and Concepts*, 247–354.

Erickson Nepstad, S., and C. Bob. 2006. "When Go Leaders Matter? Hypotheses on Leadership Dynamics in Social Movements." *Mobilization* 11 (1): 1–22. http://mobilization.metapress.com/index/013313600164m727.pdf.

Escobar, A. 2003. "Displacement, Development, and Modernity in the Colombian Pacific." *International Social Science Journal* 55 (175): 157–167.

Fernandes, S. 2007. "Barrio Women and Popular Politics in Chávez's Venezuela." *Latin American Politics and Society* 49 (3): 97–127.

FIP (Fundacíon Ideas para la Paz). 2017. *Mujeres y la economía cocalera en el Putumayo: Roles, prácticas, y riesgos*. Bogotá. http://cdn.ideaspaz.org/media/website/document/5a21a11163faf3.pdf.

Ford, L. 2019. "'Everybody Is Talking about It': Women's Tights to Take Centre Stage in 2020." *The Guardian*, 27 December 2019. https://www.theguardian.com/global-development/2019/dec/27/everybody-is-talking-about-it-womens-rights-to-take-centre-stage-in-2020.

Forst, M. 2018. *United Nations Special Rapporteur on the Situation of Human Rights Defenders: Visit to Colombia, 20 November to 3 December 2018*. End of Mission Statement. https://www.ohchr.org/Documents/Issues/Defenders/StatementVisitColombia3Dec2018_EN.pdf.

Franco Gamboa, A. 2016. "Fronteras simbólicas entre expertos y víctimas de la guerra en Colombia." *Antípoda Revista de Antropología y Arqueología* 24: 35–53.

Friedman, D., and McAdam, D. 1992. "Collective Identity and Activism: Networks, Choices, and the Life of a Social Movement." In *Frontiers in Social Movement Theory*, edited by In A.D. Morris and C. M. Mueller, 156–173. Yale University Press.

Fuentes, L. 2020. "'The Garbage of Society': Disposable Women and the Socio-Spatial Scripts of Femicide in Guatemala." *Antipode* 52 (6): 1667–1687.

Fuentes, L., and T. Cookson. 2019. "Counting Gender (in)equality? A Feminist Geographical Critique of the 'Gender Data Revolution.'" *Gender, Place, and Culture*. doi: https://doi.org/10.1080/0966369X.2019.1681371.

Gamson, W. 1990. *The Strategy of Social Protest*. Belmont, CA: Wadsworth Publishing.

———. 2015. "Defining Movement 'Success.'" In Goodwin and Jasper, *Social Movements Reader: Cases and Concepts*, 383–385.

Ganz, M. 2009. *Why David Sometimes Wins: Leadership, Organization, and Strategy in the California Farm Worker Movement*. Oxford University Press.

———. 2010. "Leading Change: Leadership, Organization, and Social Movements." In *Handbook of Leadership Theory and Practice: A Harvard Business School Centennial Colloquium*, edited by N. Nohria and R. Khurana, 527–569. Cambridge, MA: Harvard Business Press.

Gargallo Celentani, F. 2012. *Feminismos desde Abya Yala: Ideas y proposiciones de las mujeres de 607 pueblos en nuestra América*. Bogotá: Ediciones Desde Abajo.

Mac Ginty, R. 2015. "Where Is the Local? Critical Localism and Peacebuilding." *Third World Quarterly* 36 (5): 840–856.

Mac Ginty, R., and O. Richmond. 2013. "The Local Turn in Peace Building: A Critical Agenda for Peace." *Third World Quarterly* 34 (5): 763–83.

Global Network of Women Peacebuilders. 2020. *Building Peace from the Grassroots: Learning from Women Peacebuilders to Advance the WPS Agenda*. New York. https://gnwp.org/amplifying-voices-generating-ownership/.

Goetz, A. M., and R. Jenkins. 2016. "Agency and Accountability: Promoting Women's Participation in Peacebuilding." *Feminist Economics* 22 (1): 211–236.

———. 2018. "Participation and Protection: Security Council Dynamics, Bureaucratic Politics, and the Evolution of the Women, Peace, and Security Agenda." In *The Oxford Handbook of Gender and Conflict*, edited by F. Ní Aoláin et al., 119–132. Oxford University Press. https://www.oxfordhandbooks.com/view/10.1093/oxfordhb/9780199300983.001.0001/oxfordhb-9780199300983-e-10.

Goffman, E. 1959. *The Presentation of the Self in Everyday Life*. New York: Doubleday.

Gómez Carvajal, N. 2015. "'Volver a vacer' luego de sobrevivir al conflicto." *El Tiempo*, 13 September 2015. http://www.eltiempo.com/archivo/documento/CMS-16372378.

González, V., and K. Kampwirth. 2001. *Radical Women in Latin America: Left and Right*. Pennsylvania State University Press.

Goodwin, J. 1997. "The Libidinal Constitution of a High-Risk Social Movement: Affectual Ties and Solidarity in the Huk Rebellion, 1946–1954." *American Sociological Review* 62 (1): 53–69.

Goodwin, J., and J. M. Jasper. 2015. *The Social Movements Reader: Cases and Concepts*. 3rd ed. Chichester, UK: Wiley-Blackwell.

Goodwin, J., Jasper, J. M. and Polletta, F. 2001a. *Passionate Politics: Emotions and Social Movements*. University of Chicago Press.

———. 2001b. "Why Emotions Matter." Introduction to Goodwin, Jasper, and Polletta, *Passionate Politics: Emotions and Social Movements*, 1–24

Goodwin, J. and Pfaff, S. 2001. "Emotion Work in High-Risk Social Movements: Managing Fear in the U.S. and East German Rights Movements." In Goodwin, Jasper, and Polletta, *Passionate Politics: Emotions and Social Movements*, 282–303.

Gould, D. 2015. "The Emotion Work of Movements." In Goodwin and Jasper, *Social Movements Reader: Cases and Concepts*, 254–266.

Gould, R. 1995. *Insurgent Identities: Class, Community, and Protest in Paris from 1848 to the Commune*. University of Chicago Press.

Government of Canada 2017. *Canada's Feminist International Assistance Policy*. http://international.gc.ca/world-monde/issues_development-enjeux_developpement/priorities-priorites/policy-politique.aspx?lang=eng.

Guerrero, S. 2017. "Fuerza de Mujeres Wayuu gana Premio Nacional a la Defensa de los Derechos Humanos." *El Heraldo*, 19 September 2017. https://www.elheraldo

.co/la-guajira/fuerza-de-mujeres-wayuu-gana-premio-nacional-la-defensa-de-los
-derechos-humanos-404117.

Hay, K. 2012. "Engendering Policies and Programmes through Feminist Evaluation: Opportunities and Insights." *Indian Journal of Gender Studies* 19 (2): 321–340.

Herrera, N., and D. Porch. 2008. "'Like Going to a Fiesta': The Role of Female Fighters in Colombia's FARC-EP." *Small Wars and Insurgencies* 19 (4): 609–634.

Hochschild, A. 1983. *The Managed Heart: Commercialization of Human Feeling.* University of California Press.

Holston, J. 2008. *Insurgent Citizenship: Disjunctions of Democracy and Modernity in Brazil.* Princeton University Press.

Hooker, J. 2005. "Indigenous Inclusion / Black Exclusion: Race, Ethnicity, and Multicultural Citizenship in Latin America." *Journal of Latin American Studies* 37 (2): 285–310.

———. 2008. "Afro-descendant Struggles for Collective Rights in Latin America." *Souls: A Critical Journal of Black Politics, Culture, and Society* 10 (3): 279–291.

Hughes, M. 2009. "Armed Conflict, International Linkages, and Women's Parliamentary Representation in Developing Nations." *Social Problems* 56 (1): 174–204.

Humayoon, H., and M. Basij-Rasikh. 2020. *Afghan Women's Views on Violent Extremism and Aspirations to a Peacemaking Role.* Washington, DC: United States Institute of Peace. https://www.usip.org/sites/default/files/2020-02/pw_156 -afghan_womens_views_on_violent_extremism_and_aspirations_to_a _peacemaking_role-cover-pw.pdf.

Hume, M. 2009a. "Researching the Gendered Silences of Violence in El Salvador." *IDS Bulletin* 40 (3): 78–85.

———. 2009b. *The Politics of Violence: Gender, Conflict, and Community in El Salvador.* West Sussex, UK: Wiley-Blackwell.

Hume, M., and P. Wilding. 2015. "'Es que para ellos el deporte es matar': Rethinking the Scripts of Violent Men in El Salvador and Brazil." In *Violence at the Urban Margins,* edited by J. Auyero, P. Bourgois, and N. Scheper-Hughes, 93–112. Oxford University Press.

———. 2019. "Beyond Agency and Passivity: Situating a Gendered Articulation of Urban Violence in Brazil and El Salvador." *Urban Studies* 57 (2): 249–266.

Idler, A. 2019. *Borderland Battles: Violence, Crime, and Governance at the Edges of Colombia's War.* Oxford University Press.

INDEPAZ (Instituto de Estudios para el Desarrollo y la Paz). 2019. *Informe líderes y defensores de DDHH asesinados al 26 de julio de 2019.* Bogotá. http://www.indepaz .org.co/informe-lideres-y-defensores-de-ddhh-asesinados-al-26-de-julio-de-2019/.

———. 2021. *Líderes sociales, defensores de DD.HH y firmantes de Acuerdo Asesinados en 2021.* http://www.indepaz.org.co/lideres-sociales-y-defensores-de-derechos -humanos-asesinados-en-2021/.

International Crisis Group. 2020. *Broken Ties, Frozen Borders: Colombia and Venezuela Face COVID-19.* Briefing 24. Bogotá. https://www.crisisgroup.org/latin -america-caribbean/andes/colombia/b24-broken-ties-frozen-borders-colombia-and -venezuela-face-covid-19.

IPES (Instituto para la economía social). 2015. *Fortaleciendo los DDHH a través de iniciativas locales de mujeres indígenas Wayuu de Colombia.* Bogotá. http://www .ipesderechoshumanos.org/accion/fortaleciendo-ddhh-iniciativas-locales-mujeres -indigenas-wayuu-colombia/.

Jaquette, J. 1994. "Women's Political Participation and the Prospects for Democracy." Conclusion to *The Women's Movement in Latin America: Participation and Democracy,* edited by J. Jaquette, 223–238. Boulder: Westview Press.

Jasper, J. 2010. "Social Movement Theory Today: Toward a Theory of Action?" *Sociology Compass* 4 (11): 965–976.

Jokela-Pansini, M. 2016. "Spatial Imaginaries and Collective Identity in Women's Human Rights Struggles in Honduras." *Gender, Place, and Culture* 23 (10): 1465–1479.

Justino, P. 2019. "Civilian Action in Conflict Settings: The Case of Colombia." *IDS Bulletin* 50 (3): 95–113.

Kahneman, D., and A. Tversky. 1979. "Prospect Theory: An Analysis of Decision under Risk." *Econometrica* 47 (2): 263–292.

———. 1992. "Advances in Prospect Theory: Cumulative Representation of Uncertainty." *Journal of Risk and Uncertainty* 5 (4): 297–323.

Kampwirth, K. 2004. *Feminism and the Legacy of Revolution: Nicaragua, El Salvador, Chiapas.* Ohio University Press.

———. 2006. *Women and the Guerrilla Movements: Nicaragua, El Salvador, Chiapas.* Ohio University, Centre for International Studies.

Kaplan, O. 2017. *Resisting War: How Communities Protect Themselves.* Cambridge University Press.

Khawaja, M. 1993. "Repression and Popular Collective Action: Evidence from the West Bank." *Sociological Forum* 8 (1): 47–71.

Kirby, P., and L. J. Shepherd. 2016. "The Futures |Past of the Women, Peace, and Security Agenda." *International Affairs* 92 (2): 373–392.

Krause, J. 2018. *Resilient Communities: Non-Violence and Civilian Agency in Communal War.* Cambridge University Press.

———. 2019. "Gender Dimensions of (Non)Violence in Communal Conflict: The Case of Jos, Nigeria." *Comparative Political Studies* 52 (10): 1466–1499.

Krause, J., W. Krause, and P. Bränfors. 2018. "Women's Participation in Peace Negotiations and the Durability of Peace." *Empirical and Theoretical Research in International Relations* 44 (6): 985–1016.

Kreft, A.-K. 2019. "Responding to Sexual Violence: Women's Mobilization in War." *Journal of Peace Research* 56 (2): 220–233.

———. 2020. "Civil Society Perspectives on Sexual Violence in Conflict: Patriarchy and War Strategy in Colombia." *International Affairs* 96 (2): 457–478.

Kroc Institute for International Peace Studies. 2020. *Towards Implementation of Women's Rights in the Colombian Final Peace Accord: Progress, Opportunities, and Challenges.* Notre Dame, IN: University of Notre Dame, Keogh School of International Affairs. https://peaceaccords.nd.edu/wp-content/uploads/2020/11 /Towards-Implementation-of-Womens-Rights-in-the-Colombian-Final-Peace -Accord-2.pdf.

Krystalli, R. 2019. "'We Are Not Good Victims': Hierarchies of Suffering and the Politics of Victimhood in Colombia." Tufts University, Fletcher School.

———. 2020. "Women, Peace, and Victimhood." IPI Global Observatory. New York. https://theglobalobservatory.org/2020/10/women-peace-and-victimhood/#more -20687.

Krystalli, R., and K. Theidon. 2016. "Here's How Attention to Gender Affected Colombia's Peace Process." *The Monkey Cage,* 9 October 2016. https://www .washingtonpost.com/news/monkey-cage/wp/2016/10/09/heres-how-attention-to -gender-affected-colombias-peace-process/?noredirect=on&utm_term= .f167171d3d50.

Laó-Montes, A. 2016. "Afro-Latin American Feminisms at the Cutting Edge of Emerging Political-Epistemic Movements." *Meridians: Feminism, Race, Transnationalism* 14 (2): 1–24. doi: 10.2979/meridians.14.2.02.

Lemaitre, J. 2016. "After the War: Displaced Women, Ordinary Ethics, and Grassroots Reconstruction in Colombia." *Social and Legal Studies* 25 (5): 545–565.

Lemaitre, J., E. S. López, et al. 2014. *De desplazados a víctimas: Los cambios legales y la participación de la Mesa de Víctimas de Mocoa, Putumayo.* Bogotá: Universidad de los Andes.

Lemaitre, J., K. B. Sandvik, et al. 2014. *Sueño de vida digna: La Liga de las Mujeres Desplazadas.* Bogotá: Universidad de los Andes.

———. 2015. "Shifting Frames, Vanishing Resources, and Dangerous Political Opportunities: Legal Mobilizations among Displaced Women in Colombia." *Law & Society Review* 49 (1): 5–38.

Lerner, J., and D. Keltner. 2001. "Fear, Anger, and Risk." *Journal of Personality and Social Psychology* 81 (1): 146–159.

La Liga de Mujeres Desplazadas 2009. *Desde el corazón de las mujeres: Una estrategia de resistencia jurídica de la Liga de Mujeres Desplazadas.* Cartagena, Colombia.

Lobao, L. 1990. "Women in Revolutionary Movements: Changing Patterns of Latin American Guerrilla Struggle." In *Women and Social Protest,* edited by G. West and R. L. Blumberg, 180–204. Oxford University Press.

Loveman, M. 1998. "High-Risk Collective Action: Defending Human Rights in Chile, Uruguay, and Argentina." *American Journal of Sociology* 104 (2): 477–525. doi: 10.1086/210045.

Lozano, B. R. 2016. "Feminismo Negro-Afrocolombiano: Ancestral, insurgent, y cimarrón. Un feminism en-lugar." *Intersticios de la política y la cultura* 5 (9): 23–48.

Luciak, I. 2001. *After the Revolution: Gender and Democracy in El Salvador, Nicaragua, and Guatemala.* Johns Hopkins University Press.

Lynch, M. 2019. "Localizing Gender Equality after Conflict." *Peace Review* 31 (1): 83–90.

Madsen, D., and P. Snow. 1991. *The Charismatic Bond: Political Behavior in Time of Crisis.* Harvard University Press.

Maher, D., and A. Thomson. 2018. "A Precarious Peace? The Threat of Paramilitary Violence to the Peace Process in Colombia." *Third World Quarterly* 39 (1): 2142–2172.

Mahoney, J., and G. Goertz. 2004. "The Possibility Principle: Choosing Negative Cases in Comparative Research." *American Political Science Review* 98 (4): 653–669. doi: 10.2307/4145330.

Marciales Montenegro, C. X. 2013. *Violencia sexual en el conflicto armado: Los rostros Afro de la Reparación. Caso: Asociación de Mujeres Afro por la Paz (AFROMUPAZ).* Universidad Nacional de Colombia. http://www.bdigital.unal.edu.co/41944/1/04489204.2013.pdf.

———. 2015. "Violencia sexual en el conflicto armado colombiano: Racismo estructural y violencia basada en género." *VIA IURIS* 19 (2015): 69–90.

Masullo, J. 2015. "The Power of Staying Put: Nonviolent Resistance against Armed Groups in Colombia." Washington DC.: International Center on Nonviolent Conflict Press.

McAdam, D. 1982. *Political Process and the Development of Black Insurgency, 1930–1970.* University of Chicago Press.

———. 1986. "Recruitment to High-Risk Activism: The Case of Freedom Summer." *American Journal of Sociology* 92 (1): 64–90.

———. 1988. *Freedom Summer.* Oxford University Press.

McAdam, D., S. Tarrow, and C. Tilly. 2001. *Dynamics of Contention.* Cambridge University Press.

McCarthy, J., and M. Zald. 1977. "Resource Mobilization and Social Movements: A Partial Theory." *American Journal of Sociology* 82 (6): 1212–1241.

McGarry, A., and J. M. Jasper. 2015. *The Identity Dilemma: Social Movements and Collective Identity.* Temple University Press.

Meertens, D. 2001. "Facing Destruction, Rebuilding Life: Gender and the Internally Displaced in Colombia." *Latin American Perspectives* 28 (1): 132–148.

———. 2012. "Forced Displacement and Gender Justice in Colombia between Disproportional Effects of Violence and Historical Injustice." Transitional Justice and Displacement Project, International Center for Transitional Justice and Brookings-London School of Economics (July).

Meger, S., and J. Sachseder. 2020. "Militarized Peace: Understanding Post-Conflict Violence in the Wake of the Peace Deal in Colombia." *Globalizations* 17 (6): 953–973.

Melucci, A. 1988. "Getting Involved: Identity and Mobilization in Social Movements." *International Social Movement Research* 1: 329–348.

Menjívar, C. 2011. *Enduring Violence: Latina Women's Lives in Guatemala.* University of California Press.

Merry, S. 2016. *The Seductions of Quantification: Measuring Human Rights, Gender Violence, and Sex Trafficking.* University of Chicago Press.

Mill, J. S. 1843. *System of Logic, Ratiocinative and Inductive.* London: John Parker.

Moghadam, V. 1997. "Gender and Revolutions." In *Theorizing Revolutions,* edited by J. Foran, 133–163. London: Routledge.

Moloney, A. 2014. "Rape Survivors Brace as Colombia's Warlords Prepare to Leave Jail." *Thomson Reuters Foundation,* 3 June 2014. http://news.trust.org//item /20140603033635-wo8ex.

Molyneux, M. 1985. "Mobilisation without Emancipation? Women's Interests, the State, and Revolution in Nicaragua." *Feminist Studies* 11 (2): 227–254.

———. 1998. "Analysing Women's Movements." In *Feminist Visions of Development: Gender Analysis and Policy,* edited by C. Jackson and R. Pearson, 65–88. Abingdon, UK: Routledge.

Monroe, I. 2005. "Womanism." *Africana: The Encyclopedia of the African and African American Experience.* 2nd ed. Oxford University Press.

Morris, A. 1984. *The Origins of the Civil Rights Movement: Black Communities Organizing for Change.* New York: Free Press.

Morris, A., and S. Staggenborg. 2004. "Leadership in Social Movements." In *The Blackwell Companion to Social Movements,* edited by D. Snow, S. Soule, and H. Kriesi, 171–196. Malden, MA: Blackwell.

Morton, S., J. Muchiri, and L. Swiss. 2020. "Which Feminism(s)? For Whom? Intersectionality in Canada's Feminist International Assistance Policy." *International Journal* 75 (3): 329–348.

Moser, C. 2001. "The Gendered Continuum of Violence and Conflict: An Operational Framework." In *Victims, Perpetrators, or Actors? Gender, Armed Conflict, and Political Violence,* edited by C. O. N. Moser and F. C. Clark, 30–53. London: Zed Books.

Moser, C., and C. McIlwaine. 2001. "Violence and Social Capital in Urban Poor Communities: Perspectives from Colombia and Guatemala." *Journal of International Development* 13 (2001): 965–984.

Moss, D. 2014. "Repression, Response, and Contained Escalation under 'Liberalized' Authoritarianism in Jordan." *Mobilization: An International Quarterly* 19 (3): 261–286. doi: 10.17813/maiq.19.3.q508v72264766u92.

Muller, E., and K.-D. Opp. 1986. "Rational Choice and Rebellious Collective Action." *American Political Science Review* 80 (2): 471–488.

Murdock, D. 2008. *When Women Have Wings: Feminism and Development in Medellin, Colombia.* University of Michigan Press.

Narayan, D. 1997. *Voices of the Poor: Poverty and Social Capital in Tanzania.* Washington D.C.: World Bank.

Navarro, M. 1989. "The Personal Is Political: Las Madres de Plaza de Mayo." In *Power and Popular Protest: Latin American Social Movements,* edited by S. Eckstein, 241–259. University of California Press.

Ng'weno, B. 2007. "Can Ethnicity Replace Race? Afro-Colombians, Indigeneity, and the Colombian Multicultural State." *Journal of Latin American and Caribbean Anthropology* 12 (2): 414–440. doi: 10.1525/jlaca.2007.12.2.414.

Nobel Women's Initiative. 2016. "Meet Patricia Guerrero, Colombia." *Nobel Women's Initiative,* 7 December 2016. https://nobelwomensinitiative.org/meet-patricia -guerrero-colombia/.

Nordstrom, C. 2004. "The Tomorrow of Violence." In *Violence,* edited by N. Whitehead, 223–242. Santa Fe, NM: School of American Research.

Nussbaum, M. 2001. *Upheavals of Thought: The Intelligence of Emotions.* Cambridge University Press.

O'Hearn, D. 2009. "Repression and Solidary Cultures of Resistance: Irish Political Prisoners on Protest." *American Journal of Sociology* 115 (2): 491–526. doi: 10.1086/ 599249.

O'Rourke, C., and A. Swaine. 2019. "Heading to Twenty: Perils and Promises of WPS Resolution 2493." *LSE WPS Blog,* 12 November 2019. https://blogs.lse.ac .uk/wps/2019/11/12/heading-to-twenty-perils-and-promises-of-wps-resolution -2493/.

Olson, M. 1965. *The Logic of Collective Action.* Harvard University Press.

Olufemi, L. 2020. *Feminism, Interrupted: Disrupting Power.* London: Pluto Press.

Opp, K.-D. 2009. *Theories of Political Protest and Social Movements: A Multidisciplinary Introduction, Critique, and Synthesis.* London: Routledge.

Opp, K.-D., and W. Roehl. 1990. "Repression, Micromobilization, and Political Protest." *Social Forces* 69 (2): 521–547. doi: 10.1093/sf/69.2.521.

Organization of American States. 2009. "Medidas cautelares: MC 319/09; Liga de Mujeres Desplazadas, Cartagena, Colombia (18 de novimebre de 2009)." http://www.oas.org/es/cidh/mujeres/proteccion/cautelares.asp.

———. 2011. "IACHR Condemns the Murder of Keila Esther Berrio in Colombia." http://www.oas.org/en/iachr/media_center/PReleases/2011/083.asp.

Oslender, U. 2004. "Fleshing Out the Geographies of Social Movements: Colombia's Pacific Coast Black Communities and the "Aquatic Space.'" *Political Geography* 23 (8): 957–985. doi: 10.1016/j.polgeo.2004.05.025.

———. 2007a. "Revisiting the Hidden Transcript: Oral Tradition and Black Cultural Politics in the Colombian Pacific Coast Region." *Environment and Planning D: Society and Space* 25 (6): 1103–1130. doi: 10.1068/d82j.

———. 2007b. "Violence in Development: The Logic of Forced Displacement on Colombia's Pacific Coast." *Development in Practice* 17 (6): 752–764. doi: 10.1080/09614520701628147.

———. 2008. "Another History of Violence: The Production of 'Geographies of Terror' in Colombia's Pacific Coast Region." *Latin American Perspectives* 35 (5): 77–102. doi: 10.1177/0094582X08321961.

Otto, D. 2018. "Women, Peace, and Security: A Critical Analysis of the Security Council's Vision." In *The Oxford Handbook of Gender and Conflict,* edited by F. Ní Aoláin et al., 105–119. Oxford University Press.

Paarlberg-Kvam, K. 2019. "What's To Come Is More Complication: Feminist Visions of Peace in Colombia." *International Feminist Journal of Politics* 21 (2): 194–223.

Padilla, B. 2001. "Grassroots Participation and Feminist Gender Identities: A Case Study of Women from the Popular Sector in Metropolitan Lima, Peru." *Journal of International Women's Studies* 6 (1): 93–113.

Parisi, L. 2020. "Canada's New Feminist International Assistance Policy: Business as Usual?" *Foreign Policy Analysis* 16 (2): 163–180.

Parkin Daniels, J. 2020. "Colombian Death Squads Exploiting Coronavirus Lockdown to Kill Activists." *The Guardian,* 23 March 2020. https://www .theguardian.com/world/2020/mar/23/colombian-groups-exploiting-coronavirus -lockdown-to-kill-activists.

———. 2021. "'Nowhere Is Safe': Colombia Confronts Alarming Surge in Femicides." *The Guardian,* 25 January 2021. https://www.theguardian.com/global -development/2021/jan/25/nowhere-is-safe-colombia-confronts-alarming-surge-in -femicides.

Pinilla, J. J. 2000. "Corte ordena solucionar tomar de la Cruz Roja." *El Tiempo,* 27 December 2000. http://www.eltiempo.com/archivo/documento/MAM -1224943.

della Porta, D. 1988. "Recruitment Processes in Clandestine Political Organizations: Italian Left-Wing Terrorism." In *International Social Movement Research,* 155–169. Greenwich, CT: JAI Press.

Porter, E. 2016. "Gendered Narratives: Stories and Silences in Transitional Justice." *Human Rights Review* 17 (1): 35–50. doi: 10.1007/s12142-015-0389-8.

Portes, A. 1998. "Social Capital: Its Origins and Applications in Modern Sociology." *American Review of Sociology* 24 (1): 1–24.

Prem, M., et al. 2018. "Killing Social Leaders for Territorial Control: The Unintended Consequences of Peace." *Documentos de Trabajo* 016385, Universidad del Rosario, Bogotá.

Press, R. M. 2014. "Candles in the Wind: Resisting Repression in Liberia, 1979–2003." *Africa Today* 55 (3): 2–22.

Putnam, R. 2000. *Bowling Alone: The Collapse and Revival of American Community.* New York: Simon and Schuster.

Qazizai, F., and Kazmin, A. 2021. "Afghan Women Resist the Return of Taliban's Segregation." *Financial Times,* 19 October 2021. https://www.ft.com/content /d320c92f-c7a4-4277-8d6c-0c998a36b411.

Quijano, A. 2000. "Coloniality of Power and Eurocentrism in Latin America." *International Sociology* 15 (2): 215–232.

Ramírez Boscán, K. 2007. *Desde el desierto: Notas sobre paramilitares y violencia en territorio Wayúu de la Media Guajira.* Maicao, Colombia: Cabildo Wayúu Nöüna de Campamento.

Redfern, C. 2017. "'Aren't Men Just Cleverer than Women?': Building a Feminist City in the Philippines." *The Guardian,* 13 December 2017. https://www.theguardian .com/working-in-development/2017/dec/13/building-feminist-city-philippines.

Restrepo, E. M. 2016. "Leaders against All Odds: Women Victims of Conflict in Colombia." *Palgrave Communications* 2, article 16014 (16 May 2016).

Rettberg, A. 2019. "Peace-Making amidst an Unfinished Social Contract: The Case of Colombia." *Journal of Intervention and Statebuilding* 14 (1): 84–100.

Richie, J. 2003. "The Applications of Qualitative Methods to Social Research." In *Qualitative Research Practice*, edited by J. Richie and J. Lewis, 24–46. London: SAGE.

Rizzo, H., A. Price, and K. Meyer. 2012. "Anti-Sexual Harassment Campaign in Egypt." *Mobilization: An International Quarterly* 17 (4): 457–475. http://www.metapress.com/content/Q756724V461359M2.

Robnett, B. 2013. "Leadership." In *The Wiley-Blackwell Encyclopedia of Social and Political Movements*, edited by D. Snow, 1–6. Hoboken, NJ: Blackwell.

Rodriguez Castro, L. 2020. "'We Are Not Poor Things': Territorio Cuerpo-Tierra and Colombian Women's Organized Struggles." *Feminist Theory* 22 (3): 339–359.

———. 2021. *Decolonial Feminisms, Power, and Place: Sentipensando with Rural Women in Colombia*. New York: Palgrave Macmillan.

Rohter, L. 2000. "Colombians Tell of Massacre, as Army Stood By." *New York Times*, 14 July 2000. http://www.nytimes.com/2000/07/14/world/colombians-tell-of-massacre-as-army-stood-by.html.

Rojas, C. 2009. "Women and Peacebuilding in Colombia: Resistance to War, Creativity for Peace." In *Colombia: Building Peace in a Time of War*, edited by V. Bouvier, 207–225. Washington, DC: United States Institute of Peace.

Rooney, E. 2017. *Justice Learning in Transition: A Grassroots Toolkit*. September. https://papers.ssrn.com/sol3/papers.cfm?abstract_id=3051156.

Ruddick, S. 1989. *Maternal Thinking: Towards a Politics of Peace*. Boston: Beacon Press.

———. 1995. *Maternal Thinking: Towards a Politics of Peace*. 2nd ed. Boston: Beacon Press.

Ryan, C., and W. Gamson. 2015. "Are Frames Enough?" In Goodwin and Jasper, *Social Movements Reader: Cases and Concepts*, 136–143.

Sachseder, J. 2020. "Cleared for Investment? The Intersections of Transnational Capital, Gender, and Race in the Production of Sexual Violence and Internal Displacement in Colombia's Armed Conflict." *International Feminist Journal of Politics* 22 (2): 162–168.

Safa, H. 1990. "Women's Social Movements in Latin America." *Gender and Society* 4 (3): 354–369.

Sandvik, K. B. 2018. "Gendering Violent Pluralism: Women's Political Organising in Latin America." *Third World Thematics: A TWQ Journal* 3 (2): 244–259.

Sandvik, K. B., and J. Lemaitre. 2013. "Internally Displaced Women as Knowledge Producers and Users in Humanitarian Action: The View from Colombia." *Disasters* 37 (1): 36–50.

———. 2015. "From IDPs to Victims in Colombia: A Bottom-Up Reading of Law in Post-Conflict Transitions." In *International Law and Post-Conflict Reconstruction Policy*, edited by M. Saul and J. Sweeney, 251–271. Abingdon, UK: Routledge.

Sanford, V. 2008. "From Genocide to Feminicide: Impunity and Human Rights in Twenty-First Century Guatemala." *Journal of Human Rights* 7 (2): 104–122.

Schenoni, L., S. Braniff, and J. Battaglino. 2020. "Was the Malvinas/Falklands a Diversionary War? A Prospect-Theory Reinterpretation of Argentina's Decline." *Security Studies* 29 (1): 34–63.

Schroeder, K. 2006. "A Feminist Examination of Community Kitchens in Peru and Bolivia." *Gender, Place, and Culture* 13 (6): 663–668.

Schulz, P. 2020. *Male Survivors of Wartime Sexual Violence: Perspectives from Northern Uganda*. University of California Press.

Secretaría Distrital de la Mujer 2015. *AFROMUPAZ: IV Congreso de Intercambio por la Paz: En cuerpo y cara de mujer*. http://www.sdmujer.gov.co/inicio/759-afromupaz -iv-congreso-de-intercambio-por-la-paz-en-cuerpo-y-cara-de-mujer.

Shayne, J. 1999. "Gendered Revolutionary Bridges: Women in the Salvadoran Resistance Movement, 1979–1992." *Latin American Perspectives* 26 (3): 85–102.

Shayne, J. D. 2004. *The Revolution Question: Feminisms in El Salvador, Chile, and Cuba*. Rutgers University Press.

Silver, M. 1974. "Political Revolution and Repression: An Economic Approach." *Public Choice* 17: 63–71.

Simpson, K. 2007. "Voices Silenced, Voices Rediscovered: Victims of Violence and the Reclamation of Language in Traditional Societies." *International Journal of Law in Context* 3 (2): 89–103.

Sjoberg, L. 2016. *Women as Wartime Rapists: Beyond Sensation and Stereotyping*. New York University Press.

Sjoberg, L., and C. Gentry. 2015. *Beyond Mothers, Monsters, Whores: Women's Violence in Global Politics*. London: Zed Books.

Skapska, G. 1999. "Paradigm Lost? The Constitutional Process in Poland and the Hope of a "Grass Roots Constitutionalism.'" In *The Rule of Law after Communism: Problems and Prospects in East-Central Europe*, edited by M. Krygier and A. Czarnota, 149–175. Brookfield, VT: Dartmouth.

Skjelsbaek, I. 2001. "Is Femininity Inherently Peaceful? The Construction of Femininity in War." In *Gender, Conflict, and Peace*, edited by I. Skjelsbaek and D. Smith, 47–67. Oslo: International Peace Research Institute.

Snow, D. et al. 1986. "Frame Alignment Processes, Micromobilization, and Movement Participation." *American Sociological Review* 51 (4): 464–481.

Snow, D., and R. Benford. 1992. "Master Frames and Cycles of Protest." In *Frontiers in Social Movement Theory*, edited by A. Morris and C. Mueller, 133–155. Yale University Press.

Starr, L., and C. Mitchell. 2018. "How Can Canada's Feminist International Assistance Policy Support a Feminist Agenda in Africa? Challenges in Addressing Sexual Violence in Four Agricultural Colleges in Ethiopia." *Agenda-Empowering Women for Gender Equity* 32 (1): 107–118. doi: 10.1080/10130950.2018.1427692.

Stephen, L. 1997. *Women and Social Movements in Latin America: Power from Below*. University of Texas Press.

Sutton, B. 2018. *Surviving State Terror: Women's Testimonies of Repression and Resistance in Argentina*. New York University Press.

Swaine, A. 2018. *Conflict-Related Violence against Women: Transforming Transition*. Cambridge University Press.

Symmes Cobb, J., and N. Casey. 2016. "Colombia Peace Deal Is Defeated, Leaving a Nation in Shock." *New York Times*, 2 October 2016. https://www.nytimes.com /2016/10/03/world/colombia-peace-deal-defeat.html.

Tapias Torrado, N. 2019. *Situación de las lideresas y defensoras de derechos humans: Análisis desde una perspectiva de género e interseccional*. Bogotá: Instituto Capaz.

Tarrow, S. 2011. *Power in Movement: Social Movements, Collective Action, and Politics*. 3rd edition. Cambridge University Press.

Tate, W. 2007. *Counting the Dead: The Culture and Politics of Human Rights Activism in Colombia*. University of California Press.

———. 2013. "Proxy Citizenship and Transnational Advocacy: Colombian Activists from Putumayo to Washington, DC." *American Ethnologist* 40 (1): 55–70.

———. 2015. *Drugs, Thugs, and Diplomats: U.S. Policymaking in Colombia*. Stanford University Press.

———. 2016. "A Dark Day in Colombia." *North American Congress on Latin America (NACLA)*, 4 October 2016. https://nacla.org/news/2016/10/04/dark-day-colombia-0.

———. 2017. "Post-Accord Putumayo." *Journal of Latin American and Caribbean Anthropology* 22 (1): 164–173.

Taylor, V. 1998. "Feminist Methodology in Social Movements Research." *Qualitative Sociology* 21 (4): 357–379.

Taylor, V., and N. Whittier. 1992. "Collective Identities in Social Movement Communities: Lesbian Feminist Mobilization." In *Frontiers in Social Movement Theory*, edited by A. Morris and C. Mueller, 104–129. Yale University Press.

Tejedoras de Vida del Putumayo 2019. *Comunicado: Ola de violencia contra las mujeres y feminicidios en Putumayo*. http://alianzatejedorasdevida.org/2019/02/25/comunicado_-ola-de-violencia-y-feminicidios-contra-las-mujeres-en-ptumayo/#.

Theidon, K. 2009. "Reconstructing Masculinities: The Disarmament, Demobilization, and Reintegration of Former Combatants in Colombia." *Human Rights Quarterly* 31 (1): 1–34. doi: 10.1353/hrq.0.0053.

Thomas Davis, M., and J. Zulver. 2015. "Colombia's City of Women." *Al Jazeera*. http://www.aljazeera.com/indepth/features/2015/12/colombia-city-women-151211085034832.html.

Tilly, C. 1978. *From Mobilization to Revolution*. New York: Random House.

———. 2006. *Regimes and Repertoires*. University of Chicago Press.

Tripp, A. M. 2015. *Women and Power in Postconflict Africa*. Cambridge University Press.

Trisko Darden, J. T., A. Henshaw, and O. Szekely. 2019. *Insurgent Women: Female Combatants in Civil Wars*. Georgetown University Press.

Tullock, G. 1971. "The Paradox of Revolution." *Public Choice* 11 (Fall): 89–99.

UN Women. 2018. *Infographic: Women's Meaningful Participation Builds Peace*. New York. https://www.unwomen.org/en/digital-library/multimedia/2018/10/infographic-womens-meaningful-participation-builds-peace.

———. 2020. *COVID-19 and Conflict: Advancing Women's Meaningful Participation in Ceasefires and Peace Processes*. New York. https://www.unwomen.org/-/media/headquarters/attachments/sections/library/publications/2020/policy-brief-covid-19-and-conflict-en.pdf?la=en&vs=4621.

Unidad para las Víctimas. 2017. "Casos nacionales." http://www.unidadvictimas.gov.co/es/casos-nacionales/391.

———. 2018. "Mesas de Participación." http://www.unidadvictimas.gov.co/es/content/mesas-de-participación/87.

———. 2020. "Registro Único de Víctimas." https://rni.unidadvictimas.gov.co/RUV.

United Nations Security Council 2000. *Resolution 1325 (2000)*. New York. http://unscr.com/en/resolutions/doc/1325.

Verdad Abierta. 2015. "La incursión paramilitar casi acaba con los Wayuu." http://www.verdadabierta.com/victimas-seccion/organizaciones/5913-la-incursion-paramilitar-casi-acaba-con-los-wayuu.

Vergara Figueroa, A., and K. Arboleda Hurtado. 2016. "Afrodiasporic Feminist Conspiracy: Motivations and Paths Forward from the First International."

Meridians: Feminism, Race, Transnationalism 14 (2): 118–129. doi: 10.2979/meridians.14.2.08.

van der Vet, F., and L. Lyytikäinen. 2015. "Violence and Human Rights in Russia: How Human Rights Defenders Develop Their Tactics in the Face of Danger, 2005–2013." *International Journal of Human Rights* 19 (7): 979–998. doi: 10.1080/13642987.2015.1075306.

Villareal, N., and M. A. Ríos. 2006. *Cartografía de la Esperanza: Iniciativas de resistencia pacífica desde las mujeres*. Bogotá: International Peace Information Service/Corporación Ecomujer.

Viterna, J. 2006. "Pulled, Pushed, and Persuaded: Explaining Women's Mobilization into the Salvadoran Guerrilla Army." *American Journal of Sociology* 112 (1): 1–45. doi: 10.1086/502690.

———. 2009. "Negotiating the Muddiness of Grassroots Field Research: Managing Identity and Data in Rural El Salvador." In *Women Fielding Danger: Negotiating Ethnographic Identities in Field Research*, edited by M. Huggins and M.-L. Glebbeck, 271–297. Lanham, MD: Rowman and Littlefield.

———. 2013. *Women in War: The Micro-processes of Mobilization in El Salvador*. Oxford University Press.

Voge, C., and J. Zulver. 2019. "'Peace Has a Lot of Enemies Here': Colombia's Female Activists in the Firing Line." *New Humanitarian,* 28 October 2019. https://www.thenewhumanitarian.org/video/2019/10/28/Colombia-peace-women-activists-violence.

Voors, M. J., et al. 2012. "Violent Conflict and Behavior: A Field Experiment in Burundi." *American Economic Association* 102 (2): 941–694.

Waylen, G., et al., eds. 2013. "Body Politics." In *The Oxford Handbook of Gender and Politics*. Oxford University Press.

Weber, M. 1978. *Economy and Society*. University of California Press.

Webster, K., C. Chen, and K. Beardsley. 2019. "Conflict, Peace, and the Evolution of Women's Empowerment." *International Organization* 73 (2): 255–289.

Weyland, K. 2004. *The Politics of Market Reform in Fragile Democracies: Argentina, Brazil, Peru, and Venezuela*. Princeton University Press.

Whittier, N. 2015. "Sustaining Commitment among Radical Feminists." In Goodwin and Jasper, *Social Movements Reader: Cases and Concepts*, 114–126.

Wibben, A. T. R. 2020. "Everyday Security, Feminism, and the Continuum of Violence." *Journal of Global Security Studies* 5 (1): 115–121.

Wickham-Crowley, T. P. 1992. *Guerrillas and Revolution in Latin America: A Comparative Study of Insurgents and Regimes since 1956*. Princeton University Press.

Wilding, P. 2010. "'New Violence': Silencing Women's Experiences in the 'Favelas' of Brazil." *Journal of Latin American Studies* 42 (4): 719–747.

Wood, E. J. 2003. *Insurgent Collective Action and Civil War in El Salvador*. Cambridge University Press.

———. 2008. "The Social Processes of Civil War: The Wartime Transformation of Social Networks." *Annual Review of Political Science* 11 (1): 539–561. doi: 10.1146/annurev.polisci.8.082103.104832.

———. 2015. "The Emotional Benefits of Insurgency in El Salvador." In *Social Movements Reader: Cases and Concepts*, edited by Jasper and Goodwin, 143–153.

———. 2018. "Rape as a Practice of War: Towards a Typology of Political Violence." *Politics and Society* 46 (4): 513–537.

Zahra, M., and P. Sheikh Muzamil. 2020. "How Women's Roles Are Changing in Kashmir's Conflict." *New Humanitarian*, 14 July 2020. https://www .thenewhumanitarian.org/photo-feature/2020/07/14/Kashmir-military-conflict -violence-women?utm_source=The+New+Humanitarian&utm_campaign =1b02e4969f-EMAIL_CAMPAIGN_2020_09_21_Peace&utm_medium =email&utm_term=0_d842d98289-1b02e4969f-15654885.

Zulver, J. 2016. "High-risk Feminism in El Salvador: Women's Mobilisation in Violent Times." *Gender and Development* 24 (02): 171–185.

———. 2019a. "'Based in Hatred': Violence against Women in Colombia's Elections." *The Guardian*, 1 October 2019. https://www.theguardian.com/global -development/2019/oct/01/based-in-hatred-violence-against-women-colombia -elections.

———. 2019b. "Women Weaving Life in Southern Colombia." North American Congress on Latin America (NACLA). https://nacla.org/news/2019/04/11/women -weaving-life-southern-colombia.

———. 2020. "In Colombia, Pandemic Heightens Risks for Women Social Leaders." Carnegie Endowment for International Peace, 7 May 2020. https:// carnegieendowment.org/2020/05/07/in-colombia-pandemic-heightens-risks-for -women-social-leaders-pub-81736.

———. 2021. "The Endurance of Women's Mobilization during Patriarchal Backlash: A Case from Colombia's Reconfiguring Armed Conflict." *International Feminist Journal of Politics* 23 (3): 440–462.

Zulver, J., and M. Janetsky. 2020. "Colombia: How Armed Gangs Are Using Lock-down to Target Activists." BBC, 21 May 2020. https://www.bbc.com/news /world-latin-america-52661457.

Index

About the Author

JULIA MARGARET ZULVER is a Marie Skłodowska-Curie Research Fellow at the Oxford School for Global and Area Studies, University of Oxford, and the Instituto de Investigaciones Jurídicas, Universidad Nacional Autónoma de México. She earned her DPhil in sociology from the University of Oxford in 2018, where she was a Commonwealth Scholar and a Doctoral Fellow of the Social Sciences and Humanities Research Council of Canada. She engages in gender advocacy and policy work as a senior researcher at Ladysmith, a feminist research collective.

Printed and bound by CPI Group (UK) Ltd, Croydon, CR0 4YY

09/06/2025

14685740-0001